PARTNE

INTERNATIONAL

DEVELOPMENT

PARTNERSHIP FOR INTERNATIONAL DEVELOPMENT

Rhetoric or Results?

Jennifer M. Brinkerhoff

LYNNE
RIENNER
PUBLISHERS

BOULDER
LONDON

Published in the United States of America in 2002 by
Lynne Rienner Publishers, Inc.
1800 30th Street, Boulder, Colorado 80301
www.rienner.com

and in the United Kingdom by
Lynne Rienner Publishers, Inc.
3 Henrietta Street, Covent Garden, London WC2E 8LU

Library of Congress Cataloging-in-Publication Data
Brinkerhoff, Jennifer M., 1965–
    Partnership for international development : rhetoric or results? / Jennifer M. Brinkerhoff.
      p. cm.
    Includes bibliographical references and index.
    ISBN 1-58826-093-3 (hc: alk. paper)
    ISBN 1-58826-069-0 (pbk: alk. paper)
    1. Economic assistance—Developing countries—International cooperation.   2.
Non-governmental organizations—Developing countries.   I. Title.
HC60.B672   2002
338.91'09172'4—dc21

                                                2002069752

British Cataloguing in Publication Data
A Cataloguing in Publication record for this book
is available from the British Library.

5   4   3   2   1

CONTENTS

FIGURES

PREFACE

We have entered a time when international development figures prominently among policymakers, in the media, and among the general public. The complexity posed by globalization, coupled with the continuing challenges of poverty, security, and political and economic instability, necessitates creative approaches and new institutional structures to address the simultaneous needs for technical expertise and participatory, democratic practices. These challenges are intensified by the need to embrace cultural identities in the process and outcomes of international problem solving. But resources remain scarce, and policymakers and the general public continue to seek to minimize the direct involvement and funding of government bodies. In every sector and service sphere, actors are looking for the most effective and efficient means to deliver services in an increasingly interdependent world. *Partnership* has become the buzzword used to describe many of these endeavors. However, rhetoric alone will not lead to solutions, but may only make things worse as it leads to cynicism and lack of trust, discouraging actors from pursuing partnership approaches.

In this book, I seek to clarify the concept of partnership, as well as its practice, to critique our understanding and practice of partnership in international development to date, and to specify partnership's defining dimensions. Implementation guidelines outline contextual factors, which inform the decision to partner and suggest strategies for maximizing and maintaining partnership effectiveness. A more nuanced understanding of potential actors and corresponding selection criteria can assist cooperating actors to be more strategic in who they partner with, as well as how they design and implement partnerships.

One of the greatest challenges of partnership work is maintaining the balance between a focus on desired programmatic results and the necessary emphasis on process. Organizations' existing structures, systems, and rules are rarely conducive to partnership work and often present substantial obstacles to productive relationships. While agreement on the concept of partnership may be readily forthcoming, the process often breaks down during initiation and implementation. Thus, in the pages that follow, I suggest incentives and governance mechanisms to support effective partnership work. Three cases illustrate differing approaches.

Scholars and practitioners from all sectors are exploring partnership. My hope is that the policy implications, as well as the pragmatic emphasis on operationalizing partnerships, discussed in these pages will be useful to them. The term *partnership* connotes positive feelings and values. My aim in this book is to build on this potential goodwill, recognize the pragmatic contributions of its underlying values, and encourage actors to move beyond the rhetoric of partnership to actually address development challenges effectively and efficiently.

*   *   *

This book is the culmination of several years of applied and investigative work, including numerous conversations with partnership practitioners, proponents, and skeptics. It is impossible to trace the influence of so many people who stimulated my thoughts, provided examples, and sometimes pointed me in new directions. My thanks to you all.

There are several people I would like to highlight. Najma Siddiqi gave me a tremendous opportunity to explore these issues with practitioners from the World Bank and beyond. Qaim Shah was generous in providing information and answering my many questions whether from Washington, Pakistan, or Myanmar. Afzal Latif followed his lead and provided me with invaluable project documents and e-mail support. The team from International Medical Services for Health (INMED), including Linda Pfeiffer and Thad Jackson, gave generously of their time. I particularly want to thank Joyce Capelli, not only for the many hours of inquisition, despite jet lag, but also for her very heartfelt responses and the way her example and compassion continue to inspire me. Thanks to Conrad Person and Michael Bzdack from Johnson & Johnson and Bill Collins from El Paso Energy International for their thoughtful responses to my many questions. In addition to our interview, Andreas Liebenthal provided helpful feedback on Chapter 7.

Others who provided support (interviews, correspondence, materials, and/or feedback on chapters in progress) include Derick Brinkerhoff, Martin Hewitt, Nigel Twose, Jaime Kuklinski, Anthony Judge, Norman Nicholson, Aaron Williams, Art Goldsmith, and Michael Brown. I also want to thank the many practitioners who listened and gave feedback on my partnership frameworks and ideas. I would particularly like to thank those I interviewed as part of the World Bank's Learning Series on Partnerships (1998–1999). Sara Evans, my graduate assistant at George Washington University, helped with the bibliography. Very special thanks to Joshua Forrest, a superb colleague and friend, who invested a substantial amount of time and energy to provide feedback on early chapters and who encouraged me throughout.

Last on this list but first in my heart, thanks to my husband, Derick, for the depth and range of partnership we share.

1

Partnership: Promise and Practice

The mixed results of development since the 1970s, coupled with a simultaneous recognition of interdependence and resource scarcity in our globalized world, has led some scholars and practitioners to argue that development is not possible without partnership approaches and that "business as usual" cannot continue. Not only have previous approaches proved ineffective, some argue they have been detrimental.[1] The nature and scale of socioeconomic development problems are impossible to address in isolation. To solve their complexity and intransigence requires multiple actors and resources. The structure of development assistance must change to prevent a worsening of conditions and to initiate a movement toward more effective approaches. This book addresses partnership between nongovernmental organizations (NGOs), community-based organizations (CBOs), governments, donors, and the private sector for the purpose of enhancing development outcomes.

Organizations form partnerships not only to enhance outcomes, whether qualitatively or quantitatively, but also to produce synergistic rewards, where the outcomes of the partnership as a whole are greater than the sum of what individual partners contribute. Most evidence of partnership's contributions to performance is anecdotal.[2] Synergistic results are often sought and referenced, but they are rarely fully articulated and measured. Furthermore, the process of creating such synergistic rewards is more hopeful than methodical or well understood.

While partnership is being promoted in every service sphere, nowhere is the increasing need for and experimentation with partnership more in evidence than in international development.[3] And nowhere is the context for partnership more complex, with myriad potential partners who have multiple and often divergent motivations, facing the most challenging development circumstances—dire poverty, entrenched social stratification, and conflicts of many sorts. These problems are so daunting that it is obvi-

1

ous no actor can face them alone. Partnership is the topic of numerous reports, conferences, and anecdotes.[4] As with many terms in good currency, while many embrace the notion of partnership and stake a claim in its promotion, there is little agreement on what partnership means.[5] The design and management of partnerships has been little informed by theory or conceptual frameworks (Lowndes and Skelcher 1998; Lister 2000). Partnership is in danger of remaining a "feel good" panacea for governance without obtaining a pragmatic grasp of the "why" and a clearer understanding of the "how" of partnerships.

Partnership rhetoric is not serving the objectives partnership work seeks. A conceptual and practical understanding of what partnership is and how to design and implement partnerships effectively will accomplish two important objectives. First, it will establish a common language for what partnership is and how to maximize its rewards, enabling partnership actors to lobby for improved partnership practice on both practical and normative grounds. Second, it will contribute to improved partnership performance, adding substance to rhetoric, based on a clear articulation of partnership's value-added, encouraging greater commitment to and experimentation with partnership approaches, and ultimately contributing to important development outcomes.

This chapter addresses four key questions: Why is partnership so popular? How are practitioners doing in their partnership practice? What is partnership? How can partnerships be more effectively managed? The first question examines the rationale for partnership, identifying four primary reasons actors choose to partner with others. The next section provides a selected overview of the use of partnership rhetoric and results as promoted by some donor agencies (the U.S. Agency for International Development [USAID], the World Bank, and the United Nations [UN]). The review demonstrates the gap between rhetoric and actual commitment and practice, and it identifies some common administrative and political challenges to partnership work within donor agencies. Partnership is defined both in an ideal sense and as a relative practice, distinguished by two defining features: organization identity and mutuality. I argue that partnership in the ideal sense is not possible, as partnership actors may have differing conceptions of those ideals or the ideals may be unrealizable given actors' organizational constraints. The emphasis throughout the book is on partnership as a relative practice.

The last section of the chapter outlines initial lessons for effectively managing partnerships, emphasizing the softer side of partnership design and implementation. This approach encourages actors to be more proactive about establishing and reinforcing a values basis for partnership work and a corresponding partnership identity. The question of effectiveness is the primary subject of the book; therefore, the response is more fully developed in the chapters that follow.

The Why of Partnership

The most obvious motivation for establishing a partnership is the desire to enhance the effectiveness and efficiency of development efforts. Partnership can provide a means of developing strategic direction and coordination. It affords a scale and integration of interests and services that are impossible for any actor operating alone. The Barani Area Development Project (BADP), for example, integrated and coordinated the efforts of eight government departments, an NGO, and numerous village organizations in order to improve public service delivery, development outcomes, and sustainability of project efforts and institutions (see Chapter 5).

The need for partnership is most obvious in the daunting challenge of achieving sustainable development, which is predicated on the equally daunting challenge of maintaining good governance. Sustainability is increasingly viewed in a more holistic sense, which encompasses social, political, and ethical issues, all requiring strategic and operational responses. Despite differences in opinion or strategy, cooperation between NGOs and donors is recognized as "an essential prerequisite" for reaching the ultimate goal of a sustainable environment (Peterson 1997: 16). Without the cooperation of multiple and diverse actors, each with its own perspective and comparative advantages, we risk treating symptoms rather than causes of underdevelopment and becoming frustrated by systemic forces that preserve the status quo (Brown and Ashman 1996).

Partnership contributes to effectiveness by affording actors access to crucial resources—including expertise and relationships—that would otherwise be inaccessible. Those actors closest to the issue to be addressed have better information, strong incentives for assuring good performance, and lower transaction costs in bringing resources to bear. Governments and donors can access these resources via NGOs, local governments, and the private commercial sector. For example, in Brazil, multinational corporations and government agencies access the expertise and local knowledge of International Medical Services for Health (INMED) in implementing health education and improvement programs, while INMED creates new resources by harnessing opportunities for corporate philanthropy (see Chapter 6).

Similar lessons have long been acknowledged in private-sector networks where member organizations use their networks to access key technologies or other resources (Madhavan, Koka, and Prescott 1998). In this context, an organization's power is determined not by its internal resources but by the set of resources it can mobilize through its contacts. Effectiveness is also enhanced through the innovation partnership can foster. This innovation might emerge solely from the combination of different perspectives and skills or, less directly, through trust building, which allows for more effective problem solving and positive sum solutions (Peters 1998); both of these factors were instrumental in the successful process of the World Commission on Dams (WCD) (see Chapter 7).

Partnership can also enhance the efficiency of development efforts through identification and exploitation of the comparative advantages of the actors involved. Partnership rationalizes the use of resources and skills. Creativity may emerge from the assembling of diverse actors with different perspectives and expertise, resulting in efficiency improvements. For example, businesses that access the environmental expertise of NGOs and local communities are able to produce "eco-efficiencies," or savings on energy and waste (DeSimone and Popoff 2000). Similarly, partnership can reduce information and transaction costs through coordination and trust building (Börzel 1998).

Conflict, too, can form the basis for partnership. The costs of conflict in time and resources can be much greater than the costs associated with cooperation. The most obvious example is in the environmental sector, where competition over scarce resources and their protection is an ongoing moral and practical dilemma. Similar controversies surround resettlement projects. In such instances, major differences in interests and conflicting objectives can bring diverse actors together. This may be because the opposition has thwarted the parties from any action, forcing them all to the negotiating table. Or the costs of pursuing a particular agenda amid such opposition may be too great. Public relations concerns are increasingly driving the latter, especially for donors and the private sector, and they were a major force in driving both the World Bank and the large dam industry to participate in and support the WCD (Chapter 7).

The combination of these perspectives and resources can spawn creativity, yielding win-win solutions heretofore unimaginable. The conflict basis for partnership is also inherent to any good governance effort, regardless of the target organization. The potential for conflicting motivations and objectives forms the basis for accountability in upholding the pursuit of common goals, or at least agreements on goals, when diverse actors are sufficiently engaged.

Partnership can also be used strategically to open decisionmaking processes (Stoker 1997). This strategy can represent a moral dimension, where the intent is to further public interests rather than private ones, or it can be viewed pragmatically as the only means to ensure sustainability. Input from all concerned parties is essential to creating sustainable benefits.

This is particularly true in the case of the WCD, where the legitimacy of its final report is commensurate with perceptions of transparency and inclusiveness, and compliance with the WCD's recommendations remains voluntary (see Chapter 7). The benefits of increased openness and participation can contribute significantly to all of the other partnership incentives.

Regardless of the initial incentive for partnership, multiplier effects can ensue once a partnership becomes operational, further supporting the continuation, growth, and replication of partnerships. The most immediate of these effects concerns capacity. The capacity of any one actor is expanded when the resources of other actors can be leveraged for wider impact. One partner's capacity can be enhanced through the experience of working with the other partners and through training and staff exchanges. Individual partners may also benefit from access to new domains, creation of new opportunities, protection from potential threats, and improved effectiveness in achieving their own objectives, or through positive public relations and new ways to market themselves. For example, INMED Brazil was initially formalized to support INMED's partnership with Interfarma (an association of pharmaceutical manufacturers); through that initial experience, INMED developed a program design and implementation model and learned how to work effectively with multinational corporations, understanding their priorities and operating style (Chapter 6).

Another significant multiplier effect concerns the influence that each actor has upon the others. Studies show that the climate is most favorable to poverty reduction where there is a high level of interaction among the sectors, particularly between government and civil society actors (Tandon 1991; USAID 1995a). Actors can influence both the agenda of the partnership as a whole and the individual agendas of the partners. Such influence can range from NGOs promoting government responsiveness to the needs of particular constituencies, to government steering NGOs away from what it perceives as subversive activities, to the private sector influencing regulation policies. This influence is not necessarily in the interests of only one partner; allowing actors the opportunity to voice their concerns can reduce implementation problems, which benefits the partnership as a whole (see Clark 1997). For example, BADP's development of standard operating procedures and a Social Organization Unit created the space and opportunity for each partner to introduce its concerns, priorities, and technical expertise and to ensure that these would be appropriately integrated into project implementation (see Chapter 5).

The relationships cultivated in partnerships represent social capital that can be applied to other development issues, involving the same or other partners into the future. USAID found that the greater the capacity of partnerships and of individual partners themselves, the better the public dialogue with USAID and other donors will be (USAID 1997). More important for donors' objectives, this social capital is the foundation for any exit strategy. When a project is completed, the institutional capacity to sustain programs and benefits is left behind, and the society-to-society linkages the partnerships cultivated can facilitate continuing access to donor-country expertise and technology and support long-term cooperation on issues of common concern. A subtle but fundamental aspect of this social capital, extending far beyond donor interests per se, is that the greater understanding of each actor's perspective, operations, and contributions can be brought to bear on subsequent efforts, as occurred in INMED's partnerships (see Chapter 6).

From a pragmatic perspective, partnerships emerging at multiple levels entail an increasing development and specification of actors' comparative advantages and a refinement of respective roles, in order to maximize all available resources. The many benefits to partnership work outlined above can be seen as "collaborative advantages" (Huxham 1996; Kanter 1994; Doz and Hamel 1998). In general, individual actors choose to partner for one or more of the following four reasons:

1. To enhance efficiency and effectiveness through a reliance on comparative advantages and a rational division of labor. This entails incremental (though possibly dramatic) improvements in the delivery of development initiatives.
2. To provide the multiactor, integrated solutions required by the scope and nature of the problems being addressed. Without this approach, the effort would be impossible.
3. To move from a no-win situation among multiple actors to a compromise and potential win-win situation (i.e., in response to collective action problems or the need for conflict resolution). It may be possible to continue without partnership, but stakeholders would remain dissatisfied and continue to incur losses.
4. To open decisionmaking processes to promote a broader operationalization of the public good. The normative dimension of this motivator seeks to maximize representation and democratic processes; the pragmatic perspective views this as a means to ensure sustainability.

How Far Have We Come?
Donor Agencies and Partnership

So-called partnerships between resource agencies and developing country institutions have been scrutinized for some time (see, for example, Garilao 1987). Clearly the rationale and rhetoric of partnership approaches to international development have been well established. A brief overview of development activities in the 1990s indicates an increasing focus on partnership as demonstrated by conferences and workshops (e.g., the World Bank's Partnership Learning Initiative), donor policies (e.g., the requirement of local partnership for funding by the British government, European Union, and USAID's Private Voluntary Organization Matching Grant Program), and new programs and activities. Both the UN and the World Bank have established NGO liaison officers or civil society specialists in many of their departments and resident missions. Much donor partnership work is pursued on a project-by-project basis. A sampling of donor agency partnership work reveals that partnerships are also pursued as a reorientation to general operations and policymaking, and through special programmatic offices and initiatives.

Reorientation of General Operations and Policymaking

The Development Assistance Committee 21st Strategy, the UN Common Country Framework, and the World Bank's Comprehensive Development Framework and Poverty Reduction Strategy Papers offer new models for thinking about and formulating development strategy. These incorporate explicit consultation with and frequently more intense participation of the private sector and civil society, in addition to governments and donors. The frameworks seek a holistic approach to development, intended to be driven by the country in need, though who represents the country (whether government, civil society, or both) is not often clearly outlined. Each of these similar frameworks expresses the donor's perspective and desired role in the process. This puts governments in the position of having to choose among frameworks, in effect prioritizing the importance of various donors and their preferences.

Despite their rhetoric, none of the frameworks inherently guarantees a partnership between a government and the local private sector and civil society or between the donor and the host country government. The extent to which partnerships are operationalized depends on the dominant actor in each of these relationships: the government in terms of receptivity to private-sector and civil society participation and the donor in terms of allowing the government to drive the partnership process. The incentive structures to support partnership work, for both governments and donor staff, are vague at best.

Aside from these multilateral efforts, some bilaterals have promoted new partnership approaches for development strategy and implementation, including USAID's New Partnership Initiative (NPI) and, more recently, its Global Development Alliance (GDA). NPI began with a learning phase that produced a core report (USAID 1995a); related reports on democratic local governance, NGO empowerment, and small-business partnership (USAID 1995b, 1995c, 1995d); and a resource guide, which assembles the results of its learning phase and includes field-based reports on NPI pilot missions (USAID 1997). This work culminated in an intersectoral partnerships handbook (Charles, McNulty, and Pennell 1998) to support and encourage intersectoral partnership within USAID.

NPI focused on supporting and facilitating partnership work; it did not represent actual partnership engagement. No funds were designated to support partnership work at the country level. Missions had the option of pursuing an NPI approach in the selection of strategic objectives and corresponding strategies, but this was not required and no additional funds were made available to support these more ambitious, time-consuming, and costly approaches. NPI competed with other approaches and strategic objectives, and it did not often fit well with earmarked funds and programming. In addition, procurement requirements were not adjusted to accommodate partnership approaches; no special arrangements were made to facilitate partnership relations and the necessary administrative adaptations. At most, NPI recommended the creative use of existing mechanisms, such as umbrella grants. As a centralized initiative, NPI was endorsed by the USAID administrator and promoted in vague policy guidelines, but it was not necessarily supported administratively or financially.

USAID's GDA seeks to redefine how USAID implements its foreign assistance mandate and is touted as USAID's "business model for the 21st century." The alliance acknowledges the role of NGOs, foundations, corporations, and institutions of higher education in development assistance, and it seeks to marshal the resources of these diverse actors through brokering and participating in strategic partnerships. Among GDA's objectives are better coordination, leveraging private financing, and enhancing policy reform through advocacy (USAID 2001).

The GDA and its programs are still at the earliest stages of implementation. However, strategic questions are already emerging. For example, partners will want to ensure that their participation is valued beyond the material resources they provide. This requirement highlights the issue of strategy development and program design and the potential constraints that congressional oversight may pose to partnership approaches in these areas. Congress and the U.S. public demand more than haphazard development programs, negotiated on a case-by-case basis with available partners and their particular comparative advantages and interests. The GDA guidelines repeatedly call for flexibility in considering alliances that may not fit neatly into agency strategic objectives. How such flexibility will be maintained, particularly in a results-driven environment, remains to be seen. The GDA received a $20 million budget allocation for its incentive fund for fiscal year 2002. Its first year's performance will prove critical to its ability to attract future funding.

Specialized Offices and Initiatives

Donors' partnership work is also demonstrated in specialized offices and initiatives, including those that encompass learning, and partnering with the private sector and NGOs. The World Bank has engaged in several learning initiatives related to partnership work, among them the Learning Series on Building Effective Partnerships to Meet the Challenge of Equitable and Sustainable Development, which consisted of two workshops (in 1998). The first focused on collecting the lessons learned from officials within the Bank who had engaged in partnership work; the second, drawing upon this information, sought to provide training to those interested in pursuing partnership work. Publications included proceedings of the two events and a collection of case examples (Coston 1999). More recently, the World Bank sponsored the Internet-based Forum on Partnering with Civil Society, which had global participation from practitioners and scholars. These dialogues are useful opportunities to exchange ideas; however, they tend to preach to the converted without having concrete impact on World Bank procedures and modes of operation.

Another learning initiative, Partnerships for Poverty Reduction (1996–1998), sought to promote a partnership approach to poverty reduction efforts in Latin America and the Caribbean. The program itself was a partnership between the World Bank, the Inter-American Foundation, the UN Development Programme, and national committees of six participating countries. Participants developed and disseminated hundreds of best-practice case studies. The analysis of the program and the lessons learned there identifies the outcomes of and enabling environment characteristics for partnerships for poverty reduction (Fiszbein and Lowden 1998). It is a useful beginning for selling the partnership approach, though it does not include analyses that would inform partnership practice.

Donors' cooperation with the private sector is not new; however, it is increasingly couched in partnership rhetoric, and specific partnership initiatives are emerging. For example, the International Finance Corporation–facilitated program Business Partners for Development (BPD) aims to study and promote good examples of trisector partnerships (business, government, and civil society) around the world. BPD organizes partnerships into four clusters: youth development, water and sanitation, natural resources, and road traffic safety. Its activities in each of these include direct input to focus projects, national roundtables and workshops, expert study visits, training, research, and communications. BPD's Knowledge

Resource Group collects, analyzes, links, and disseminates the lessons learned from these partnerships (World Bank 1999). While BPD has successfully secured broad and diverse participation, it is unclear how the various interests of participating private-sector organizations, international NGOs, and donors are balanced, particularly in service to local development needs.

Much of the recent expansion of the UN's partnerships with the private sector is in response to Secretary-General Kofi Annan's public appeal in January 1999 for business to "do its part by demonstrating good global citizenship wherever it operates." The secretary-general proposed a "global compact," in which businesses would abide by principles espoused in the international agreements on human rights, labor, and the environment. The global compact invites private-sector partnerships with the International Labour Organization, UN High Commissioner for Refugees, and the UN Environment Programme (UN 1999). Such private-sector partnerships suffer from some of the same concerns as their World Bank counterparts. There are few, if any, guarantees that these partnerships will serve and support local organizations, including government development strategies, local business, and civil society. Memoranda of understanding are often vague skeletons, lacking the substance of significant commitment to identifiable outcomes. The UN as a whole has limited ability to fund, promote, coordinate, and implement private-sector partnerships.

One of the most extensive areas for partnership initiatives is donors' work with NGOs. Each donor agency has a long, often problematic history of relations with NGOs. Specialized initiatives and offices often reflect these histories. The evolution of the World Bank's cooperation with NGOs resembles a schizophrenia of sorts. On the one hand, the World Bank has responded to NGO criticism and advocacy, resulting in various committees and policy efforts (see Fox and Brown 1998). On the other hand, the World Bank claims to want to promote cooperation with NGOs to enhance the effectiveness of development efforts. This schizophrenia is revealed in the continuously vague mission of the World Bank NGO and Civil Society Unit, which is expected to act as the interface between the Bank and the NGO community, an external focus, while promoting operational work with NGOs and training and supporting resident mission civil society specialists, an internal orientation.

There is a long-standing criticism of the World Bank's cooperation with NGOs: NGOs who participate on the World Bank–NGO committee and in policy review processes tend to be a select group. They are not viewed as representative of the NGO community broadly defined, and no objective selection criteria support their participation as sector representatives (to the exclusion of other interests as individual organizations). This selection process suggests that the Bank may be working with organizations with which it has become relatively comfortable over time. Cooperation with NGOs is marginal, selective, and sometimes forced solely by the desire to quiet critics in support of public relations.

Perhaps the most lofty partnership rhetoric comes from the UN. According to the secretary-general, a true partnership between NGOs and the UN is "not an option; it is a necessity" (Annan 1998a). He also specifically identifies UN-NGO partnerships as essential to enforcing the Universal Declaration of Human Rights (Annan 1998b). The UN's various summits (such as the Rio Earth Summit, 1992, and subsequent summits on population, urban development, gender, and social development) established partnership as the central approach to achieving Agenda 21 targets for sustainable development. Partnership is also the espoused approach for meeting the Millennium Development Goals.

Criticism of the UN's relationship to NGOs can be scathing. In a critique of the secretary-general's report on the UN's work with NGOs, Annan was blasted for making lofty speeches about NGOs as "indispensable partners" while increasing restrictions on their involvement through new rules, regulations, and fees (Deen 1999). NGOs complain that security measures, introduced before September 11, 2001, are increasingly scrutinizing them, their members' entry to UN buildings, and even documents carried in and out of UN facilities (Global Policy Forum 1999). NGOs were excluded from the "Vienna Plus Five" human rights summit (in 1998). According to some NGOs, global policy discussions have shifted to special sessions of the General Assembly or other UN venues, with greater restrictions on NGO access (Global Policy Forum 1999). Some NGOs see the current situation "as a game in which all the moves are being determined by the UN— with the NGOs forced into a basically reactive posture waiting the next moves from a rather slow moving intergovernmental animal" (Judge 1999b).

Such animosity is less apparent in relations between USAID and its NGO partners.[6] USAID's Office of Private and Voluntary Cooperation (PVC) has played a key role as the primary interface between the agency and its NGO partners, including facilitating the inclusion of NGOs into agency policymaking. This inclusion has encompassed, among other things, PVC facilitation and participation in the Advisory Committee on Voluntary Foreign Aid (ACVFA). ACVFA comprises NGO and research institution representatives. Its mandate is to "provide well informed and constructive advice to USAID's Administrator on the range of issues and challenges that affect the relationship between the official foreign assistance program and the work of the private voluntary community" (ACVFA 1997: v).

ACVFA worked hard to identify and facilitate resolution of important administrative barriers to partnership work, as well as to promote a better understanding within the agency about NGOs, their strengths and operations. Like many donor agencies, USAID requires NGOs to register in order to receive funds or other forms of assistance; historically this process has been onerous, particularly for local NGOs. While ACVFA made progress in streamlining the requirements for international NGOs, its progress with respect to local NGO registration has been slower. ACVFA was originally founded to support U.S. NGOs' work with, and funding support from, USAID. This mission arguably limits how representative it is of both local and U.S.-based international NGOs. ACVFA's advocacy within USAID can be said to be self-interested, limiting its credibility and effectiveness.

Review of the Practice

Regardless of the particular donor agency, partnership work necessarily varies with the partnership and project officers involved. Work with external actors is typically structured through requests for applications (e.g., with USAID) or defined program areas and objectives. The mutual design of partnership work is often limited, potentially by more than donor priorities and objectives. Some partnership initiatives encourage the use of more flexible mechanisms (e.g., USAID umbrella grants). However, the use of such mechanisms competes with other priorities, particularly administrative requirements and time specifications, which support results management. In addition, these mechanisms are often reinterpreted by USAID project officers. For example, NGOs complain that cooperative agreements are implemented no differently than contracts. In most cases, donors do not provide additional funding to support the time, relationship building, and pilot efforts that partnership work often requires.

Because partnership work is frequently pursued at the discretion of individual project officers, its success depends on these officers' creativity, risk tolerance, political clout, and persistence in identifying and promoting the mechanisms and support systems necessary for partnership work. A recent review of successful World Bank partnership work reveals that while some task managers take risks and invest the effort to pursue genuine partnership approaches, they continue to be plagued by onerous administrative procedures, competitive bidding requirements, and limitations in information disclosure. In most of the cases reviewed, task managers were required to negotiate new models and legal agreements for collaborative work, which required lengthy approval processes sometimes delaying project implementation by as much as one to two years (Coston 1998c, 1999).

Such efforts presume entrepreneurial, high-capacity staff and systems. However, donor officials and offices interfacing with partners are often insufficiently prepared to cope with the volume and variety of partners, and this limited capacity is exacerbated by understaffing and lack of training specific to partnership work (see, for example, UN 1998). At the UN, the secretary-general has recently added a new component on cooperating with civil society to the training curricula of the UN Staff College (Annan 1998a). However, additional training will not be sufficient either to cope with the volume, diversity, political controversy, and potential infighting within the NGO community, or for the funding and administrative support mechanisms necessary to partnership work. Critics are also calling for a more systematic review of and investment in electronic mechanisms for information dissemination, consultation, and other forms of participation, though to date these needs have not been recognized by the secretary-general or explored in any meaningful way (see Judge 1999a).

Donors' partnership work is also challenged in its lack of coordination, which makes systematic support more difficult. For example, the varied experience within the UN system implies that the organization has the flexibility necessary for innovation but remains inconsistent due to lack of coordination and corresponding inefficiency (Rice and Ritchie 1995), and an absence of clear guidelines for UN officials (UN 1998). A recurring obstacle to UN-NGO partnership work is the lack of uniform rules and procedures for NGO participation throughout the UN system. USAID's experimental efforts, while promising, remain uncoordinated, haphazard, and, for the most part, rhetorical because they are inadequately funded.

Moving Beyond Rhetoric

While partnership rhetoric is strong, the effectiveness, efficiency, and credibility of the practice are less certain. Given the partnership trend and each donor's effort to promote and embody it, there is no dearth of approaches to consider. In fact, the diversity of partnership approaches is less indicative of the varied developing country contexts than it is of the numerous, often overlapping, and sometimes contradicting donor initiatives promoted (Nicholson 1999). Unspecified and overly ambitious expectations of partnership, coupled with the overuse of partnership rhetoric and inconsistent practice may lead to an abandonment of partnership work altogether and a forfeiting of its potential value-added.

However, partnership rhetoric could be a potential launching point for accountability and revised practice. Conceptual refinement will help to identify essential targets for accountability and analysis when evaluating the authenticity of partnership rhetoric. Further refinement of the concept and examination of the practice of partnership will assist actors to improve progress in creating effective partnerships. This effort begins with defining partnership.

What Is Partnership?

Most people will agree that "partnership" conjures a positive reaction, implying a desirable, values-laden type of relationship. Partnership principles seek to articulate these values and suggest how they can be operationalized. The type of partnership that proponents would ideally seek encompasses a range of partnership principles including mutual trust, respect, accountability, and influence, with mutual determination of ends and means (Malena 1995; Fowler 1995b). Practitioners from all sectors increasingly recognize many of these partnership principles. They are often found in public relations materials. In essence, they constitute a generally accepted partnership rhetoric. Many of the principles are difficult if not impossible to quantify and measure, and perspectives on their operationalization (and realism) vary, justifying their inclusion in the definition of an ideal type, as opposed to a standard practice. The ideal type of partnership and its results can be summarized as follows: Partnership is a dynamic relationship among diverse actors, based on mutually agreed objectives, pursued through a shared understanding of the most rational division of labor based on the respective comparative advantages of each partner. This relationship results in mutual influence, with a careful balance between synergy and respective autonomy, which incorporates mutual respect, equal participation in decisionmaking, mutual accountability, and transparency.

There are three obvious problems with such ideal-type definitions: (1) they may never be fully operational; (2) they may not be universally appropriate; and (3) their justification is subjective. While some of the values promoted by NGO advocates may be instrumental, their range and depth can complicate or render impossible their operationalization, especially when they are justified exclusively on moral grounds. The lofty combination of normative requirements as espoused in partnership principles may be impossible to achieve, whether due to organizational or political constraints. As a consequence, it may be more appropriate to describe partnership practice on a relative scale, referring to the extent to which an interorganizational relationship is operating like a partnership. Henceforth, unless otherwise noted the term *partnership* refers to this relative practice.

Defining Dimensions of Partnership

Literature and experience combine to suggest two relevant dimensions for defining partnerships. Mutuality encompasses the spirit of partnership principles; and organization identity captures the rationale for selecting particular partners, and its maintenance is the basis of partnership's value-added.

Mutuality.   Mutuality can be distinguished as horizontal, as opposed to hierarchical, coordination and accountability and equality in decisionmaking, rather than the domination of one or more partners. Additional principles include jointly agreed purpose and values and mutual trust and respect. Mutuality refers to mutual dependence and entails respective rights and responsibilities of each actor to the others (see Kellner and Thackray 1999). These rights and responsibilities seek to maximize benefits for each party, subject to limits posed by the expediency of meeting joint objectives. Embedded in mutuality are a strong commitment to partnership goals and objectives and an assumption that these joint objectives are consistent and supportive of each partner organization's mission and objectives. In defining mutuality in the context of intersectoral partnerships, James Austin adds "value balance." When partners generally benefit equally from their relationship, partnerships tend to be more enduring (Austin 2000) and high performing (Kanter 1994).

Mutuality also refers to interdependence, as opposed to sequential dependence. This implies a greater degree of process integration in the joint value to be produced by a partnership, and it contrasts with simpler models of supplier or production contracting. Relative integration necessitates more frequent interaction, communication, and decisionmaking, both formal and ad hoc, throughout the stages of program design, implementation, and evaluation. Mutuality means that all partners have an opportunity to influence their shared objectives, processes, outcomes, and evaluation.

Organization identity.   Organization identity generally refers to that which is distinctive and enduring in a particular organization. The creation and maintenance of organization identity is essential to long-term success. Successful organizations do not maintain organizational systems, processes, and strategies as much as they maintain continuity of core beliefs and values across time and contexts (Gioia, Schultz, and Korley 2000). In fact, successful organizations change in response to turbulent environments precisely in order to maintain their identity over time (Gagliardi 1986). This adaptability can lead to organizations entering into partnerships to pursue their missions more effectively. The key for maintaining organization identity is to maintain core values and constituencies.

Organization identity can be examined at two levels. First, *the maintenance of organization identity is the extent to which an organization remains consistent and committed to its mission, core values, and constituencies.* This includes accountability and responsiveness. Constituencies are distinguished from stakeholders more generally. The most important stakeholders are those who possess power, legitimacy, and urgency (Mitchell, Angle, and Wood 1997). Those stakeholders with the most immediate access to power and urgency are often partner organizations who control important resources or may provide access to important opportunities. With respect to organization identity, the emphasis is on stakeholders with legitimacy. Legitimate stakeholders are the constituents for the value that the partner organization currently produces. They may be beneficiaries, individual contributors, staff, or other supporting organizations. These are the stakeholders with whom the organization has an implicit contract to provide value in accordance with its mission and core values.

Second, from a broader institutional view, *organization identity refers to the maintenance of characteristics—particularly comparative advantages—reflective of the sector or organizational type from which the organization originates.* This aspect of organization identity is related to the selection of different organizational partners. Presumably a partner is selected on the basis both of its expertise and mission as an individual organization and of those characteristics deriving from its nature as a particular sectoral organization. The most common exception is when government or donors seeking efficient service deliverers contract with nonprofits when they could have as easily contracted with a private commercial entity. Besides being central to partnership effectiveness, the maintenance of organization identity is necessary to partner commitment (Huxham 1993) and sustainability (Frumkin and Andre-Clark 2000).

Partnership's Value-Added

While the rationale for a partnership approach may be apparent, actors too often engage and initiate partners without considering the changes in their own behavior necessary to make partnerships effective. Partnership is a strategic option that produces benefits commensurate with risks and investments. Actors unwilling to take those risks tend to pursue partnership benefits through conventional approaches (e.g., contracts) under a new label; most interorganizational relationships are not partnerships. While the partners may in fact benefit from these relationships, chances are that the benefits are not equally shared; damage to actors' organization identity may ensue; or, at a minimum, the opportunities and advantages afforded by a partnership approach are lost. In order to overcome the challenges to a partnership's operationalization, and deepen the realization of its principles, actors must be convinced of partnership's value-added.

Partnership's value-added is rooted in its defining dimensions. Organization identity is the impetus for initiating a partnership strategy. Partnerships with other actors are pursued because these actors have something unique to offer, whether resources, skills, relationships, or consent. If organization identity is lost, comparative advantages are also lost; the organization loses legitimacy in the eyes of its defined constituencies, and its effectiveness wanes. Absorption, co-optation, bureaucratic creep, or the infiltration of one organizational culture into another can all lead to a diminished capacity of a partner to maximize its contribution in the longer run. Without organization identity, there is no longer a strong rationale to justify the extra effort required for a partnership.

Mutuality can reinforce organization identity.[7] The opportunity to participate in a partnership and influence it equally means that each actor can more easily protect its organization identity, and hence the efficiency, effectiveness, and synergistic rewards of the partnership. At the outset, no single organization can understand the implications of its or the partnership's actions for members' organization identity. Mutuality at least affords partner organizations the opportunity to consider and explain these implications and potentially defend their distinctive advantages, skills, and legitimacy— all of which are necessary for the partnership's success. By maintaining organization identity organizations can enter into more than one partnership.

From a normative perspective, mutuality implies fairness and equity, which maximize responsiveness to each actor's constituencies and organizational needs. From a pragmatic perspective, mutuality affords opportunities for partner organizations to contribute their skills and other advantages as needed. With mutuality, these partners can more easily raise new ideas and propose new, more effective approaches. Actors know when their own advantages and potential contributions may be most relevant. Mutuality enables partners to contribute to the partnership with fewer constraints (e.g., approvals, scrutiny, regulation, and other forms of interference) and greater legitimacy. In addition, when each actor has agreed to them and feels a sense of ownership, mutuality can help to ensure acceptance of the partnership's policies and procedures and to ease their implementation.

Partnership: An End or a Means?

Partnerships represent both an end and a means. As an end, partnership is the expression of values. NGO advocates are the primary promoters of this perspective.[8] These advocates critique donor and government practices, urging a larger role for NGOs and civil society, and recommend that partnerships should seek to maximize equity and inclusiveness. In a democratic fashion partnerships should mobilize, legitimate, and engage all parties potentially affected by or contributing to a particular development effort. Partnership, these advocates argue, is the most ethically appropriate approach to sustainable development. This perspective encompasses the normative view of participation and empowerment and promotes partnership values and principles of mutual influence, equality, and reciprocal accountability.

Partnership's values are also instrumental. As promoted in the strategic management literature, these values inform program design and implementation, and they promote flexibility and responsiveness to dynamic environments.[9] Incorporating values into development efforts can provide opportunities for capacity building, empowerment, and local ownership, all of which are essential to self-reliance and sustainability. Decisions about partnership structure and management have normative implications because they embody values. These values can contribute to efficiency and effectiveness.

As a means, partnership may be instrumental in meeting other objectives, such as efficiency and effectiveness. When needs require multiorganizational response, complexity increases substantially. No one organization is in a position to understand all the intricacies and interdependencies of international development challenges or to command the necessary information, skills, and relationships to address them. Partnership is a rational and highly appropriate response to this complexity. Its effectiveness depends on each partner organization recognizing the bounds of its own rationality and drawing on its partners according to their strengths.

Partnership is driven both by normative values and for its instrumental value. These perspectives are not necessarily contradictory. The perspective here emphasizes the pragmatic view. First, the normative perspective may be unrealistic from an operational, resource, or political perspective when its aims reach beyond the practical advantages of partnership. Second, the normative perspective can also be promoted to the advantage of one actor or stakeholder (typically the civil society actors or for public relations purposes), potentially at the expense of the others (contradicting the general spirit of partnership). Third, partnership's added effort and risk must be justified in order for more powerful organizations to forfeit power, and these organizations are typically ones that value efficiency and effectiveness and are driven by economic outcomes rather than normative ones.

Lessons for Managing Partnerships

The following lessons point to the instrumentality of values and various rationales for their promotion in the partnership context. Generally, they suggest three responses to resolving partnership challenges: (1) incentives and sanctions to appeal to the self-interest of the parties, including instrumental rationality; (2) the cultivation of a values base for partnership work and the promotion of moral incentives; and (3) a careful combination of formal and informal structure and processes. Additional lessons for managing partnerships follow.[10]

Partnership as a Learning Organization

The most successful organizations tap people's capacity for learning and commitment at all levels of the organization. Individuals working in learning organizations are characterized by personal mastery, that is, high skill proficiency, as well as a personal vision that relates directly to their work within the organization. Such individuals will be intensely committed, yet objective and patient in pragmatically pursuing their personal and organizational vision. These individuals, as well as the organization as a whole, are outward looking rather than internally focused. Learning organizations are built on systems thinking that explicitly acknowledges interdependencies. Finally, learning organizations successfully build a shared vision among their employees, in part through team learning, or "thinking together" (Senge 1990; see also Bauman, Jackson, and Laurence 1997). The learning organization model's outward orientation is frequently the means by which partnership needs and opportunities are identified and pursued. Its systems thinking further reinforces acknowledging the importance of other actors and interdependencies.

Informal Processes

Particularly in complex environments, responsiveness, problem solving, and motivation require informal structures and processes. Informal organization is an effective and least-cost means to coordinate multiorganizational systems (Chisholm 1989). Formal systems often create gaps between the formal authority to make decisions and the capacity to do so. Overlooked is the need for specific technical information, as well as the understanding of relevant contexts, in order to make effective decisions. Coordination of multiorganizational systems can be achieved through a system of informal channels, behavioral norms, and agreements. These mechanisms often develop as needed, deriving from everyday processes of mutual adjustment. Nevertheless, an explicit recognition and cultivation of informal mechanisms may be necessary, both to counteract the perception that control and formalization are needed in order to coordinate projects and to avert the general penchant (particularly in complex environments) to centralize systems. These informal mechanisms lay the foundation for more formal processes of coordination, as they help cultivate consensus about how best to coordinate and meet shared objectives. As the informal mechanisms emerge, consensus, mutual understanding, and trust are built through trial and error. This process and the resulting consensus are particularly important to multiorganizational systems characterized by highly diverse organizational members, who may share a history of conflict or distrust.

Informal mechanisms enable complex multiorganizational systems to respond to needs and environmental changes in the most efficient way. Accordingly, participation in decisionmaking and implementation is not predetermined by an organizational chart or standard operating procedures, specified in advance and based on limited information and understanding. Rather, it is determined by the need at hand and the skills and resources available. Informal organization allows for autonomy of participating organizations and can thus contribute to flexibility and representativeness. These are often eliminated or, at best, diminished under more formal arrangements and consolidation.

Governance Mechanisms: The Importance of Culture

Much of this informal organization is represented by shared behavioral norms. In essence, these represent the culture governance mechanism. Governance mechanism refers to the approach and enforceability of rules and associated desired behavior. Governance requires recourse in the event that rules are broken or expectations are not met. Governance mechanisms include market, bureaucratic, or culture approaches, or some combination of all three.[11] The most effective organizations combine these three mechanisms (see, for example, Coston 1998b; Peters 1998). However, culture mechanisms are often undervalued. Under these mechanisms, enforcement and compliance are based on trust, and expectations are rooted in a sense of belonging to the team. Effective partnerships incorporate these mechanisms into partnership design and management through the creation and promotion of a partnership identity and an associated organizational culture with incentive systems specific to the partnership's objectives and values.

Values, Commitment, and Organization Citizenship Behavior

Individuals pursue not only pleasure and utility but also morality.[12] Consequent motivators include values, personal moral standards, social obligations, and normative rules. Such motivators are consistent with informal and culture mechanisms, and they suggest the need for a more explicit recognition of the values dimension of partnership work. The kind of personal mastery promoted by the learning organization model also presumes that individuals will place the greater good of the organizational effort above their own self-interest, or at least work to align these objectives.

Commitment and the concept of organization citizenship behavior further reinforce these values dimensions and suggest ways to operationalize them. Chris Argyris (2000) distinguishes external commitment (activated by management policies and practices that enable employees to do their job) from internal commitment (activated because completing a job is intrinsically rewarding). Internal commitment is not possible when objectives, goals, and approaches are defined for the employee. Internal commitment supports greater participation and a sense of employee ownership within organizations. While there are practical limits to participation, it can be extended to at least a core group of employees and partner organization representatives. Other mechanisms to promote internal commitment include the cultivation of a partnership identity and associated organization culture that builds upon values and related incentive systems, as above.

Organization commitment is an attitude, while organization citizenship behavior (OCB) is an action (Organ 1990). OCB refers to extra-role behavior that goes beyond explicit instructions or requirements for the good of the organization. OCB results first from individuals' disposition; and, second, from the organizational context. In order to sustain individuals' propensity to engage in OCB, they must perceive the organization's objectives as worthy of effort and the organization context and management as fair. This analytic perspective supports an emphasis on values within partnerships, to recruit and inspire individuals with an OCB disposition. It further suggests incorporating transparency and mutual accountability to support a shared perception of fairness.

The Dynamic Nature of Partnership

Partnership requires different governance mechanisms at each stage. According to Vivien Lowndes and Chris Skelcher (1998), culture mechanisms are most appropriate to the prepartnership or initiation stage, where informality, flexibility, and trust are key. Bureaucratic mechanisms are necessary at the creation and consolidation stage of partnership, where structures and process are formalized through sometimes binding agreements. Market mechanisms support the contracting relationships of the implementation or program delivery stage, with culture mechanisms supporting the generation of ideas, feedback, management, and expenditure decisions. Culture mechanisms serve to maintain commitment, community involvement, and staff employment at the termination stage.

These stages take place in a dynamic environment where power relations are continuously shifting, alternately stimulating cooperation and competition, trust and defensiveness. Much of the competition and defensiveness derives from resource dependency, necessitating a careful approach to financing that is explicit enough to preempt conflict, yet flexible enough to encourage collaboration and sharing. The most vulnerable points to conflict are found at the convergence of different governance mechanisms. These vulnerabilities require both "rational" instrumental processes—such as assigned roles and responsibilities, standard operating procedures, and reporting requirements—and "nonrational" integration processes—such as organization culture, rituals and non-task-oriented discourses (Machado and Burns 1998).

Summary of the Analytic Perspective

Decisions regarding how to structure and manage partnerships are never value-neutral. The democratic values promoted with partnership approaches can serve both normative and pragmatic ends. The most effective partnerships will likely be structured and managed based on the learning organization model, where interdependencies are explicitly acknowledged and rationally addressed through a reliance on each partner's comparative advantage and individuals are motivated through values, a cultivated connection between personal vision and partnership objectives, and psychological and social incentives. Partnership structure should incorporate and even emphasize (1) informal structure and processes as well as formal ones, including a partnership identity and associated organization culture; (2) culture governance mechanisms, as well as market and bureaucratic mechanisms, with flexibility to adjust their relative balance as the partnership evolves; (3) both moral and material incentives; and (4) transparency and accountability to support perceptions of fairness.

Overview

The following chapters discuss the context of partnership work, providing a framework for assessing environmental hostility; describe the actors in partnerships, and the various contributions and challenges associated with partnering with them, providing selection criteria for addressing these; and identify the trade-off decisions and strategy influences for partnership design, maintenance, and evaluation. Three case examples are then developed: the Barani Area Development Project in Pakistan; INMED's *Healthy Children, Healthy Futures* program in Brazil; and the World Commission on Dams. Each illustrates a different type of partnership, with correspondingly varied objectives and approaches. These include partnerships for public service, corporate social responsibility, and conflict resolution. The three cases vary in scope (local, provincial, and international), participants (governments, NGOs, donors, and the private sector), and objectives (improved public services and community empowerment, the private provision of public goods, and conflict resolution). The concluding chapter reviews the book's findings, confirms partnership's increasing relevance in a globalized world, and discusses broader implications for future partnership work.

Notes

1. Under the New Policy Agenda, for example, donors look to nongovernmental organizations (NGOs) as implementers of donor-driven development policy, thereby bypassing government and co-opting NGOs, often destroying their organization identity and comparative advantages in the process (Hulme and Edwards 1997a; see also Beckmann 1991). This policy erodes the sovereignty of poorer governments and heightens tension between them and NGOs, in effect working against good governance and the strengthening of civil society (Fowler 1992, 1997).

2. Some research supports partnership's contribution to improved performance (see, for example, Ellinger, Keller, and Ellinger 2000). There are also exceptions among private-sector alliances, where increased efficiencies can be quantified (see Shah and Singh 2001).

3. For example, a recent report of the Rockefeller Brothers Fund's Global Interdependence Initiative calls for a retooling of traditional assistance organizations and the exploration of new mechanisms of cooperative engagement (Mazur and Sechler 1997).

4. See, for example, ACVFA 1997; Alexander n.d.; Nelson 1996; Overseas Development Council and Synergos Institute 1995; UN 1998; Watanabe 1998; and World Bank 1996, 1997.

5. Even in the private sector, partnership is considered "the buzzword of the 1990s" (Woodward 1994) and "one of the most overused and abused terms" (Pollack 1995).

6. USAID refers to international development NGOs as private voluntary organizations (PVOs).

7. Mutuality's reinforcement of organization identity is not guaranteed. Sarah Lister's (2000) work on power relations in partnership work implies that mutuality can also afford opportunities to influence needs, perceptions, and ultimately behavior, which may compromise organization identity in the long run.

8. See, for example, Garilao 1987; Van der Heijden 1987; Malena 1995; Fowler 1995b, 1999; Bush 1992; and Smillie 1995.

9. See, for example, Brinkerhoff 1991, 1997; and Goldsmith 1996.

10. These are taken from collective action theory. In particular, see Olson 1965; Etzioni 1991; Mansbridge 1990; Frank 1990; and Börzel 1998.

11. See Ouchi 1979, 1980. Bureaucracy here should not be confused with structure; rather, it refers to an approach for influencing behavior through established rules and procedures. These governance mechanisms have also been referred to as price, authority, and trust (Bradach and Eccles 1991).

12. See, for example, Etzioni 1988, 1991; Frank 1990; and Scott 1995.

2

Opportunities and Constraints in the Partnership Environment

Environmental factors influence the extent to which partnership is desirable or feasible. In development contexts there are many factors and actors at play at various levels, each of which affects the others to greater or lesser degrees. Interdependence between the environment and an institution—in this case a partnership—and among different actors or stakeholders exists regardless of whether or not it is formally recognized and addressed. This chapter reviews the environmental circumstances that can influence partnership effectiveness and ease of implementation, and identifies specific features that contribute directly or indirectly to environmental hostility.[1]

The partnership environment consists of both the broader development context and the immediate partnership environment. The scope and location of a particular partnership determine the parameters of both. The broader context represents those external conditions, incentives, and policies that indirectly influence the partnership's systems, operating costs, and effectiveness. The immediate partnership environment directly affects the inputs, processes, and outputs of partnership systems. Factors that directly contribute to environmental hostility can also determine the feasibility of partnership initiation and design.

Factors in the broader context that are conducive to partnership may be rare in any development context and are usually beyond the scope of any one partnership to create. Many of these factors have been identified and targeted in donor strategies. In the more immediate partnership context, participating organizations may have greater opportunities to influence conducive factors, whether this means cultivating them in preparation for or during implementation of partnership work or in negotiating exceptions. Some factors specific to a partnership can be controlled somewhat through partnership design and management.

Indirect Environmental Influences

Indirect factors entail governance issues and legal frameworks, institutional dynamics, and general environmental characteristics. A number of these factors influence environmental hostility in the broader context of partnership work (Figure 2.1).

Governance

Countries that have embraced the new governance model (see Coston 1998b), which incorporates democratic governance and a rationalized government, provide a more conducive environment for partnerships. Democratic governance, the rationalization of government, and decentralization strengthen various sectors, enhance social capital, and, in some instances, determine the will to partner. For example, in Latin America representative democracy has expanded; consequently, the participation of citizens and civil society is recognized as both a means and an end of development work. Decentralization has created the potential for both partnerships and government partners at the local level. Economic reforms have enabled the emergence of a new, autonomous private sector (see Fiszbein and Lowden 1998). In short, adoption of the new governance model in Latin America has created space, incentives, and capacity for partnerships.

Democratic governance emphasizes transparency, accountability, and responsiveness. Effective partnership work requires transparency, and a democratic culture can reinforce its expectation and practice. Although rare in most developing countries, accountable and responsive government legitimizes the role of different actors in development decisionmaking and affords recourse in the event that agreements are violated. This type of governance enables civil society and the private sector to engage in advocacy, lobbying, and mobilizing demand for goods, services, and policy. These roles bring civil society and private-sector actors into contact with government as legitimate development actors and potential partners. Since participation is often legislated under democratic governance, these actors are further legitimized and empowered. In the absence of democratic governance, the existence and enforcement of the rule of law can be questionable, undermining the confidence needed to invest in development processes; there are no checks on corruption; and actors outside of government may not be viewed as legitimate actors, may be persecuted for their efforts, and will likely have minimal access to policymakers.

Progress toward the rationalization of the state can best be measured according to the extent to which the various sectors work together, or at least interact, and government recognizes the importance of the other sectors and provides appropriate legal frameworks to support their work. A

Figure 2.1   Factors Influencing Environmental Hostility:
The Broader Partnership Context

	Factors Contributing to Low Hostility in the Environment	Factors Contributing to High Hostility in the Environment
Democratic governance	Transparency, accountability, and responsiveness to citizens. Civil society and private-sector actors are recognized as legitimate development actors.	Questionable rule of law, corruption, minimal access to policymakers.
Rational government	Existing tradition of government working with other sectors. Other sectors are viewed as legitimate deliverers of public goods and services.	Resistance to institutional pluralism. Government continues to control, regulate, and produce public services without cooperating with other sectors. Possible competition, rivalry, or repression of other actors' activities.
Decentralization	Governance authority devolved to those closest to the issues being addressed. Potentially greater flexibility and local government capacity to engage with other development actors.	Limited access to government actors with decisionmaking authority. Government partners are limited in their ability to partner or in their understanding of the local context. Potentially greater uncertainty of government commitment and follow-through.
Legal frameworks	Legal frameworks legitimize the participation and facilitate the work of the private sector and civil society in development and governance.	Legal frameworks set limits on private-sector and civil society activities and revenue generation and/or are potentially onerous in terms of administrative burden and associated costs.
Institutional capacity and linkage	Each sector has an established record of capacity in meeting development objectives. Bridging mechanisms between the sectors exist.	One or more of the sectors exhibits limited capacity. Absence of bridging mechanisms between the sectors.
Stability	Economic, political, and sociocultural environments are relatively stable.	Economic, political, and sociocultural environments are unstable.
Flexibility	Economic, political, and sociocultural features permit and/or support systems change.	Economic, political, and sociocultural features do not permit and/or support systems change.
Artificiality	Low levels of distortion within economic, political, and sociocultural dimensions.	High levels of distortion within economic, political, and sociocultural dimensions.

rationalized state acknowledges the comparative advantages of other sectors or actors and seeks to work with them. Such states are willing to work with other sectors and will likely consider those relationship types that will prove most effective and efficient. Partnership promoters are more likely to find ready listeners within such governments. Especially under these circumstances, donors can facilitate the interaction between NGOs and governments by including NGOs in the design, planning, and monitoring of development projects (Box 2.1). Alternatively, government may continue to control, regulate, and/or produce public goods and services without acknowledging the potential contribution of other sectors. Government may view the activities of other actors as competitive or threatening, resulting in inefficiency and potential overregulation or suppression. Resistance to institutional pluralism produces hostilities and distrust that can make partnership negotiation prohibitive or rivalrous, where governments may be reluctant or refuse to follow through on partnership agreements.

Decentralization is essential to enhancing not just efficiency and effectiveness but also participation and responsiveness. Decentralization is conducive to partnership work when it entails administrative, financial, and political dimensions, corresponding to a transfer of functional responsibility, access to resources, and accountability (Van Sant 1996). Administrative decentralization enables those governments closest to the needs to be addressed to determine priority projects, goods and services, and approaches. Financial decentralization facilitates the selection and implementation of those projects and can present opportunities for local governments to support partnerships financially. Both administratively and financially, decentralization can create potential partners and significantly enhance their capacity to engage in partnership work. Political decentralization and its corresponding accountability is particularly conducive to partnership work as it transfers the accountability of local officials from an upward

---

Box 2.1   Family Group Practice Associations in Central Asia

In Kazakhstan and Kyrgyzstan, government and society are slowly beginning to experiment with private associations and NGOs for support and provision of health services (D. Brinkerhoff 2002). Privatization and a diminished role for the state opened space for experimentation. Family Group Practice Associations (FGPAs) are supporting family group practices in service delivery, in addition to implementing some regulatory and quality assurance and monitoring functions. However, the fledgling FGPAs are cautious in pursuing donor intentions of advocacy, and a legacy of deference to central government persists. The legitimacy of truly independent, representative FGPAs remains to be seen.

direction, toward the center, to one that is outward to citizens and service customers. This enhances both the incentives for transparent and accountable partnership work and the likelihood that local governments would entertain partnership options. Decentralization grants local governments flexibility, affording opportunities to recognize and incorporate local knowledge and expertise and to pursue cost savings and effectiveness enhancement through various forms of privatization. These benefits of decentralization depend on a country's historical and sociopolitical context (Box 2.2). In some instances, decentralization can contribute to the capture of governance processes and outcomes by local elites (see Migdal 1988; see also Frischtak 1994).

Under centralized systems, development actors (especially local ones) will have difficulty accessing government decisionmakers, and those decisionmakers may not readily understand or prioritize local needs and feasible approaches to addressing them. Partnership initiatives at the local level will also require additional layers of approval and face greater uncertainties in government follow-through, owing to shifting political climates and competing priorities and interests. Limited local government responsiveness and capacity provide fewer options for recourse in the event that government partners breach their partnership agreements.

A rational government implies acceptance of institutional pluralism at a minimum. Governments that are relatively rationalized also provide legal frameworks to support and facilitate the activities of other development actors, or at least to remove bottlenecks to their work. There are many studies and development initiatives concerning appropriate legal frameworks

---

Box 2.2   The Chalatenango Environmental Committee, El Salvador

In El Salvador, the Chalatenango Environmental Committee (CACH) assembles local government and nongovernmental agencies for the purpose of promoting environmentally sustainable development in the Chalatenango Department (FUNDE 1997). Decentralization has empowered local government agencies to participate in and contribute to the partnership, while legitimizing the activities of nongovernmental members. Many of these NGOs were, until recently, the only environmental actors in the half of the department that was divided by the civil war.

CACH's work has been greatly complicated by the absence of national environmental policies, which could provide incentives, enforcement, and general guidelines to support its efforts. However, the current NGO legal framework enabled CACH to operate without formal legalization. While there is some disagreement on the merits of this structure, those who favor CACH's flexible approach to date count this unencumbered structure as an important asset.

for sustainable development (see, for example, USAID 1997). The legal frameworks supporting an enabling environment typically include the freedoms of speech, press, assembly, and association, as well as laws and regulations specific to the NGO and business sectors (see, for example, International Center for Not-for-Profit Law 1997). These laws and regulations can impose or remove operating costs related to income and duty taxes, limits on revenue generation, and administrative costs for initial registration and regulation compliance.

Legal frameworks specific to particular institutional or substantive sectors may be nonexistent or repressive (as in Box 2.2). NGO legal frameworks have been particularly problematic in many developing countries, as NGOs are a new phenomenon for many governments emerging from socialism, and these governments may perceive such institutional actors, whose very name implies an antigovernment stance, as a threat. Legal frameworks can prevent development activities altogether by either outlawing them or creating overly onerous administrative and financial requirements. Indirectly, legal frameworks can impose additional operating costs on partnerships, influence opportunities for interorganizational alliances, and determine the range and potential capacity of partner organizations.

Institutional Capacity

Existing capacity, an established track record of meeting development objectives, and institutional linkages among the sectors can demonstrate the potential for partnerships and inspire confidence in their potential effectiveness. Capacity and experience can determine the range of potential partners from which to choose and the type and extent of resources that can be applied to partnership objectives. Experience with partnership work can also provide examples and lessons. Potential partners can judge the potential comparative advantages of each sector based on their capacity and experience, informing a rational division of labor, and can articulate partnership motivators based on these perceived advantages.

The established legitimacy of the various sectors can inspire the confidence needed to take the risks and absorb the costs of partnership work. Partners are more willing to take risks when they know the other sectors are capable of actualizing particular comparative advantages and have a track record of following through on similar agreements (Box 2.3). Existing bridging mechanisms represent established social capital, an important resource demonstrating intersectoral trust and cooperation.

Generally, the stronger the state, the stronger the NGO sector tends to be (Annis 1987; Bebbington and Riddell 1997). Additional factors indicating the strength of an NGO sector include NGO independence and diversity; representativeness; participation in governance and development, either

---

Box 2.3   The Malawi Social Action Fund

The Malawi Social Action Fund incorporates a sponsored subproject (SSP) designed to address the social needs of the most vulnerable groups in Malawi (orphans, street children, the handicapped, people with HIV/AIDS, and the elderly). Given these specialized needs, the SSP partners with NGOs already working with these groups. In doing so, it seeks to leverage their expertise, information, and contacts, by providing funding, capacity building, and sectoral support to further enhance their work and scope (Da Silva 1998; Coston 1999).

---

independently or with other actors; access to diverse funding sources; opportunities for capacity building; and the existence of umbrella organizations.

Government capacity entails not only the capacity to develop policy (including legal frameworks) but also the capacity to enforce it (rule of law). In addition, the effectiveness of local government partners depends on the resources and authority they wield (see Box 2.2). Government capacity is also reflected in the perceived legitimacy and amount of corruption in the government; the existence of effective career structures and competent staff in the civil service; frequency of staff turnover; and the degree of jealousy between government and officials from the private and NGO sectors (see Clark 1997; Fiszbein and Lowden 1998).

Private-sector capacity refers to the strength (resources, market share, profit) and diversity (goods and services provided, geographic dispersion) of private-sector actors, as well as the linkages between them and other institutional actors. Strength and diversity determine the potential resources that can be applied to partnership objectives. Local private-sector actors with links to multinational corporations can bring additional resources and attention to partnership efforts. Private-sector linkages to government actors can also be beneficial as long as they are not associated with patronage systems that compete with partnership objectives. An existing tradition of corporate philanthropy and foundations can represent a willingness to entertain partnership possibilities and a track record that will inspire confidence in other partners (Box 2.4).

In the absence of high-capacity sectors and bridging mechanisms between them, partnerships take greater risks in terms of feasibility and operating costs. Working with actors with limited capacity and little to no track record requires a much more extensive trial-and-error process with greater investments in capacity enhancement. Furthermore, a lack of bridging mechanisms may signal broad distrust among the sectors, possibly even hostility. Partnership promoters will not have access to bridging mechanisms to initiate dialogues regarding the potential for partnership or for exploring the range of potential partners available (Box 2.5).

General Environmental Characteristics

Environmental stability affords greater certainty in establishing and maintaining partnership structures and processes. While adjustments will always be necessary in response to changes in the environment, stable environments imply that these changes will be less severe and less frequent. For example, routine enforcement of legal frameworks can contribute to environmental stability as these frameworks provide certainty regarding the

---

Box 2.4   Acesita in Brazil

Corporate philanthropy is on the rise in Brazil, as state-owned enterprises privatize, devolve themselves of public-service responsibilities, and subsequently recognize the need to take some action to restore selected services and support other actors in these efforts. Like most state-owned enterprises, Acesita (Itabira Special Steels Company) had a long tradition of social development (Fischer and Faria 1999). Following privatization in 1992, Acesita established the Acesita Foundation for Social Development, with the aim to promote regional development. The foundation built upon Acesita's previous experience in social development but also needed to adapt to a private-sector, corporate philanthropy model, one that would support the mission of Acesita itself. This entailed identifying key areas of support (education, culture, community action, and the environment), cultivating partnerships, and building relations with targeted community members and government officials.

Box 2.5   The Grassroots Initiative Project, Mali

A lack of bridging mechanisms may signal a role for donors in initiating dialogues and facilitating relationships. In the World Bank's Grassroots Initiative Project in Mali, the Bank had to intervene on several occasions to facilitate dialogue between the government and NGO sectors for more effective service provision at the grassroots level (De Leva 1998). The project aimed to maximize resources, share knowledge and skills, build capacity, and reach poor communities more effectively. The initial distrust among the sectors required multiple meetings and negotiations. NGOs boycotted the first planning meeting, organized by the World Bank, questioning the Bank's role as convenor. After much negotiation and a participatory approach to meeting planning, the Bank facilitated the formation of a joint government-NGO Steering Committee and the production of a jointly developed Manual of Procedures to inform the day-to-day multisectoral implementation.

legality and consequences of partnership activities. The influence of democratic governance on environmental stability is inconclusive. On the one hand, democratic governance implies enforcement of the rule of law and accountability and recourse if corruption exists or there are deviations in the application of the law. On the other hand, democratic governance entails access to and influence on policymakers by special interests and elections, which can rapidly change the rules of the game.

Environmental flexibility determines the ability of actors to establish and pursue partnerships. It represents the extent to which experimenting with new approaches and institutional arrangements is culturally and politically acceptable. Environmental flexibility enables partners to select the most feasible and efficient options for design and implementation. It also determines the ease with which new administrative procedures or exceptions to existing ones can be negotiated (Box 2.6). Ideally, decentralization can provide flexibility to local government to recognize the potential for, support, and directly engage in partnerships. Rigidity in the environment can impose costs for compliance with sociocultural or political norms, prevent partnerships from responding to needs and environmental changes in the most rational way, and potentially divert scarce resources to the point where the benefits no longer justify the costs.

Artificiality represents the extent to which resources outside the immediate environment are available. Such resources distort the actual costs of partnership initiation and implementation, and its independent feasibility. Subsidies for inputs make partnerships vulnerable to their removal. Subsidies can come from government, but artificiality most often derives from donor interventions. When these distortions are not the result of specific partner relationships and agreements, partners are more limited in influencing their continuation and may not even recognize the resulting vulnerability they face. Artificiality can encourage overexpansion and

---

Box 2.6   Civil Society Program, USAID South Africa

In the continuing postapartheid transition, South Africa has been characterized by a flexible environment. This environment enabled the USAID Mission to South Africa to introduce a Civil Society Program design process, which emphasized learning and participation (USAID/SA 1999a, 1999b). The process targeted options and support for formulating partnerships between the public, NGO, and private sectors for public service delivery and quality-of-life improvements. The process was highly participatory and inclusive, with each sector committed to supporting its aims, expressing willingness to participate in and eventually adapt its procedures to accommodate partnership efforts.

external dependency. All donor interventions create artificial systems, though the degree of artificiality may vary. For example, interventions may range from seed grants to the creation of a separate project implementation unit. Distortion results when external funding delinks supply from demand, undermining local ownership and efficient pricing. It also occurs when systems are created that bypass indigenous arrangements, again undermining local ownership and distorting incentives. Donors can also introduce policy distortions. Donors provide incentives for government to become more open, transparent, and supportive of other development actors. Under such circumstances, partnership actors can be overconfident in the goodwill of government actors to follow through on partnership agreements if these incentives are removed (see Box 2.1).

Direct Environmental Influences

Additional features specific to particular partnerships more directly influence environmental hostility. These include factors related to involved actors, both individuals and organizations; the specific partnership objective; stakeholders; and general contextual features (Figure 2.2).

Partnership Actors

The specific partnership environment may present significant opportunities for effective partnership because of the possibility of dynamic, entrepreneurial, and potentially charismatic personalities with the capacity to champion the partnership effort. Championing capacity entails not only communication, negotiation, and organizational skills but also perceived legitimacy among potential partners and stakeholders (Box 2.7). The immediate context may also present particularly salient drivers to inspire such individuals to champion partnership approaches. For example, in a partnership whose objective is conflict resolution, those parties who are incurring the greatest losses may be more likely to promote and invest in the partnership process. The strength of the incentives and the dynamism, commitment, and capacity of the champion will influence the partnership initiation and design process, the extent to which partners and individuals within these organizations embrace and support the partnership, and ultimately its maintenance and effectiveness.

Preexisting linkages and relationships provide immediate opportunities to explore the potential for partnership among actors; they facilitate the identification of common problems and joint solutions. Existing bridging mechanisms can be used to initiate and design the partnership and to resolve conflicts once the partnership is established (Box 2.8). In addition, these linkages represent social capital in the form of trust among potential

**Figure 2.2   Factors Influencing Environmental Hostility:
The Immediate Partnership Environment**

	Factors Contributing to Low Hostility in the Environment	Factors Contributing to High Hostility in the Environment
Partnership champions	Dynamic, entrepreneurial, and potentially charismatic actors: • Exist and • Recognize strong drivers for themselves individually and/or for their organizational objectives and • Choose and have the capacity to champion and continuously promote the partnership within partner organizations, among partners, and with potential partnership stakeholders.	Dynamic, entrepreneurial, and potentially charismatic actors: • Do not exist or • Do not recognize sufficient drivers for themselves individually and/or for their organizational objectives or • Choose not to or lack the capacity to champion and continuously promote the partnership within partner organizations, among partners, and with potential partnership stakeholders.
Institutional linkage	Preexistence of strong and supportive relationships among partners; partners know and understand each other's mission and track record.	Partners have no previous experience relating or working together and are unfamiliar with each other or have had negative experiences interacting or working together in the past.
Partner organizations	Organizations with identified comparative advantages: • Exist. • Have the capacity to fulfill the requirements of the partnership. • Have a strong organization identity. • Do not have constituents or stakeholders whose interests may conflict with partnership objectives. • Have an existing positive relationship with targeted stakeholders and are viewed as legitimate actors. • Are interested and available to partner, recognizing strong drivers to participate in the partnership. • Have agreement among organization members regarding partnership participation and vision. • Share a common vision (with other potential partners) for the partnership objective. • Are compatible with other partner organizations in terms of corporate values and approaches.	Organizations with identified comparative advantages: • Need to be created. • Do not have high capacity to fulfill the administrative and technical requirements of the partnership. Capacity building is necessary. • Do not have a clearly defined mission, stakeholders, or understanding of their comparative advantages. • Have constituents or stakeholders whose interests may conflict with partnership objectives. • Have no previous relationship with targeted stakeholders and/or are not viewed as legitimate actors. • Require convincing regarding the merits of partnership and the need to make it a high priority. There is a need to identify and articulate partnership drivers. • Lack agreement within their organization regarding partnership participation and mission. • Have contradictory priorities and vision for the partnership. Additional accountability mechanisms may be required.

(continues)

Figure 2.2   Continued

	Factors Contributing to Low Hostility in the Environment	Factors Contributing to High Hostility in the Environment
		• Have inhibiting contradictions or conflicts with other partner organizations with respect to values and approaches.
Partnership objective	Minimal challenges to vested interests.	Challenging to entrenched vested interests and patronage systems.
	Implications for fewer government agencies.	Entails working with multiple government agencies.
	Partnership outcomes will be directly felt at the local level and can be readily identified.	Partnership outcomes will have an indirect impact on local quality of life; attribution is difficult and impacts are difficult to identify.
	Ready demand for the good or service to be produced.	Low level of demand for good or service; demand creation is necessary.
Partnership stakeholders	Relatively homogeneous, organized, and have influencing capacity.	Diverse, with potentially conflicting interests, unorganized, and/or lack influencing capacity.
Legal Frameworks	Partnership and its chosen activities are legal, and legal framework is flexible. Partners have discretion in the design and structure of the partnership.	The partnership and/or its chosen activities are illegal or overregulated. Legal framework sets limits on partnership design and structure.
Stability	Minimal staff turnover within partner organizations.	High staff turnover within partner organizations. Little continuity in informal agreements and understanding among partners.
Flexibility	Stakeholder interests and demands remain relatively stable.	Stakeholder interests and demands change radically and frequently in response to environmental changes.
Artificiality	Partner organizations are flexible in pursuing new structures and procedures and/or making adjustments in existing ones to support the partnership and partner organizations' identity.	Partner organizations adhere to rigid administrative and structural requirements that inhibit the efficiency and effectiveness of the partnership and may compromise partner organizations' identity.
	Low levels of distortion. The partnership is characterized by local ownership and mutual agreements and relationships.	High levels of distortion. Donors, or other outsiders, continuously facilitate the process.

Box 2.7 Poverty Reduction in Ramón Abdala Neighborhood, Argentina

The success of the poverty reduction partnership in the Ramón Abdala neighborhood in Rosario de la Frontera, Argentina, is largely credited to the local chairwoman of the Red Cross. The Red Cross is the designated coordinator of the partnership due to its track record, credibility with the various stakeholders, and consequent convening power. More specifically, the chairwoman personally negotiated working agreements among community residents, with other neighborhoods, and with experts and representatives of the other partner organizations. The lack of rivalry within the partnership is attributed to the recognition and respect that each partnership member has for the Red Cross chairwoman (Nassif and Mussi 1997).

Box 2.8 West Bank and Gaza Health Education Project

The West Bank and Gaza Health Education Project benefited from existing collaboration between an NGO, the American-Jewish Joint Distribution Committee (JDC), and the Palestinian Authority (Isofo 1998; Coston 1999). JDC and the Palestinian Ministry of Health (PMOH) developed a joint proposal for World Bank funding under the West Bank and Gaza Education and Health Rehabilitation project. JDC had already done the groundwork on health education needs, activities, and approaches and shared this information with the World Bank during its appraisal mission. JDC and PMOH maintained a daily working relationship, sharing responsibility for all planning, evaluation, reporting, and fundraising aspects of the project. The relationship was built upon preexisting personal and professional contacts. The World Bank took a hands-off approach, disbursing funding to the Palestinian Authority; PMOH then interacted directly with JDC. There was no formal agreement between the World Bank and the NGO.

---

partners and can bridge gaps of wealth, power, and culture (see Waddock 1993).

The more partners know and understand each other's mission and track record in advance of the partnership, the less learning and trust building has to occur in the context of partnership initiation, design, and implementation. Positive previous experience and mutual understanding can help to avert misunderstandings, identify opportunities and constraints within and among the organizations to support partnership work, recognize how and when each partner can contribute to partnership objectives, and design ways to protect each organization's identity. Previous understanding and experience can improve the learning curve and provide a better foundation for negotiation on each of these points.

Development actors select partner organizations on the basis of comparative advantages deemed necessary or helpful to meet common objectives. The extent to which organizations with desired characteristics, or at least the potential to build them, exist within the environment directly determines the potential for effective partnerships. Where desirable organizations or characteristics do not already exist, they can be created in the context of partnership work, though this complicates implementation and adds to operating costs. Partner organization capacity refers not only to technical comparative advantages and skills but also to relationships and administrative and absorptive capacity.

In order to maximize partnership value-added, partner organizations need to have a strong organization identity at the outset, or, if an organizational partner is created in the context of a partnership, organization identity must be cultivated and prioritized. Without this feature, the relationship may remain beneficial but will lose partnership's value-added as the organization becomes absorbed or co-opted by more powerful partners. Such occurrences have been regrettably common in irrigation management, where governments or donors attempt to create irrigation associations, sometimes without attention to ownership issues, local incentives, and broad participation in planning and management (see, for example, Ascher and Healy 1990; Merrey 1986; Chambers 1988). Organizations with a strong identity at the outset will be more likely to negotiate a partnership that will be less compromising to this identity, and these organizations will be better prepared to explain and defend their identity as the partnership evolves.

One component of organization identity is a clearly defined constituency to which the organization is accountable. Partnerships will be easier and more efficient in their implementation where these constituencies are shared among the partners or at least their interests do not directly conflict with partnership beneficiaries and stakeholders (for a contrary example, see Box 2.9). The extent to which partner organizations have an existing, positive, and legitimate relationship with partnership stakeholders will similarly ease the partnership's design and implementation.

The partnership environment will be less hostile if each partner perceives an interest in participating and is available to do so. The partners need to perceive that potential benefits merit the investments and potential risks, both generally and with respect to partnering with particular organizations. These benefits, or drivers, also relate to the depth of actors' belief in a partnership's potential value-added. Agreement on partnership participation and vision within the organization reduces transaction costs by eliminating or reducing the need to constantly renegotiate responsibilities, monitor actions, and impose sanctions when organization members are noncooperative or sluggish in fulfilling their partnership responsibilities. It also facilitates the identification of the most efficient approaches and divi-

---

Box 2.9   The World Bank's Africa Environment Consultative Meetings

The purpose of the World Bank's Africa Environment Consultative Meetings
is to learn how better to access all the development forces available in order
to address the daunting environmental problems in Africa (Mercier 1998;
Coston 1999). The World Bank and participating NGOs share a concern for
the environment. However, the Bank's primary constituency is African governments, and NGOs must remain accountable to their constituents who
expect environmental issues to come first no matter the costs. Contentious
projects have interrupted the dialogue between the Bank and NGOs, and there
is a continuous tension between NGOs' advocacy and watchdog role and the
concern that the World Bank will be perceived as trying, or will in fact try, to
co-opt these NGOs. In response, the meetings and learning process have been
very informal and voluntary, flexibly responding to emerging issues.

---

sions of labor within the organization (see Box 2.10 for a contrary example).

Shared vision can reduce the need for extensive confidence-building
and accountability mechanisms, and it can facilitate negotiation of the par-
ticulars of partnership implementation. Partners' pursuit of individual
objectives does not necessarily compromise this shared vision. Combining
self-interested goals with broader, shared goals can enhance the likelihood
of success (Kolzow 1994), as self-interest enhances a partner's drivers and
commitment (Box 2.11).

Organization compatibility is defined in terms of compatible values,

---

Box 2.10   The World Bank's Governance and Anti-Corruption Program

The World Bank's Governance and Anti-Corruption Program was complicated by dissension within participating organizations (Langseth 1998; Coston
1999). While the task manager viewed partnership as a special relationship,
requiring extra trust and flexibility, Bank procedures did not support this
view, instead treating partners the same as any other contractor. At one point,
the Bank called a moratorium on one partner's contract until an internal
report and analysis of its expenditures could be produced; such reporting had
not originally been required, in favor of a more trusting partnership model.
Some dissension also existed within another partner organization. The organization is a loosely structured federation with member chapters in many of the
targeted countries. The international headquarters would have preferred sanc-
tioning these member chapters and selecting individual implementers instead
of the World Bank negotiating and contracting with their selected implementers directly.

**Box 2.11   The Bahia School of Arts and Crafts
and the Odebrecht Foundation, Bahia, Brazil**

A Brazilian partnership between a nonprofit school and a corporate foundation began as an effort for the school to obtain funding to rebuild its physical
infrastructure following a fire (Fischer and Falconer 1999). The foundation
was seeking to reconcile the external pressures to restore the historical center
of the city of Salvador, Bahia, with the heated internal debate of whether to
invest in an existing institution or build a new one to pursue the foundation's
mission to "educate young people for life" through the provision of vocational training. The foundation and the school established a partnership that
incorporated reconstruction of the physical building (satisfying external pressure), while reinvigorating the school's programs, approach, and philosophy
through the introduction of the foundation's underlying philosophy and business approach (satisfying, to a degree, parties from both sides of the internal
debate).

---

cultures, and objectives; compatibility of management philosophy and
techniques, such as attitudes toward teamwork and employee empowerment, results orientation, and so forth; demographic similarity, that is, sym-
metry in terms of the importance of each organization to the other; and
organizational environments supportive of the partnership effort (Lambert,
Emmelhainz, and Gardner 1996). The chances of beginning with compara-
ble organization structures and procedural values are slim, particularly in
development projects where the organizations involved differ dramatically.
The most important features of organization compatibility for a partnership
environment are shared values and compatible approaches.

Compatibility does not mean similarity. Organizations that share a particular ideology and provide similar types of service can also be the most
difficult to coordinate (Peters 1998). This may be related to turf battles (see
Savoie and Peters 1998), or it may be because, despite working in the same
policy area, the organizations differ in their perspectives on service delivery. Differences among partner organizations can produce creative tension
and are often the basis for the partnership and its resultant synergy (Box
2.12). Variance among the organizations in terms of their expertise,
resource bases, and administrative and management systems can contribute
favorably to partnership effectiveness (see World Bank 1996).

Partnership Objectives

Policies and programs inevitably produce winners and losers. Challenging
vested interests can transform the most powerful players in a particular

---

Box 2.12   CARE and Cable & Wireless

CARE, a U.S.-based NGO, engages in both relief and development work internationally. In order to enhance its humanitarian relief and emergency response, it entered a partnership with Cable & Wireless to develop specialized telecommunications kits for use in emergency situations. CARE was able to articulate clearly the particular needs for communications equipment under emergency situations and to outline the challenges that can emerge, potentially disrupting or limiting communications options. Cable & Wireless contributed its own communications technical expertise to develop portable kits. The partnership included the secondment to CARE of one of Cable & Wireless's senior emergency response specialists. Benefits to the private company continue, as they seek to become the leader in the emergency telecommunications market, and, through CARE's experience, have the opportunity to test and adapt their emergency products under the most demanding circumstances (Nelson 1996).

---

context into the greatest losers. Some argue that the social sectors (see World Bank 1996) or society-wide concerns (Garrison 1999) may entail fewer challenges to vested interests, but the number of challenges will depend on the specific partnership objectives. Local partnerships may encounter a longer and more intense history of patronage relationship between government and local powerholders.

Similarly, the fewer government agencies implicated in a partnership effort, the greater the ease with which the partnership can be negotiated and implemented (see Mawer 1997). This simplifies coordination and approval. There may be instances, however, where the number of government agencies involved can be managed through coordinating mechanisms within the government, for example, by partnering with a special coordinating unit (Box 2.13).

Partnerships with the potential for immediate impacts are also more easily negotiated and implemented. Partner organizations and other stakeholders can more readily gauge the value of their participation and are thus more likely to be committed and invest in partnership success. While partnerships often emerge because of the complexity and required long-term response of particular development challenges, partnership objectives and strategies can still be structured to ensure short-term tangible gains.

Because local impacts are relatively easier to recognize and measure, it may be easier to build support and momentum for partnerships that operate at the local level where attribution is often less complex (see Coston 1998b; Fiszbein and Lowden 1998). This is seen, for example, in several slum rehabilitation efforts in Latin America (see Bilbao and Pachano 1997; Nassif and Mussi 1997; Universidad de West Indies 1997). In these cases,

---

Box 2.13   The Fondo de Inversion Social, Bolivia

Many social investment funds operate through partnerships with identified government implementation units. In Bolivia, the Fondo de Inversion Social, a local development fund, aims to support decentralization. The Vice Ministry of Popular Participation, a central agency, oversees the fund. Local governments develop five-year plans to support investment decisions. Local government matching funds are required for selected social sectors. An oversight committee, composed of community representatives, ensures that the local government's development plan reflects community priorities; it has the authority to freeze the transfer of funds from the central government if the plan does not respond to community demands. The vice ministry assists both the local government and the communities in this process. The vice ministry's sectoral-neutral nature minimizes the possibility of sectoral distortion or bias in planning and investment, and supports its mediation between local and central government, the local government and local communities, and among investment priorities and associated ministries (Parker and Serrano 2000).

---

residents could immediately see and benefit from the impacts of the partnerships, enhancing their commitment and participation.

The nature of public services and development is such that not all beneficiaries will readily recognize the merits of the good or service provided. To the extent that constituents recognize the value of the effort and the need addressed as salient, partner organizations will not need to cultivate demand or commitment and will likely work with a constituency prepared to cooperate, provide necessary information, and possibly act as an additional partner (see Box 2.14 for a contrary example).

Box 2.14   Housing Partnerships in Venezuela and Jamaica

Several housing partnerships in Latin America illustrate the added complexity of the need to cultivate demand. In the Santa Cruz Barrio, Caracas, Venezuela, the Low-Income Housing Foundation (Fundación Vivienda Popular) had to convince residents of the need to organize before it could act as an intermediary on their behalf to secure credit and discount building supplies (Bilbao and Pachano 1997).

In Jamaica, the demand for slum rehabilitation was complicated by the fact that residents were often squatters. They needed to be convinced of the security and value of investing their own resources to obtain land tenure (Universidad de West Indies 1997).

General Environment

Legal frameworks establish the legality of a particular partnership and its activities and can determine how it is designed and structured. For example, some partnerships will require formal registration, whereas others may have the opportunity to operate less formally (see Box 2.2).

Environmental stability in the immediate partnership environment includes factors within partner organizations (primarily staff turnover) and with respect to partnership stakeholders (relatively stable interests and demands). High staff turnover incurs not only the standard costs of retraining in particular skill areas but also the less predictable costs of time, training, and interaction for new staff to get to know partner organizations and their representatives, to understand potentially new or unique approaches, and to become inculcated into the organization culture that encompasses the partnership identity. Staff turnover can terminate a partnership or its successes by directly impacting the soft side (relationships and partnership organization culture) or the hard side (the actual work and its processes) of partnership work. Changing interests and demands can introduce conflict among stakeholders, between partner organizations and stakeholders, and among partner organizations, as each tries to express and respond to adjusted preferences.

Flexibility in the immediate partnership context refers to whether or not partner organizations are prepared to make the necessary adjustments for mutuality and protection of their partners' organization identity. Flexibility can sometimes be gauged by a partner organization's track record and the rigidity of its current systems, though not always. Organizations entering into partnerships sometimes recognize the experimental nature of partnerships at the outset and are prepared and willing to make radical changes in order to explore their benefits. Intraorganizational flexibility to support interorganizational partnerships is demonstrated by a partner organization's willingness to accommodate new procedures and mechanisms or to make exceptions in existing ones and by its willingness to accommodate their partners' concerns more generally, including being accountable to respective constituencies and protecting organization identity (Box 2.15).

Artificiality can entail donor pressure or influence to engage otherwise unwilling "partners" in a partnership effort. The degree of artificiality can range from the provision of initial incentives (for example, project funding) to the necessity and enforcement of continuous incentives to keep the partners engaged. As a partnership evolves, if partners are unable to recognize the merits of the partnership aside from these incentives, artificiality persists and the partnership's successes and existence will be vulnerable should those incentives be removed (Box 2.16).

Box 2.15   India Population Project VIII

The World Bank's India Population Project VIII faced serious environmental hostility at the outset because the Bank did not have systems and procedures sufficiently flexible to accommodate the proposed partnerships with local community organizations. Exceptions were eventually negotiated, but the process was an onerous one, entailing a long learning and negotiation process, culminating in a legal agreement that still needed to be amended twice. Review processes were simplified and exceptions negotiated to accommodate sole-source contracts and reimbursement of operating costs (Fogle 1998; Coston, 1999). This process was taxing for the task manager who needed to champion personally each step while constantly reassuring partner organizations.

Box 2.16   World Bank–Sponsored Social Funds in Uganda and Bangladesh

The Ugandan Program for the Alleviation of Poverty and the Social Cost of Adjustment, initiated in 1990, was a social investment fund designed to address the immediate needs of the most vulnerable population (Hino 1996). From the start, other donors viewed the program as a public relations exercise for the World Bank and questioned the effectiveness of funding NGOs through government. The program further suffered from a lack of counterpart financing from the government of Uganda. Participating NGOs were subject to funding delays, onerous administrative procedures, and requirements for competitive bidding. NGOs often created high expectations among the residents, and with the termination of funding, many left without notice to local governments, informing residents that the project's services were now the responsibility of local governments.

   In another World Bank project, the Fourth Population and Health Project in Bangladesh (Hino 1996), termination of funding led to the disbanding of self-help groups. While government and NGOs worked together on the project, this was done more on a case-by-case basis, in accordance with the project design and incentives. Regulations for government-NGO relations remained nonexistent. Many government officials viewed NGOs as competitors with government, found NGO staff's higher salaries demoralizing, and perceived that NGOs prioritized donor responsiveness above local accountability. In short, it is possible that donor distortions could have worsened relations between government and NGOs.

Summary and Next Steps

Even with a strong will on the part of participating actors, partnerships are subject to environmental factors. Environmental factors—both in the broader and in the immediate context—can present opportunities for partnerships, facilitating design and implementation, or threats to partnerships, rendering them unfeasible or prohibitively complex or costly. Identifying relevant environmental factors can assist partnership actors to assess the feasibility of proposed efforts; identify potential obstacles or hindrances and prepare to strategically address them; conduct a preliminary cost-benefit analysis to ensure a partnership is worth the effort; cultivate more facilitative factors, at least in the immediate environment where actors may have more influence; and structure partnerships in ways that minimize environmental hostility.

We turn next to a more detailed discussion of partnership actors. Chapter 4, on managing for partnership results, will combine environmental factors and characteristics of actors to develop a model for strategically managing partnership initiation, design, and maintenance.

Note

1. Portions of this discussion build on Brinkerhoff and Goldsmith 1992.

3

Choosing the Right Partners for the Right Reasons

Partnerships bring together a variety of actors. In international development, the most common potential partners are representative individuals and agencies of national and local governments, NGOs, local communities and community-based organizations (CBOs), the private sector, and international donors and development agencies. Selecting organizations among these types of actors will depend on the context, objectives, and interests of the particular actors.

A primary driver for partnerships is the need to access key resources to reach objectives, when those resources are lacking or insufficient within one actor's reserves. Such assets can include hard resources such as money and materials, as well as important soft resources like managerial and technical skills, information, contacts, and credibility within a specialized area. While each actor has its unique portfolio of assets and skills, particular sectors do have general comparative advantages. Actors are often prescribed potential roles according to these presumed comparative advantages.[1] For example, national governments can provide important legal and institutional frameworks for partnership work, in addition to financial and material resources; local governments can provide financial and material resources, as well as offering implementation support on the ground; NGOs often play an important intermediary and social mobilization role vis-à-vis local communities; local communities and CBOs can mobilize local resources and engender local ownership; the private sector can contribute financial, technical, and managerial resources; and international donors and development agencies can fulfill a facilitating role in addition to providing financial and technical support.

Each type of actor poses particular potential challenges to partnership work. Actors' expectations, political and technical constraints, and organizational structures and processes can influence the effectiveness and efficiency of partnership work. To minimize these challenges and to assure each actor can make its expected contribution, partnership actors can apply selection criteria.

Despite their significant potential benefits, partnerships necessarily involve vulnerability and risk. Actors have the potential to grow and learn in positive ways or, especially for less powerful partners, to fall into dependence and lose their organization identity. General risks, common to all partners, are inherent to the politics of partnership. Partnerships force actors to compromise on objectives and processes. Despite careful selection criteria, actors can never be assured that their selected partners will not in some way create controversy. In partnerships, actors put their own reputation and resources on the line, at the mercy of the politics and capacity of other actors they cannot fully control. Actors cannot always be assured of the legitimacy or integrity of their partners. More powerful organizations may intentionally overexert their power, driving the process, destroying the spirit of partnership (along with many of its benefits), and co-opting and compromising the organization identity of their partners. Organization identity can also be lost unintentionally and more subtly through incremental compromise.

Following is an overview of each type of actor, its presumed comparative advantages, its most commonly prescribed roles, the possible challenges it poses, corresponding proposed selection criteria, and its potential benefits and risks from partnerships. These profiles are not likely to describe accurately and completely the reality for any one organization; rather they represent observed tendencies and potentialities.

Nongovernmental Organizations

NGOs have evolved into strategically managed development specialists, treading the fine line between knowing the technical language and processes of the development industry and maintaining responsiveness to developing country clientele and individual contributors. In the following discussion, unless otherwise noted, NGOs are presumed to comply with the stereotypical altruistic model. NGOs are presumed to be well intentioned, serving a defined constituency. While this assumption does not hold universally, it is the basis from which NGO advocates and donors most often derive assumptions of the comparative advantage of these organizations.

Comparative Advantages and Roles

The depth and universality of NGO comparative advantages have been greatly exaggerated. Donors and practitioners are increasingly questioning assumptions about NGO cost effectiveness, particularly of local NGOs, which often lack capacity; and NGO effectiveness, legitimacy, and credibility, as they often emerge or change agendas in response to available funding. Nevertheless, presumed comparative advantages may still represent the general potential of NGOs, if not the actuality of all organizations.

At the macro level, NGOs may have on-the-ground contacts that enable an accurate understanding of the development context, and they can introduce this in-depth understanding into decisionmaking. Their flexibility enables them to access a variety of players and gather information on those players' views and interests. NGOs can raise issues and concerns that might otherwise be neglected. NGOs can enhance transparency and accountability. They can cultivate and provide an interested and informed constituency to influence decisions and to facilitate implementation and the monitoring of results. They can foster public debate by disseminating information to their constituencies, by organizing public consultations, by ensuring adequate representation of affected parties, and by serving on official commissions and decisionmaking bodies (Clark 1997) (Box 3.1).

NGOs can deliver services, mobilize productive energy and resources, and provide feedback to donors and governments. In addition to providing technical expertise, NGOs can articulate beneficiaries' needs to other part-

---

Box 3.1   NGOs and Poverty Reduction Strategy Papers

NGOs and civil society organizations are considered key players in the World Bank/International Monetary Fund's proposed Poverty Reduction Strategy Papers (PRSPs) (Development Committee 1999). The PRSP process is designed to support debt-relief efforts for countries that qualify. Loan repayment is diverted to support national poverty reduction strategies. The design of PRSPs is intended to emphasize country ownership (rather than being donor driven) and broad participation of stakeholders, including the poor, civil society organizations, private-sector actors, and government. How the process will be operationalized in each country depends on the local conditions, priorities, and actors involved.

In Bolivia, the Catholic Church spearheaded an ambitious process of national discussion and debate. Jubilee 2000 planned for seventeen regional forums during February 2000, after which regional delegates would attend a national workshop in March 2000. Themes included macroeconomic issues and civil society participation, to ensure that civil society positions would inform the PRSP process whether they were included in the government's plans for consultation or not.

Seven NGO networks recruited an interdisciplinary team to produce a ten-page document outlining proposals for debate and discussion at the Jubilee 2000 regional workshops; it was also publicized for a broader public hearing. A final document was produced after the regional forums for the Jubilee 2000 National Forum at the end of April (Anonymous 2000).

ners, provide communities with information about the partnership and its objectives, organize communities to take advantage of the partnership benefits, deliver services to less accessible populations, and serve as intermediaries to other actors. NGOs can provide bridges between higher authorities and poor communities, the state and businesses, and businesses and local communities. NGOs can support local communities in forming and managing their own representative bodies, as well as providing significant technical and managerial capacity building specific to the partnership's objectives. NGOs can greatly contribute to the consensus building and commitment necessary for partnership success, promoting equity and ownership in the process.

NGOs may have specific advantages in helping partnerships form among actors with histories of conflict or mistrust. Their potential independence provides a degree of neutrality, flexibility, and hence credibility that other actors may lack. Due to their accumulated experience working with a variety of actors, NGOs may bring a broader understanding of various perspectives and operating procedures. Local NGOs' particular comparative advantages include managing local conflicts and fostering joint learning (Box 3.2).

Challenges and Selection Criteria

NGOs do not always possess the comparative advantages partners expect; if they do, they may quickly lose them if extra care, time, and resources are

---

Box 3.2   The Coatepeque Foundation, El Salvador

A partnership for poverty alleviation and local development for the Lake Coatepeque basin in El Salvador faced considerable conflict and skepticism in addressing housing issues (Najarro 1997). The displacement of families due to armed conflict led to overcrowding and environmental degradation in the Los Planes zone, where settlers reduced a two-way street to one lane for two-way traffic. A local NGO foundation assisted in organizing the local population into its own community development association and facilitating agreement among residents regarding housing solutions. The partnership resulted in the construction of fifty-three new houses, in a new location with electrical power service. This experience laid the groundwork for continued partnership between the local foundation, the community-development association, and other actors (public and private) brought in by the foundation. Residents and the foundation learned to trust each other and to believe in the potential for improved living conditions through joint efforts. Residents subsequently participated in a broader partnership for the construction and management of a public bath house.

not invested to protect them. NGO comparative advantages also create challenges. For example, close constituency relations may generate tension between the partners' potentially conflicting priorities and operational procedures. Partners may assume an understanding of NGOs that does not reflect reality. The sheer volume and diversity of NGOs makes selection problematic, and competition within a particular NGO sector further exacerbates a neutral understanding of the organizations' respective strengths and weaknesses. One of the most intractable challenges may be NGOs' organizational capacity.

Selection criteria can be used to minimize the occurrence or resulting expense from these challenges, and to maximize NGO contributions. Selection criteria can be contradictory. Potential partners need to carefully prioritize the desired characteristics of an NGO partner, recognizing that the NGOs available will ultimately determine selection. Proposed NGO selection criteria are:

- Organization identity: articulated definition of development, mission, institutional goals, and constituencies; and evidence of desired comparative advantages.
- Technical and institutional capacities specific to the partnership, including analytic capacity, relations with key stakeholders, and credibility and legitimacy with key stakeholders.
- Legal status and good government relations.
- Management systems and absorptive capacity.
- Compatibility with other partners in regard to priorities, activities, and methodologies.
- Track record.

If a partner is looking for comparative advantages deriving from NGOs' philanthropic origins, the NGO should be able to articulate clearly its definition of development, mission, institutional goals, and identified constituency. Legal status or recognition may not be relevant if special arrangements can be negotiated with government agencies as part of a pilot or demonstration effort. Management systems and capacity can be developed in the context of a partnership—implying that other criteria may take precedence, but sufficient absorptive capacity must exist at least to initiate the partnership. Many scholars and most donors advocate selecting NGO partners based on their track record (Hodson 1997; Hino 1996; UN 1998). This is somewhat controversial in that it implies a barrier of entry to qualified NGOs who may have limited experience. Partners will need to carefully balance evaluation of an organization's track record with other priorities for specific skills, contacts, and relationships.

Benefits and Risks

NGOs' possible benefits include enhanced effectiveness, influence, and capacity. These benefits may be expected or unintentional by-products of partnership work. In the environment sector, for example, NGOs' successful partnerships with business have created greater environmental education and consumer support for environmental goals, "giving teeth" to voluntary initiatives (Murphy and Bendell 1997: 225) (Box 3.3).

Partnerships enable NGOs to scale up their own work and scope. Through them, NGOs can build trust with communities even outside the intervention, and NGOs may acquire a new dimension to their work that can enrich their core activities. Major impact is predicated on NGOs' ability to cultivate close personal contacts with the powers-that-be (Bratton 1990), and partnerships can provide such opportunities. NGOs can expand their sphere of influence through networking and broadened access to financial and information resources. Such influence can be project specific, for example, seeking to inject a more participatory focus into project design; sector specific, promoting a more favorable policy environment for NGOs generally; or NGOs can use partnerships to forward their own vision of development. Participating in partnerships can generate understanding of NGOs and their work by a broader array of potential stakeholders. More specific capacity benefits include experience and skills in working in contractual or other administrative arrangements; enhanced understanding of how other sectors operate; useful and practical knowledge from training and skill transfer; and additional material support (financial and in-kind), which can release existing resources to be applied to other activities.

These benefits are not without potential costs. Many NGOs may lose their organization identity through a gradual and subtle "hardening of the

---

Box 3.3   The Marine Stewardship Council

The Marine Stewardship Council (MSC) is a formalized (NGO) partnership. The MSC started as a joint initiative between the World Wildlife Fund for Nature (WWF) and Unilever, a multinational corporation that buys and manufacturers fish products. With a shared goal of ensuring the long-term viability of fish populations, WWF and Unilever initiated the MSC in 1996. The MSC developed a broad set of principles and criteria and a related standardized certification program. The MSC logo certifies, through independent certification bodies, that fish products originate from sustainable, well-managed sources. The MSC logo will serve to educate consumers and give them an option to support the promotion of "responsible, environmentally appropriate, socially beneficial and economically viable fisheries practices" (MSC 2000).

arteries," as NGOs bureaucratize and become risk averse or reluctant to bear the costs of listening to their constituencies. This is particularly documented with respect to donors (Hulme and Edwards 1997b: 278). The process begins with the acceptance of donor money; progresses to the adoption of donor techniques for programming, implementation, monitoring, and evaluation; and begins to affect staff composition—recruitment, selection, and valued skills; until the entire organization culture is eventually attuned to donors (Box 3.4). This process can also occur when NGOs work with government (Lipsky and Smith 1989–1990), or businesses (Murphy and Bendell 1997). It often entails the introduction of administrative requirements for which NGOs are sometimes ill prepared or overburdened, or results in skewing the incentives and priorities of day-to-day service. Introducing new technologies and management practices can alter an NGO's ability to tap "the altruism and energy" of those committed to the NGO's mission (Bush 1992: 404–405). Financial dependence and its outcomes also weaken an NGO's constituency relations and legitimacy. NGOs are likely to neglect these priorities as they vie for partners' attention and support.

Box 3.4   Sarvodaya in Sri Lanka

The introduction of a donor consortium (1985) to support Sarvodaya in Sri Lanka essentially transformed Sarvodaya from a people's movement to a donor instrument (Perera 1997). The consortium was formed with good intentions and was perceived by Sarvodaya as an opportunity to engage in long-term planning with a committed three-year budget and a more systematic monitoring and evaluation plan. Only a year after approval of the first three-year plan, the donor consortium requested submission of another plan, subject to approval. The consortium imposed complex, top-down financial and administrative control systems, and Sarvodaya became subject to numerous and frequent external monitors, evaluators, consultants, and experts. Resulting decisions, which distanced Sarvodaya from its original mission and identity, included the separation of eight districts from the primary movement and eventual termination of programming in the area, the separation of social programs from economic programs, and the gradual reduction of development education centers from 360 to one. In addition, the donor consortium imposed a top-heavy administration of English-speaking professionals (at much higher salaries than non-English-speaking community development workers), requested Sarvodaya to convert volunteers to paid workers, provided and cultivated a reliance on vehicles, and mandated reduction of Sarvodaya villages from 8,600 to 3,000 in 1982 and to 2,000 by 1994. In short, "what started off as a partnership based on dialogue had, by the mid-1990s, become a subcontractorship based on commands and sanctions" (Perera 1997: 166).

Partners may have a tendency to exaggerate the capacity and effectiveness of NGOs in meeting certain objectives, essentially setting these organizations up for failure. NGOs may be asked only to contribute resources and skills in service delivery and project implementation, not their analytical perspectives in project design (Clark 1991), which would enable NGOs to serve their constituents more effectively and protect their organization identity. Partners' priorities and agendas can conflict with those of NGOs and can shift somewhat arbitrarily. Preferences for short-term planning and efforts conflict with NGOs' longer-term commitments to their constituencies. Overfunding can breed waste and corruption, and human capacity in time and effort is inevitably diverted from other organizational priorities (Fowler 1997). Because of their own administrative requirements and organizational constraints, donors and governments tend to restrict flexibility, and they require substantial investments of time to negotiate contracts and solve problems of rules and regulations. Finally, NGOs and their organization identity may suffer from funding and implementation delays rooted in partners' organizational constraints and priorities (Hodson 1997; Robinson 1997).

Community-Based Organizations

Typically CBOs are less formal, more localized NGOs. They are often not legally registered with governments, though they can be. Some of the same comparative advantages, roles, benefits and risks, challenges, and selection criteria that apply to NGOs may apply to CBOs. When CBOs are involved in partnerships it is often to organize partnership beneficiaries, with the assistance of an NGO intermediary.

Comparative Advantages and Roles

As the most common conduit for local participation, CBOs potentially contribute the best that participation has to offer: stimulation of initiative, entrepreneurship, and rapid technology transfer (see USAID 1995c). CBOs are tapped for partnerships because of their location and relationship with targeted constituencies. Their local focus presents particularly important comparative advantages: stronger incentives for solutions, more accurate information, and lower costs in marshaling resources. CBOs represent human and institutional capital, potentially capable of contributing public regulation and authority. In exercising these, CBOs are able to cultivate and rely on social norms as the least expensive and potentially most effective governance mechanism. Through relationships of trust and reciprocity,

CBOs can facilitate tapping into local resources; these might be monetary or in-kind, particularly in terms of community labor (Box 3.5).

In partnerships, CBOs are called on to organize participation, condition social behavior, and assist in allocating resources. CBOs represent constituencies and regulate locally managed processes and resources. They also act as intermediaries with unorganized constituencies, assisting partnerships to build local trust and commitment to and ownership of partnership processes and outcomes.

Challenges and Selection Criteria

The challenges to working with CBOs are related to capacity and social and political dynamics. Most CBOs are relatively weak in terms of resources and institutional development. In some cases, CBOs are created specifically for a particular partnership. This requires financial, technical, and sometimes in-kind investments. As local organizations, CBOs are subject to the social and political dynamics inherent to their local context; they are often vulnerable to political co-optation by local elites and other stakeholders.

It is difficult to know how representative CBOs are. Even when diverse interests are represented, the potential for internal social conflicts is great; this is particularly the case as partnerships try to expand or target broader objectives—both geographically and substantively—than a sole-interest CBO can easily address (see Bratton 1990). CBOs are not immune from pursuing self-interest, both their members' and as organizations. This implies that some CBOs may exist for the sole purpose of accessing external resources, whether or not they intend to distribute those resources equitably and in the service of partnership objectives. CBOs can create smoke-

---

Box 3.5   The Carvajal Foundation, Colombia

In Colombia, the Carvajal Foundation facilitated the formation of community development associations, which then took responsibility for overseeing the community construction of infrastructure projects in the country's largest substandard settlement (Aguablanca, Santiago de Cali). Residents must pay for all materials (over two years), which are delivered to the community through the Community Action Board. The Cali Municipal Companies provides the community with the design, technical advisory services, and work inspection; the community hires a registered construction foreman and provides the labor. The community development association is integral to securing effective supervision by the community and ensuring the timely construction of quality works (Carvajal Foundation 1997).

screens of pseudoparticipation, where partners are led to believe their objectives are being met when in fact the traditional politics of local institutions are left intact (Elliott 1987).

Some of the most important challenges can be only partially addressed through selection criteria. Various selection criteria must be carefully weighted to reflect the partnership's highest priorities. Tools for selecting CBOs for particular development objectives have been developed; checklists can address institutional capacity, representativeness, and unity of purpose (see, for example, Fowler 1995a). The NGO selection criteria noted above generally apply to CBOs. However, given the most commonly prescribed CBO roles, and given that capacity can be built in the context of partnerships, partners may choose to weight institutional capacity as relatively less important than representativeness, relationships, legitimacy, and track record. Proposed selection criteria for partnering with CBOs are:

- Representativeness.
- Legitimacy and local accountability.
- Track record.
- Political or social constraints.
- Transparency.
- Potential to access comparative advantages and institutional capacity required by partnership.
- Institutional capacity.

Benefits and Risks

The greatest potential partnership benefits for CBOs are improvements in the quality of life of the individuals, families, and groups that both comprise CBOs and are represented by them. Partnerships can provide CBOs with manpower, technology, and institutional relationships. Partnerships often invest in CBO capacity building for the purpose of implementing partnership objectives. This entails identifying and cultivating leaders, providing technical assistance and managerial support, and linking CBOs to other actors and sectors, including the various partners. These investments can have multiplier effects for CBOs and their objectives. Partnerships create conditions in which organizations are given resources and stimulus to grow, which in turn can assist the CBO to be a collective actor in the context of the partnership and beyond. The resources, skills, and experience gained through a partnership can subsequently or simultaneously be applied to other community-based initiatives, both at the local level, and in broader policy arenas.

The most important partnership risk to CBOs is that, like other NGOs, they can suffer distancing from their constituencies. One might assume that because CBOs are often composed of representatives of these constituencies, the possibility of compromising those ties is minimal. However, representatives may become acculturated to the language and technologies of larger institutional partners to the point where priorities may shift or rationales for decisions are not easily explained, and the organization can lose the trust and confidence of its constituency (Box 3.6).

If the CBO's contextual constraints are not understood, the CBO and its representatives risk social and political oppression and possibly violence. Empowerment, which threatens the status quo of power relations, can be dangerous. Especially when CBOs are created for a partnership, they can become the mere implementers of objectives, policies, and programs not of their own making and possibly not even in their best interest. If the legitimacy of a CBO or its representatives is called into question, individuals risk being ostracized from their own communities, or subject to social sanctions.

Box 3.6   The Pico Union Neighborhood Council, Los Angeles

The Pico Union Neighborhood Council's (PUNC's) participation in the Neighborhood Development Program in Los Angeles inadvertently led to the transformation of PUNC from an informal, militant advocacy CBO, to a formal community-development organization directed largely by professionals (Cooper 1980). With good intentions, the University Extension Office of Urban Affairs, University of California at Los Angeles (UCLA) provided technical assistance to assist PUNC in meaningfully participating in and promoting its vision of neighborhood development to the Community Redevelopment Agency (CRA) of Los Angeles. The technical assistance began as simple training sessions on planning concepts, governmental decisionmaking processes, the Housing and Urban Development Act of 1968, the CRA, federal housing programs, and the problems of the public schools in the area. Eventually, council members were introduced to a specialized vocabulary and, through joint meetings with CRA and UCLA consultants, they began to understand the professional subculture of community development. In the meantime, attendance at more general neighborhood meetings rapidly diminished as residents struggled to relate to the new vocabulary, thought process, and subculture. Upon recommendations, PUNC introduced professional, salaried positions, secured meeting space, and eventually formalized as an incorporated nonprofit organization (with UCLA consultants providing technical and legal assistance). While this enhanced the CRA's view of PUNC as a viable and credible community development organization, it also produced outcomes indicative of PUNC's distancing from its constituencies: PUNC became less dependent on residents for support and participation; active community involvement evolved into passive approval of PUNC's efforts; and tasks became more technical and concentrated, enabling fewer people to participate.

Governments

Government often represents the most potent concentration of political and economic power and thus may need to be included, consulted, or at least informed, regardless of potential comparative disadvantages. Formal partnerships with governments tend to occur more frequently at local levels (see, for example, Peterson 1997).

Comparative Advantages and Roles

Government possesses particular comparative advantages inherent in its bureaucracy and large scale, the particular tasks it performs, and the resources it controls. In the partnership context, government can provide essential resources, including finance, material support, and possibly legitimacy.[2] It can also provide important services, such as administrative, supervisory or oversight, coercion, information, and research services; technical assistance; training; and promotion. Its scale, institutional longevity, and continuing presence offer the potential for broadening, sustaining, and replicating partnership efforts. Government can provide a check on elite control and support equity objectives. Government can act as an enabler of partnerships, providing important support systems.

Governments have convening power and can heavily influence other stakeholders, for example, providing forums for coordination and promoting the participation of various actors and the inclusion of diverse perspectives. Government agents are potential arbitrators among stakeholders. This influencing power can greatly contribute to coping with vested interests among powerful stakeholders (assuming the same stakeholders have not captured the government and its agents). Governments are also in a unique position to facilitate contacts and relationships within government and among other actors. Governments can contribute their discretionary powers in engaging citizens and other stakeholders in participatory processes; local governments in particular can motivate and facilitate citizen participation (Box 3.7). Finally, governments can set the policy agendas that inspire, make possible, or facilitate partnerships and their objectives, enabling stakeholder mobilization.

Challenges and Selection Criteria

The inability of governments to recognize their own limitations and the comparative advantages of other actors can pose the greatest bottlenecks to partnership work (Fiszbein and Lowden 1998). Mutual distrust and jealousy among the various sectors can be deep-rooted. In some cases, the suspicion of foreign agendas and potential overthrow may be severe.

Box 3.7   The Mobile Health Clinics Program, Venezuela

In Maracaibo, Venezuela, the mayor initiated a mobile health clinics program (Hernández, Portillo, and Méndez 1997). The program contracted a private company to manufacture the mobile units, and then established a civil contract for a civil association to deliver health services utilizing the mobile unit. Since its inception in 1993, the program has grown to encompass multiple partnerships with private companies, neighborhood associations, NGOs, and government agencies. The needs addressed have expanded from direct health issues to encompass sanitation, electrification, agriculture, and latrines. In each case, the mobile health clinic recognizes a problem facing the community it serves, works with the community, and then approaches relevant government agencies, NGOs, and private-sector actors for assistance with community-led solutions. In this sense, the program can be seen as the initiator and broker of partnerships. As a government program, it faces fewer obstacles in negotiating and attaining support from other government agencies at the local and national levels.

The Maracaibo municipality has been able to access significant national government support through various departments of the Ministry of Health. The program provides a ready infrastructure to absorb technical support from regional and national public bodies. It also represents one of the great success stories of operationalizing the Municipal Law, which transfers responsibility for health services to the municipality.

Governments may also need to overcome other assumptions about NGOs, for example, that they are ineffective and too costly. As a result of these challenges, government may be prone to overregulate NGOs, as well as the development process and the partnership itself, potentially reducing efficiency and effectiveness.

Governments require time and energy investments to negotiate appropriate mechanisms for the transfer of funds to other partners, particularly NGOs (Hino 1996). The tendency to overregulate, lack of institutional capacity, and insufficient political will can lead to implementation and funding delays. Governments also have the potential to threaten the continuation of partnerships by canceling long-term commitments if the political situation changes. Inherent to its nature as a publicly accountable bureaucracy, government is likely to be slow and cumbersome. Governments' conventional tools are coercion and money, neither of which is likely to elicit voluntary social energy (Brown and Korten 1991), which can be vital in reaching partnership objectives.

The institutional capacity of governments varies a great deal and is likely to be questionable in most government settings. Most developing and transitioning governments are in the midst of radical reforms, as they are being asked to pursue political transitions, economic transitions, or both.

Government functions and responsibilities are in flux; a particular regime may not survive through the implementation or even planning of a partnership, and the morale of government employees is likely to be extremely low. Partners will need to take great care to avoid asking governments to perform roles for which they lack capacity. This may be particularly true at the local level, where national government may pose another challenge by promising or mandating the participation of local governments in a partnership without providing the resources for them to do so. Finally, governments may lack legitimacy and may be corrupt.

Partners do not have many options in selecting from among government bodies, unless they have flexibility in terms of the agency or location. Selection criteria can facilitate decisions as to whether or not governments should be engaged under various circumstances, and they can inform choices when this flexibility exists. Crucial to these decisions is determining the extent to which government partnership is necessary. Other relationship options can be explored, ranging from keeping government informed, to seeking consent, to less formal agreements to cooperate. General selection criteria for government partners are:

- Political viability.
- Policies, with respect to sector objectives, types and specific potential partners, partnership objectives, development priorities, and participation and democratic processes.
- Track record: history of cooperation, previous experience with potential partners and stakeholders, administrative bottlenecks (implementation and funding delays), and follow-through on commitments.
- Degree of corruption: in government overall and in individuals occupying critical positions for the partnership.
- Administrative procedures: general degree of red tape and procedures and regulations relevant to partnership objectives and actors.
- Political will to support the partnership: in government overall and in individuals occupying critical positions.
- Institutional capacity: both generally and specific to proposed partnership role.

Benefits and Risks

Government's greatest partnership benefit is the potential to contribute meaningfully to development objectives, improving the lives of citizens, and engendering stability and potential government legitimacy. Partnerships can help government to "sell itself" in terms of elections and maximizing tax receipts (Fiszbein and Lowden 1998). Government can gain both in institutional capacity to fulfill its mission and in credibility as an honest broker. The latter is particularly important as many governments suffer from reputations of corruption and inefficiency, or they may be newly elected and seeking to establish credibility (Box 3.8).

Governments can also benefit from enhanced effectiveness and efficiency owing to information and technological advantages and cost savings through the mobilization of external resources, including beneficiary contributions. Multiplier effects are also possible; for example, local partnerships can have demonstration effects with limited investments, providing techniques, approaches, and incentives to pursue partnerships in other contexts. Through partnerships, governments can explore unconventional or unproven approaches and share the risk with other actors. By accessing other actors, perspectives, and approaches, governments can also learn new technologies and means of addressing development challenges. These benefits, as well as the relationships and social capital developed through partnerships, can be leveraged for other development initiatives.

Some of these benefits are particularly important to local governments. Many local governments have insufficient resources to credibly pursue development objectives and are very limited in their ability to collect taxes. In addition to developing local support, demonstrated successes through

---

Box 3.8   The Bulgarian Association for Building Partnership

In Bulgaria, a newly elected reformist regime built upon a partnership in progress (Brinkerhoff and Brinkerhoff 2001). In early 1997, USAID began collaborating with the Bulgarian Association for Building Partnership (BAP) in an effort to create a policy dialogue process involving stakeholders in Bulgaria's small and medium enterprise (SME) sector, for the purpose of improving laws and policies that promote competitive private-sector growth. The BAP developed an SME action plan and a coalition-building campaign that led to a coalescing of support for SME reform nationwide from over fifty private-sector groups. In the meantime, public outrage over government failures led to the collapse of the socialist government and a reformist government came to power in spring 1997. The new regime was much more open to change and subsequently adopted the BAP platform as part of its economic restructuring package submitted to the National Assembly in the summer of 1997. The success of the coalition-building campaign and the new government openness led to the formation of an SME policy-reform network that linked civil society and the state. A "trialogue" strategy evolved, bringing together business associations, policy think tanks, government officials, and parliamentarians. The government also initiated participatory regional town-hall meetings, managed by joint civil society–government working groups. These initiatives enabled the government to acquire essential input regarding the policies necessary to support SMEs.

partnerships can call attention to a particular local government, earning officials recognition from government superiors and potentially enhancing relations with and support from central government (see Box 3.7).

Governments also face risks. First, they may be asked to work with perceived enemies of the state who pose political threats to their legitimacy. Second, the initiation of participation can be akin to opening Pandora's box; government may not have the capacity to respond to the extent and diversity of demand that results, potentially precipitating government failure or a collapsed or failed state (Eriksson 1998; Zartman 1995). Third, by legitimizing the participation of NGOs and the private sector, governments risk further diverting donor funding and technical assistance from government. This can in turn provide incentives for highly skilled officials to move into NGO and private-sector positions. Fourth, sometimes entering into partnerships means having to respond to pressure exerted from donors via NGOs, or as some call it, "NGO colonialism" (Beckmann 1991). Finally, governments may fear that if they open the door an inch, it will be kicked in. Precedents may be set, making it increasingly difficult for governments to backtrack from the inertia of participation in decisionmaking. Each partnership experience can serve to further empower government critics and constituents, complicating a government's preferred agenda and challenging its capacity to respond to citizens and critics.

Donors

Donors can include multilateral and bilateral agencies, as well as private foundations. As each private foundation is unique, and even in the aggregate their contributions to development assistance are no match to official funding, the emphasis here is on official development assistance through multi- and bilaterals.

Comparative Advantages and Roles

The most obvious comparative advantage donors have is the wealth of resources they apply to fund development projects and programs, and to provide technical assistance in the development, implementation, and evaluation of these efforts. These resources enable both a scale of development work that is otherwise impossible and the potential to replicate partnership successes. Their enormous resource base (relative to other actors) enables donors to become development specialists, often investing in research to explore the best alternatives for addressing development challenges in various contexts.

Donors have significant convening power; they have the potential capacity to bring all stakeholders to the table even in highly conflictive situations (see Box 2.5). Donors can ensure that all relevant stakeholders are represented, including beneficiaries, those who will be most affected by development efforts, and NGOs. They have an enormous influence on various actors, providing important incentives to achieve agreement and to follow through on policies, programs, and implementation. In particular, donors have significant bargaining power with governments. They can be important in negotiating approvals and support systems for partnership work (Box 3.9). They can also exert pressure to improve the enabling environment for NGOs and to promote greater transparency and democratic processes.

If this pressure is supplemented with continuing efforts to strengthen government, donors can significantly contribute to institutional capacity throughout a particular country and meaningfully improve relations between government and civil society. Donors can strengthen the institutional capacity, representativeness, and technical capacity of local NGOs, and they can make certain that NGOs' expertise and local information are considered in government policy and program decisionmaking (see Box 2.1). In promoting partnerships, donors provide opportunities for the various sectors to learn about each other and work together toward common goals.

Collectively, donors provide an important contribution when they coordinate among themselves so as to avoid replication, confusion, and, most important, competition for local capital (social and institutional in particular). Such coordination can lead to engaging a variety of donors in partnership work, to access greater resources (including funding); local experi-

---

Box 3.9   The Pakistan National Drainage Project

Given the multiplicity of factors, interests, and players, the World Bank believed it would be impossible to pursue a drainage agenda in Pakistan's Indus Valley without the participation of all stakeholder groups. To overcome resistance and secure cooperation and participation from these stakeholders, the Bank attempted to provide a vision to which the diverse stakeholders could subscribe through the National Drainage Project. The vision presents potential improvements in the previous approach such that each stakeholder perceived benefits. The Bank facilitated agreement among donors not to offer any more irrigation and drainage assistance unless the government of Pakistan agreed to the terms (particularly institutional reforms) proposed by the project. Stakeholders were made to feel that if they did not participate, they would be left out of the "only game in town" (Wambia 1998; Coston 1999).

ence, contacts, relationships, and credibility; and particular technical niches.

Challenges and Selection Criteria

Challenges associated with donors mostly derive from their institutional and administrative procedures. Donors typically have a fast pace and expect to see results according to a timeline determined in advance. Cooperative agreements, particularly partnerships, can require an enormous amount of negotiation, involving lawyers, layers of approval, and additional costs in time and money. Since donors have strict accountability to their contributing governments, they are not typically set up with the kind of flexibility and openness required for partnership work. Once consensus is reached and approvals for agreements and procedures are obtained, donors may still not provide the appropriate incentives to staff to follow through on these agreements (Bebbington and Riddell 1997; see also USAID 1995a). This can lead to serious funding and implementation delays.

Donor representatives sent to negotiate partnership agreements are not always the same individuals with authority to approve them. Negotiation and approval processes, as well as partnership design, require greater up-front investments in time and money than do more traditional development projects (Box 3.10; see also Box 2.15). While partnership relationships ideally occur at the institutional level, in practice they are most often rooted in relationships between individuals. There are ways to broaden these relationships, but ultimately individuals will continue to play key roles. Given

---

Box 3.10   The India Population Project VIII

The World Bank's India Population Project VIII suffered from delays at the start. While the loan agreement was signed in 1991, initial funds were not disbursed until 1994. The original project language included a component of working with NGOs, primarily in the delivery of vocational education for women. However, by the time funds were disbursed, the language was antiquated and the new task manager needed to explore how best to implement the initiative. Acquiring earmarked trust funds for this effort, she hired a consultant to explore the issue. Contracts for the NGOs had to be crafted carefully to preserve the NGOs' autonomy, to be acceptable to the Bank, and to include measurable outcomes. Particular care had to be taken to ensure that the allocated funding for this partnership component did not exceed the transaction costs. Through a long learning and negotiation process, the legal agreement for the project was amended twice (Fogle 1998; Coston 1999).

this feature of partnership work, the greatest challenge posed by donors is frequent staff turnover and reassignment.

Donors may intentionally overexert their power, driving the process and destroying the spirit of partnership (along with many of its benefits), co-opting and compromising the organization identity of its partners, and even threatening national sovereignty (Hulme and Edwards 1997a). More commonly, the negative impact on partners' organization identity is caused by donors' lack of understanding of partners, their strengths and weaknesses; and the constraints posed by donors' administrative procedures and requirements and accountability to their own constituents. The volume of resources and power a donor controls can influence incentive structures, diverting attention from values-based motivations, and, in the worst cases, inciting competition and corruption. Proposed donor selection criteria are:

- Willingness to jointly develop partnership objectives and processes.
- Willingness and ability to work in partnership: flexibility, responsiveness, and process approach.
- Authority of donor representative.
- Compatibility with objectives and value-orientation of partners.
- Sufficient resources required (financial, material, technical).
- Experience in the proposed context.
- Long-term commitment to constituencies.
- Appropriate expectations of partners.
- Willingness to build the capacity of partners.

Benefits and Risks

Through partnerships, donors can adapt programs to local conditions, leverage resources, and attain more significant impact. Partnerships can be key to donors' exit strategies. They can create social capital that donors can continue to access and apply to other development initiatives. Partnerships enable donors to reach communities and address issues that would otherwise be impossible or problematic. They further contribute to donors' own technical expertise and understanding, which can be applied elsewhere. Partnerships also create goodwill not only among participating stakeholders but also within the publics upon whose political support many donors rely.

However, partnerships often entail significant investments in capacity building for organizations that may be subject to high turnover. The provision of technical support, training, and skills transfer can make staff attractive to other potential employers. Partnerships also require lengthy negotiations; despite hefty expenses for these, partnerships may not always come to fruition. Even if they do, they may require more time than other project approaches to produce quantifiable results. This can make donors vulnerable to stakeholder criticism, for example, from the legislatures that authorize and fund them.

Private Sector

The private sector is the fastest growing source of development funding. Corporate philanthropy now seeks to match the corporation's comparative advantages (skills, knowledge, and experience) to needs rather than focusing on needs for which the corporation has no specific advantage. Increasingly, corporations are also looking to partner with other organizations and sectors to leverage their contributions and build relationships that may prove valuable to other objectives. Corporate philanthropy is required for doing business in particular countries or localities, as local governing structures increasingly assert their bargaining power (see Passow 1995). Corporate philanthropy has become more generous in terms of volume and direct engagement, while at the same time, potentially more self-interested.

Comparative Advantages and Roles

Private-sector contributions to development can include investment and income flows, employment, goods and services, infrastructure (both physical and institutional, including inputs to financial, legal, and regulatory systems), technology, standards and business practices, local business development, and building bridges between large- and small-scale businesses (Nelson 1996). Businesses provide an important demonstration of initiative, entrepreneurship, and responsibility. They can also enhance economic participation and opportunity, and they potentially promote a more equitable income distribution, in turn supporting social and political stability (Box 3.11). This latter advantage most often accrues when businesses partner with government and civil society (Brown and Korten 1991).

The private sector's partnership roles can be as varied as the individual businesses that comprise it. Private-sector actors can contribute essential resources and skills specific to partnership objectives and facilitate partnership development and maintenance. The private sector's skills include those specific to the corporation's industry (e.g., infrastructure, information technology, biochemical), functional and organizational skills (e.g., marketing, budgeting, forecasting, public relations, research and development), and more general management and communication skills. These actors can also provide access to key networks of individuals and organizations who might otherwise be inaccessible or ignored but who can make important

---

Box 3.11   Homegrown (Kenya) Ltd.

Homegrown (Kenya) Ltd., a private horticultural business, worked with small farmers in Kenya to help them access supermarkets in the United Kingdom. Supermarkets dominate sales of horticultural produce and require documentation of where a good was produced and how (e.g., welfare of the workers, responsible farming practices, and protection of the environment). Homegrown uses local farmers as outgrowers, buying materials (seeds, chemicals, fertilizers, and protective clothing) in bulk, and providing these in the form of financing until repayment is possible, once production starts. The Homegrown crop-protection unit organizes outgrowers into regular planting regimes to smooth variations in supply. Crop yields are collected every week, with weekly payment to the farmers, and transportation costs are absorbed by Homegrown. Homegrown provides all the verification for marketing the farmers' goods to the UK supermarkets. Homegrown trains the farmers on the necessary practices and supervises compliance with the corresponding Homegrown Code of Practice. The partnership also relies on the Germany bilateral GTZ for agricultural technical assistance and works with NGOs to raise AIDS awareness and address other quality-of-life issues for the small farmers. Through the partnership, Homegrown acquires production and small farmers gain access to otherwise inaccessible markets and a dependable income. It is estimated that Homegrown employs 620 people in Kenya, supporting roughly 6,000 dependents, and annually invests $1.6–1.8 million in rural areas, stimulating the development of the rural economy (Evans 1999).

---

contributions to development processes. In addition to direct technical contributions, private-sector actors can transfer skills and build capacity of other partners and constituencies. This is often accomplished through volunteer or release time of corporate employees. Employees' resources can have an enormous impact on development objectives (Box 3.12).

Challenges and Selection Criteria

Potential partners may be uncomfortable with companies benefiting from philanthropic work. There is also still a body of thought within the business sector that refutes philanthropic rationales, arguing that companies' ultimate purpose in society is the pursuit of profit and its only obligations are to its shareholders (see Sternberg 1994: 41). Some corporations persist in questioning the credibility and capacity of particular NGOs, especially former critics. These actors may need to be convinced that the risks to partnering with the private sector do not outweigh the potential benefits. NGOs put their own reputation on the line and may unknowingly contribute to systems to which they are morally opposed when partnering with donors,

---

Box 3.12   The Instituto Radiofónico Fe Alegría, Venezuela

The aim of Instituto Radiofónico Fe Alegría (IRFA) is to provide adult education and literacy and technical secondary school training for adults (over fifteen years old) who were unable to complete basic education programs. From 1975 to 1990, the adult education program was offered only by radio. Since then, IRFA has entered multiple partnerships with communities and private companies to offer an on-site curriculum. Private companies provide premises and human resources (coordinators, and volunteers to act as guides) for operating the system. IRFA contributes printed materials, radio lessons, training for coordinators, testing and review, and application to the Ministry of Education for certification. Some companies limit enrollment to employees, as part of their human-resource development objectives, while others explicitly promote participation from the broader community (Luengo and Ponce 1997).

---

government, and the private sector. This is particularly true when NGOs engage with companies whom they have perceived as adversaries in the past (Murphy and Bendell 1997).

Private-sector organization culture emphasizes a monetary bottom line and short-term profits. This raises the possibility that private-sector partners may want to disengage from partnership work prematurely. Since philanthropic work is not companies' core activity, they also cannot be expected to be immediate specialists. However, private-sector actors may approach development challenges with naïve cowboy gusto, as this is a new arena for many of them.

Proposed selection criteria to inform decisions to enter a partnership with particular private-sector actors include:

- Support for corporate citizenship: guiding values and principles, voluntary codes of conduct, and citizenship track record and experience.
- Reputation and good or neutral standing with key stakeholders: labor and environmental policies; local and global history and practice.
- Expected benefit: direct interest and benefits that are easily identified and articulated.
- Corporate commitment and recognition of expected benefits.
- Command of required resources and skills.
- Employee volunteer or release time.
- Capacity to contribute effectively.
- Agreement on necessary time frame.

Benefits and Risks

Globalization poses challenges to both corporate competitiveness and corporate governance. Companies are faced with greater accountability to a larger number and greater diversity of stakeholders (including environmental, social, and human rights activists) on a broader range of issues. Partnerships can support all four necessary components for achieving corporate competitiveness and good corporate governance: reputation management, relationship management, responsiveness to systems and service needs, and resource efficiency and enhancement (Nelson 1996).

Boycotts have demonstrated the important power of moral authority and the potential to sway the public and consumers to detrimental effect on profit (for example, grapes in California, tuna from Mexico, and global boycotts on Nestlé). Many businesses recognize a link between reputation and profit, and they weigh the perceived risks when contemplating alternative business strategies and the perceived benefit in considering corporate citizenship strategies.[3] The assessment of a company's ethical capital may increasingly determine the extent to which it can avoid costs from overregulation and legal challenges and ultimately earn a license to operate in new and emerging markets. For many companies, philanthropic partnerships are a risk-management strategy. Not surprisingly, most corporations' participation in partnerships will be well advertised (Box 3.13).

Partnerships afford access to key players in government and among financing institutions (such as the International Monetary Fund) and enhance negotiating power and goodwill. Partnerships can foster more communication, improved relations, and sometimes conflict resolution with a company's critics. The relationships developed through partnership work

---

Box 3.13   Denny's and Save the Children, USA

In the United States, Denny's sought to overcome the reputational damage of a federal discrimination suit by partnering with Save the Children, an international, child sponsorship NGO. Denny's became Save the Children's largest corporate sponsor, committing to raise $750,000 through its network of 1,600 restaurants, 70,000 corporate and franchise employees, and approximately one million daily customers. Denny's servers wore Save the Children ties, and each company-owned restaurant and participating franchisee sponsored a child, sold Save the Children ties and note cards, and engaged in other local fundraising activities. The partnership was publicly announced on National Children's Day, October 9, 1994. Denny's also sponsored a children's art contest with ample press coverage of its ceremonies for the national winners. The tie or T-shirt featuring the artwork was sent to local reporters, editors, and producers and to fifty selected media celebrities (Sagawa and Segal 2000).

can be leveraged to gain market entry into new and emerging markets, to build or sustain market share and customer loyalty, to promote and enhance brand image, and to gain access to market intelligence. Partnerships can enhance a company's understanding of and relationships with consumer and employee communities, needs, and interests (see Kanter 1995) (Box 3.14).

Improved relationships can reduce input and transaction costs, increase process efficiency, and improve the quality of products and services. Partnerships improve companies' ability to access high-quality resources such as employee motivation and commitment, customer loyalty, and enhanced understanding and information from various stakeholders. Organizational learning from partnership work can include new technologies and solutions; experience with the way different sectors operate, their strengths, weaknesses, opportunities, and constraints; new managerial processes and organizational structures; and a spirit of innovation and initiative that incorporates flexibility, responsiveness, and a commitment to maximizing benefits to all concerned. All of these experiences and benefits can be applied to core business, enhancing corporate competitiveness and improving corporate governance.

The greatest potential risk for private-sector actors is their bottom line. With respect to reputation, the public, particularly civil society organizations (CSOs) and activists, is sometimes intolerant of businesses profiting from philanthropic work, though this is changing in some circles. Since target issues and communities have so much to gain from partnerships that engage the private sector, the selection process can ruffle feathers—there are always winners and losers. In addition, partners may speak out or act in ways that can be detrimental to a corporation's reputation.

Partnerships are typically designed to address problems that are beyond the scope of any one actor; they may be the most intractable problems, requiring long-term investments. Businesses tend to engage in long-term planning but with an emphasis on short-term results and earnings.

Box 3.14   Slum Rehabilitation, Jamaica

In Montego Bay, Jamaica, a company's participation in a partnership for slum rehabilitation helped it to better understand informal communities and how they affect the employees who live there. Another private-sector partner reports direct benefits to the improved living conditions in the slums because his employees "come to the workplace more relaxed; their productivity is high; they're clean and have hygienic standards because they are coming from hygienic surroundings" (Universidad de West Indies 1997: 8).

There is a reasonable risk that the partnership will not accomplish what it set out to do within a "reasonable" time frame. Stockholders may lose patience with these investments, and if the media begins to tout "failure," the company will need to do damage control with respect to both its core business and its morally motivated stakeholders and critics. While development work can be an important motivator for corporate employees, it also risks distracting them from core business.

Partnership Actors: To Partner or Not to Partner

The most salient factors influencing partnership partner composition are the partnership objectives, corresponding necessary inputs, comparative advantages and drivers of various sectors, and the particular drivers for individual organizations and actors. The variation in these factors confirms the continuing diversity of partnerships both in the types of partners represented and their prescribed roles. Selection criteria can assist partnership actors and initiators to maximize the benefits and minimize the challenges posed by each potential partner. Partnerships may pose risks to actors, some of which are based on their sectoral origins and traditional role in society. Because partnerships entail costs as well as benefits, it is helpful to enumerate both sets of potential outcomes and conduct cost-benefit analyses to inform decisions to enter into partnerships. Cost-benefit analyses can also assist actors in determining whether or not a partnership is the most cost-effective relationship option and how to structure and sequence the partnership initiation and implementation. Additional inputs and considerations for the latter challenge are taken up in Chapter 4.

Notes

1. These presumptions and prescriptions are frequently normative; there is a fair share of government and donor bashing, as well as biases of NGO praise or criticism.

2. The comparative advantage of government legitimacy has been contested. In some circumstances, government participation can lend considerable status and legitimacy to a particular development effort (see Fiszbein and Lowden 1998), while in others the opposite case may hold.

3. The Harris Reputation Quotient, for example, rates companies annually, enabling them to compare their reputation to that of competitors (Harris Interactive 2002).

4

Managing for Partnership Results

There are multiple reasons why organizations choose to partner. The principles of partnership are many and sometimes contradictory; they may even be impossible to achieve. The best circumstances for pursuing a partnership approach may never exist in the development context, and some conducive factors may conflict with others, making the classification of contextual features highly subjective. Also, the types of partner organizations and their possible configurations vary with many motivations to partner (often conflicting) and a complex range of potential challenges posed by each. Partnerships constitute heterogeneous relationships that encompass diverse technologies, with multiple specialties (or divisions of labor). The question of *how* best to partner is not a simple one, and it is largely compounded by the reality that partnerships entail change.

Partnership design and implementation are determined by objectives, context, preferences, and the strategies actors employ to address them. Chapter 2 addressed contextual factors that directly and indirectly influence partnership implementation and effectiveness. Chapter 3 presented two strategies actors may employ to determine components of partnership implementation: cost-benefit analysis and partner-selection criteria. This chapter will address partnership design, implementation, and coping strategies, and it will specify the parameters over which actors must decide. Figure 4.1 illustrates the relationship among objectives, environmental hostility, preferences, and selected strategies.

Both individual organizations' partnership objectives and the overall partnership objectives are rationally determined based on an organization's mission and sociopolitical context. They are also informed by the organization's preferences regarding how it should pursue that mission. While objectives are likely to vary among partners, partners typically find common ground in the partnership or programmatic objectives, or they negotiate until they do. Selected objectives will drive preferences for certain

Figure 4.1   Interrelationship Among Objectives, Environmental Hostility, Preferences, and Strategies

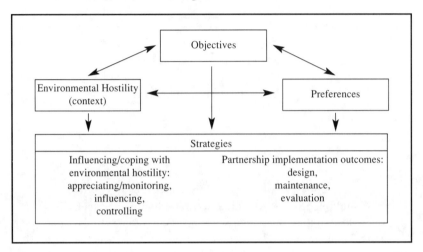

strategies and approaches, based on the trade-offs they imply. Objectives also directly determine the range of possible strategies. Particular objectives may create or reduce environmental hostility (see Chapter 2). The reverse, however, is also true: environmental hostility influences the selection of objectives. The environment can make some objectives illegal, impossible, or prohibitively complicated or costly.

Selection of coping and implementation strategies also entails trade-off decisions. Trade-offs exist in the relative weight of the various factors contributing to strategy selection and in strategy options. Whether explicitly or not, these trade-offs are decided through cost-benefit analyses, which take actors' preferences into account, and negotiation among partner organizations.

The Parameters of Preferences

Preferences are driven by an actor's tolerance for sharing power; willingness to adapt and be flexible in the interest of maximizing partnership efficiency and effectiveness, including ensuring partner organization identity; and trust and confidence in its partners.

Sharing Power and Adapting to Partnership Needs

Actors' tolerance for sharing power and their willingness to adapt derive from the personalities of participating individuals (typically beyond the control of partnership actors); the organization's culture; and the organization's requirements for stakeholder accountability and constituency relations. Some organizations are more risk-averse than others. Organization leaders may actively encourage and reward participation, innovation, and risk taking, or they may prevent or discourage it. Management practice and structure provide clues to whether an organization's culture will be more or less tolerant for sharing power and adapting. For example, is the organization structured around teams? What is the span of managers' control? Are meetings open and participatory? What is the degree of information sharing within and outside of the organization? Organizations' internal relations tend to be reflected in their interorganizational relations (Forester 1993). Organizations that are relatively more mechanistic in structure will be less tolerant of sharing power and less willing to adapt for the sake of partnership effectiveness, while organizations that are more organic will tend to be flexible and more tolerant (see Burns and Stalker 1961). Figure 4.2 summarizes parameters contributing to low and high tolerance for power sharing and willingness to adapt.

Flexibility and tolerance are also determined by an organization's stakeholders and constituencies. The constraints of internal stakeholders will depend on the degree of consensus within the organization to support the partnership and its particular approach. Contradicting external stakeholder relations requirements would mean willingly compromising organization identity. Constituency needs and concerns, and particularly formal accountability criteria, set limits on how far organizations can go in sharing power and adapting practices and structures to accommodate a partnership. Partnership actors need to manage these relationships strategically to cultivate broad support for the partnership and ensure a common understanding of the need for power sharing and adaptation.

Trust and Confidence

Trust and confidence are both the target of strategy and the determinants of strategic preferences. Trust is voluntary and linked to shared values (Tonkiss and Passey 1999). Confidence is based on rational expectations, rather than ethics, and is typically grounded in institutional arrangements, such as contracts, regulations, and standard operating procedures (Luhmann 1988). Initial trust and confidence levels are determined by environmental hostility (for example, the existence of rule of law, the quality of intersectoral relations, and previous experience among the actors). Trust may or may not develop over time, as partner organizations and individuals gain understanding and accumulate experience through repeated interaction. Strategies for enhancing trust include making values explicit, broadening the scope of participation to cultivate internal commitment, and carefully crafting and reinforcing the partnership organization culture.

Figure 4.2   Tolerance for Sharing Power and Willingness to Adapt to Partnership Needs

Low Tolerance/Willingness (mechanistic organization)	Continuum	High Tolerance/Willingness (organic organization)
Rigid division of labor based on functional tasks.	◄———►	Fluid division of labor based on specialized knowledge and experience.
Emphasis on application of specialized techniques to complete the task.	◄———►	Emphasis on application of knowledge to contribute to organizational effectiveness.
A priori task assignment with coordination at each level of hierarchy.	◄———►	Continual redefinition and adjustment of individual tasks through interaction.
Precise definition of rights, obligations, and technical methods of each functional role.	◄———►	Individual responsibility for contributing to overall organization effectiveness.
Dedication to a defined functional position.	◄———►	Commitment to organization's mission.
Hierarchical control, authority, and communication.	◄———►	Network structure of control, authority, and communication.
Reinforcement of hierarchy through exclusive knowledge of actualities at the top.	◄———►	Knowledge about the organization's technical nature and effectiveness can be located anywhere in the network.
Vertical interaction.	◄———►	Fluid interaction, contingent on the information and skills required at the moment.
Governance through issuing instructions and decisions by supervisors.	◄———►	Emphasis in communications on information and advice (not instructions and decisions).
Local and technical knowledge more highly valued than general, universal knowledge.	◄———►	Innovation, creative thinking, and knowledge of interdependence highly valued.
Decisions made through hierarchy.	◄———►	Decisions made through participation.

Confidence can be developed through transparency and accountability mechanisms, as well as by specifying contracts, roles and responsibilities, and standard operating procedures.

Effective partnerships require both trust and confidence. The tension between trust and confidence is reflected in the trade-offs between formal and informal processes, governance mechanisms, and breadth and depth of representativeness and participation. Confidence can substitute for trust to a point, but trust can be more efficient and effective, utilizing culture governance mechanisms (the mechanism with the lowest transaction costs). Organizations and individuals with a low tolerance for sharing power and low willingness to adapt for partnership effectiveness and partner organization identity requirements are likely to rely more on confidence measures than trust building and maintenance (Box 4.1). Confidence and trust do not conform to a linear model, though trust is typically enhanced over time. Like standard operating procedures, confidence-building mechanisms serve to enhance efficiency and reduce transaction costs. These mechanisms can be developed through trust-building approaches, with active and broad participation based on consensus. Confidence mechanisms can serve as an initial substitute for trust, but neglecting simultaneous trust-building measures or overrelying on confidence mechanisms can potentially undermine and prevent trust building, raise transaction costs, and weaken organization commitment.

Strategies to Address Environmental Hostility

The Appreciate/Influence/Control (A/I/C) model is the basis for environmental response strategies (see ODII 2000; Smith 1991). Appreciation

---

Box 4.1   Trust and Confidence Alternatives

The Women's Enterprise Management Training Outreach Program (WEM-TOP). WEMTOP emphasized trust building from the outset. The first Training Needs Analysis workshop became a venting session for NGOs to criticize and express frustration with the World Bank. The World Bank task manager considered this "a necessary ventilation . . . [and] a rare face-to-face opportunity with a donor to level the ground for debate and collaboration" (Viswanath 1995). The demonstrated willingness to listen and respond to NGO concerns was the first step in building credibility. Together, the World Bank task manager and Udyogini (the NGO partner organization) crafted and agreed to a detailed memorandum of agreement. This entailed six months of joint work, with negotiations and iterative clearance from the World Bank Legal Department. The end result deviates from the Bank's contractual and legal norms. The document is responsive to NGO concerns and culture in its wording; and its terminology emphasizes the partnership role of Udyogini, rather than treating it as a contractor (Viswanath 1995; Coston 1999).

The World Bank's India Population Project VIII. While special arrangements were also made for the NGO partnership component in the World Bank's India Population Project VIII, the emphasis was much more on confidence establishment than on trust building. Exceptions were made based on rational principles of efficiency and effectiveness, not necessarily for relationship building. Care was taken to ensure that the wording of the contract and procedures did not create transaction costs that would exceed the allocated funding. It was on this basis that the review process was simplified. The contract emphasizes specification of measurable outcomes rather than spelling out relationship parameters (Fogle 1998; Coston 1999).

implies understanding and monitoring, in order to anticipate and respond to changes in the environment and to reclassify factors deemed beyond actors' control and influence, where possible, and determine influencing and controlling strategies. Influencing encompasses incentive systems, exchanges, and proactive negotiation. In addition to assuming responsibility generally, controlling occurs when agreements and processes are standardized and formalized. For example, organizations use selection criteria to control their selection of partners. Partners' preferences will determine which factors are subject to negotiation and influence and which can only be appreciated.

Figures 4.3 and 4.4 delineate strategies to address environmental hostility, identifying whether or not particular factors can typically be appreciated, influenced, or controlled. Factors in the broader development environment are beyond the scope of individual partnerships but are frequently targeted by donors and sometimes governments' reform initiatives. Factors at other levels can be addressed by partner organizations and partnership organizers or facilitators. These strategies imply ideal responses and

Figure 4.3   Strategies for Addressing Hostility in the Broader Development Environment

Level/Target	A/I/C[a]	Actors: Partnership Members, Donors, and Government
Legal frameworks and the rule of law	A/I	Partnership members appreciate: monitor for relevant changes (opportunities and threats); donors and governments influence: apply pressure or initiate policy change processes.
Democratic governance	A/I	Partnership members appreciate: monitor for relevant changes (opportunities and threats); donors and governments influence: apply pressure or initiate change processes.
Rationalization of the state	A/I	Partnership members appreciate: monitor for relevant changes (opportunities and threats); donors and governments influence: apply pressure or initiate change processes.
Intersectoral relations	A/I	Partnership members appreciate: monitor for relevant changes (opportunities and threats); donors and governments influence, including incorporating CSOs in the design, planning, implementation and monitoring of development projects.
Environmental stability and flexibility	A/I	Partnership members appreciate: monitor for relevant changes (opportunities and threats); donors and governments influence: apply pressure or initiate actions to prevent upheavals and promote adaptation.
Environmental artificiality	A/I/C	Partnership members appreciate: monitor for relevant changes (opportunities and threats); donors and governments control or influence: apply pressure or make decisions and take action to avoid contributing to artificiality.

Note: a. A/I/C is Appreciate/Influence/Control.

Figure 4.4   Strategies for Addressing Hostility in the Immediate Partnership Environment

Level/Target	A/I/C	Actors: Partnership Members
Partnership champions	I/C	Identify and solicit participation of entrepreneurial actors, within and outside of the organization as needed.
	I	Identify and sell individual and organizational drivers for partnership effort.
	I	Maintain and adjust incentive systems to sustain the internal commitment of partnership champions.
Institutional linkage	I/A	Identify or create bridging mechanisms between sectoral actors; appreciate their absence when creation is not possible.
	I	Maintain and nurture existing mechanisms through stakeholder relations.
	I/A	Identify and influence (as possible) transaction costs of local institutional frameworks.
	I/A	Identify local power relations, co-opt and/or negotiate exceptions as possible.
Partner organizations	C	If necessary, create organizations with which to partner.
	A	Appreciate the organization identity and unique contributions of each partner; identify these and assure mutual understanding.
	I	Continuously monitor the implications of the partnership for the partners' identity. Make these known and lobby for and make adjustments as needed.
	A/C	Appreciate physical proximity, prior history of working together, and shared high-value end-users or incorporate these into selection criteria.
	A/C	Appreciate partner organizations' stakeholders and constituents; identify and make these and related implications explicit; or control for incompatibilities through selection criteria.
	A/I	Monitor partner organizations' stakeholder and constituent interests; identify and sell partnership drivers accordingly.
	I	Continuously identify and sell partner organization drivers for the partnership effort among partner organizations.
	I	Cultivate and continuously promote a shared partnership vision within partner organizations (among organization members), and among partner organizations.
	I/C	Negotiate adaptations to enhance compatibility of partnership partners (ongoing as needed) and/or control through selection criteria.
	I/C	Assure partners have needed capacity, skills, and characteristics: build capacity as possible, within resource limits; incorporate these into partner selection criteria.
	A/I	Monitor changing capacity needs and implement capacity-building measures accordingly.
	A/C	Appreciate, where necessary, the absence of partners with an understanding of local dynamics and history of working in the local context, and monitor to identify alternative sources of local expertise; or identify and engage such partners (selection criterion).
	A/I	Assure individuals occupying key roles in partner organizations have requisite skills for partnership success; build capacity as appropriate and possible, given resource constraints (continuing); minimize turnover among key players; and negotiate with partner organizations regarding their relevant personnel as possible or appropriate.

(continues)

Figure 4.4   Continued

Level/Target	A/I/C	Actors: Partnership Members
	I	Cultivate and maintain shared values among partners and individuals, create and promote a common partnership culture.
	C	Establish agreement on joint objectives.
Partnership objective	A/C	Appreciate environmental hostility deriving from objectives and monitor for relevant opportunities or threats; or select (control) objectives with minimal challenges to vested interests, implications for fewer government agencies, and partnership outcomes with ease of attribution.
	I	Adapt objectives, as needed and agreed, in response to external opportunities and threats and internal strengths and weaknesses.
	I/C	Cultivate demand for partnership outcomes, as necessary, and monitor and expand demand as needed; or select objectives/services/products with a ready demand.
Partnership stakeholders	A/I	Appreciate and monitor for relevant changes (opportunities and threats); or cultivate new stakeholders, where possible, influencing the relative balance of interests and diversity as needed.
	I	Organize stakeholders as needed.
	I	Empower stakeholders to enhance the influence of those who are supportive of the partnership effort.
	I	Continuously sell the merits of the partnership and the requirements for sharing power and adapting as needed.
Legal frameworks	A/I/C	Appreciate legal frameworks, and monitor for and respond to emerging opportunities and threats; lobby influential actors to modify or grant exceptions to inhibiting features of legal frameworks; and/or select partnership and structures that conform to legal frameworks.
Stability	A	Appreciate staff turnover within partner organizations; monitor to anticipate and respond to changes.
	I	Influence turnover within own organization; provide incentives and institutional support to key individuals.
	I	Promote incentive systems, partnership culture, and fairness to maintain internal commitment and OCB.
	A/I	Appreciate changing stakeholder interests and demands; monitor for emerging opportunities and threats; influence stakeholder interests and demands, where possible, by selling the partnership, its benefits and outcomes.
Flexibility	A	Appreciate nonnegotiable partnership procedures/approaches (i.e., those that contradict partner organization identity or conflict with stakeholder/constituency interests); monitor for emerging opportunities and threats.
	C	Develop alternative arrangements or coping mechanisms for nonnegotiable procedures/approaches.
	I	Negotiate exceptions and adaptations in partner organization structures and procedures.
Artificiality	I/C	Cultivate and continuously promote local ownership (e.g., through participation) and mutual agreements.
	A/I	Appreciate when artificiality is necessary for partnership formation and implementation, and monitor for emerging opportunities and threats, but try to influence its impacts by creating alternative incentives.

encompass trade-off decisions in resource allocation and investment, individual organization preferences, and negotiated agreements. Addressing environmental hostility begins with partnership initiation and design, and it is a continuing management responsibility, integral to both maintaining partnerships throughout their institutional duration and contributing to the sustainability of their benefits.

Partnership Design and Implementation Decisions

Objectives, environmental hostility, and preferences determine how partnerships are designed, maintained, and evaluated. Within these activities, partners identify options, weigh trade-offs, and make decisions.

Design

While much of partnership's complexity is unavoidable, trade-off decisions can lead to more efficient complexity, which balances the need for responsiveness and flexibility with the minimization of transaction costs. Decisions based on authority, formalization, hierarchy, and centralization can reduce complexity and transaction costs, but they can also compromise partnership effectiveness, as these structural features tend to reduce flexibility and responsiveness. This trade-off parallels that between confidence and trust. Design trade-offs are resolved at various levels of partnership governance. The degree of autonomy and formality at each governance level varies and may determine the extent to which any one partner is in charge at a particular moment. One option is to maintain flexibility and responsiveness at the operational level, which can reduce reporting and other transaction costs by relying more on trust. This is often more feasible if governance at higher levels is more formally agreed, instilling confidence.

Organizational possibilities can range from completely informal to fully institutionalized. Decisions regarding design trade-offs and their organizational (structure and process) solutions are informed by actors' preferences and objectives in determining how to maximize opportunities provided through the partnership, while minimizing the risks to partners, stakeholders, and constituencies. Partnership design builds on clear goals, explicit distribution of authority, and a specified division of labor. Design trade-offs encompass structure and its degree of integration and formality; the relative weight of various governance mechanisms (bureaucracy, market, and culture); incentive systems and values; representativeness and participation; and accountability and transparency.

Integration and mediation.   General characteristics of partnership structure include pluriformity, or the extent to which the partnership can be viewed as a single entity or a collection of autonomous organizations; interdependence and self-containment, or the capacity of partners to shield themselves from the influences of the partnership; and formality (Peters 1998). Pluriformity, interdependence, and self-containment are features of both design and evolution. Partners may choose to begin as a more pluriform, less interdependent partnership, which, if proven successful, may evolve into a more uniform, integrated partnership. Such an evolution can be based upon incremental successes, the partners' growing level of comfort and trust, project or funder requirements, or legal and cultural constraints that prevent continued or expanded work without more formal agreements.

Ronald Burt (2000) posits that networks that are dense and hierarchical do not perform as well as more loosely affiliated, heterogeneous networks do. The more opportunities for structural holes—that is, information diffusion where individual actors act as bridges between diffuse sources of information—the more likely the network is associated with good performance, assuming those structural holes are adequately exploited. This makes logical sense in that the network has access to more information, for example, on needs and interests, effective methods, constraints, and new technologies. Given the challenges and complexity of collective action, partnerships will often require more formal structures than Burt's application to networks might suggest. However, his theory does support an approach that would minimize hierarchy and control and embrace differences and creative tension.

The degree of environmental hostility may determine the potential for high integration. For example, legal frameworks may not support integrated structures; constituents/stakeholders of partner organizations may not tolerate it; or the nature of partnership objectives may preclude it due to complexity, such as the number of actors implicated or the geographic and substantive spread of the issue to be addressed. Integration entails power sharing and substantial organizational adaptation. Effective integration can instill confidence through established structures and procedures. More loosely organized partnerships may produce the benefits of more structural holes, but they will also require significant trust among partners; for example, actors must trust that the information available through these holes is consistently and broadly shared for the benefit of partnership objectives. Trust also implies a relationship based on mutual understanding that enables partners to recognize potentially strategic information and opportunities. Integration trade-offs are summarized in Figure 4.5.

The definition of a partnership's structure and coordination may include the establishment of mediators or mediating bodies. The most effective partnerships rely upon mediators (see, for example, Nelson 1996; Fiszbein and Lowden 1998), sometimes without fully realizing it. Mediators establish bridges and negotiate between partners regarding dif-

Figure 4.5   Integration Trade-offs

Low Integration	Continuum	High Integration
Maintenance of a range of information, knowledge and skills (structural holes).	←——————→	Similarity over time.
Maximization of opportunity.	←——————→	Maximization of predictability within the system.
Maximization of effectiveness through responsiveness.	←——————→	Maximization of efficiency through standardization.
Reliance on trust.	←——————→	Reliance on confidence.

ferent motivations, needs, and resources, and they facilitate a sense of equity and partnership identity, especially when partners are unequal in power and resources. Mediators may also organize meetings, monitor and promote partnership principles, ensure partner capacity, prepare partners for the impacts of partnership activity, and make certain that different views are represented. Mediators can be individuals or groups from any one of the partner organizations or sectors, academic institutions, or external stakeholder groups and specialists. The need for and role of mediators will likely change as the partnership evolves, depending on the extent of trust and confidence built over time.

The use of a mediator may substitute for some trust and confidence among partner organizations, but it requires significant trust and confidence in the mediating actor and the processes employed. Mediators can address partner organizations' intolerance for sharing power and reluctance to adapt, sometimes substituting for these by providing a buffer, such as fulfilling administrative requirements, reformatting reports, or negotiating adjustments necessary for partnership effectiveness. Mediators are particularly important when partner organizations lack experience with and understanding of each other; have a history of conflict, competition, or opposition; or are diverse, numerous, or geographically dispersed.

Degree of formality.   Partnerships are often created to maximize the informational, skill, and resource opportunities described in Burt's theory of network structure. Once partnerships are formed, however, James Coleman's (1988, 1990) perspective on social capital—a denser network of relationships can engender trust—becomes relevant. The challenge is to attain the appropriate balance between the advantages of a dynamic partnership, which continuously seeks and exploits new opportunities for information and intelligence gathering (a diffuse, nonhierarchical network), and a deeply rooted partnership based on trust and expected norms of behavior (a dense, closed network). The latter does not necessarily justify formalization and economic and bureaucratic sanctions. To the contrary, efficient partnerships seek to maximize low-cost governance mechanisms, and effective partnerships find ways to remain flexible and responsive to emerging opportunities, which implies relying on informal processes. Effective partnerships require a careful combination of formal structures, which facilitate coordination, and informal processes, which allow for responsiveness in the systems governing internal and external relations.

Distrust or lack of experience among partners and dynamic internal environments may lead to preferences for relatively more formality. Because of partnership's complexity, there is a tendency to overemphasize structure and process formalization. Formalization can produce confidence to substitute for lack of trust. However, overly specified plans tend to emphasize accounting over accountability (Fowler 1997), promoting bureaucratic expediency rather than focusing on impact and effectiveness. Even when partner relationships are very good on an interpersonal level and things seem to be working well, it may be important to put agreements in writing—including those related to underlying philosophy—in the hopes of withstanding staff turnover and changing climates.

The degree of formalization is also dependent on the task or function at hand. Formalization facilitates the pursuit of selected common goals—reducing transaction costs in responding to repeated tasks—and the control of anticipated consequences. A formalized structure reduces the need to develop ad hoc understandings and engage in constant negotiation and bargaining (Peters 1998). Formalization is required to ensure financial accounting; and transparency often necessitates the formalization of agreements and reporting requirements. When significant resource commitments are introduced, even previously informal organizations tend to formalize. Institutionalizing lessons learned through partnership work also typically rely on formal processes, such as the development of standard operating procedures.

Hierarchy and formalization cannot eliminate the pursuit of self-interest and power plays; formal requirements and procedures can lead to project delays and implementation obstacles; and formalization does not necessarily reduce complexity. One important response to coping with complexity is to rely on informal processes. Without the constraints of formal rules of assignment and responsibility, informal relations can provide for information exchange, communication, and the exercise of influence. Furthermore, informal relations build trust by promoting mutual information exchange and reduce transaction costs by providing a basis of common knowledge, experience, and normative orientation (Börzel 1998). Informal processes provide for flexibility and opportunities for creativity not constrained by rigid bureaucratic requirements; they enable partners and their staff to respond to opportunities as they arise. Less formalization affords partner organizations greater leeway to protect organization identity and respond to their own constituencies.

Effective partnerships employ a "dialectical mode of organization" (Machado and Burns 1998: 379), combining formal and informal systems and procedures. Typically, the most powerful partners—donors, governments, and large corporations—operate on the basis of hierarchy and formality. For this reason, the merits of informality and flexibility require proactive attention. Formalization trade-offs are summarized in Figure 4.6.

Governance mechanisms. The application of market mechanisms in partnerships is most evident in the use of contracts and exit strategies. Some partnerships are set up through a contracting arrangement that specifies a price (financial, material, or otherwise) based on the delivery of determined goods or services (i.e., the contribution of specified comparative advantages). In addition, an important mechanism of accountability in partnerships is the opportunity for partners to exit the relationship if it is not implemented as agreed or if results are not as expected. The parameters of exit may be defined in contracts or other initiating agreements; while exit may be an option, it may not be without a price. The downside of price or market mechanisms is that they neither encompass nor promote trust.

Bureaucratic mechanisms can be used to define roles and responsibilities based on comparative advantages and the agreed contributions to be made by each partner. Bureaucratic mechanisms can also provide for or mandate opportunities for exit and voice for all partners and constituencies. These mechanisms define the parameters of representation and participation, and create forums for regularly providing input into decisions, for instance, through establishing meeting schedules and special events. They are also the means to establish and promote transparency, access, and dis-

Figure 4.6   Formalization Trade-offs

Low Formalization	Continuum	High Formalization
Trust.	◄———►	Control/confidence.
Efficiency in governance mechanisms.	◄———►	Higher transaction costs of governance mechanisms.
Flexibility and responsiveness to dynamic external environment.	◄———►	Predictability and stability within dynamic internal environment.
Effectiveness in responding to nonroutine tasks and unanticipated challenges.	◄———►	Efficiency in standardization of procedures for repeated tasks and anticipated challenges.
Tasks: innovation and protection of organization identity.	◄———►	Tasks: financial accounting, transparency, and learning.

semination of information. Bureaucratic governance mechanisms are most important when establishing a partnership (see Lowndes and Skelcher 1998), both in terms of defining its structure and the respective roles and responsibilities of partners, and in terms of partnership design, including standard operating procedures, lines of accountability, reporting and information exchange, and representation and authority.

Culture mechanisms are a powerful source of influence and control that are often undervalued. Repeated communication and interaction create the foundation for learning who to trust, what the consequences of behavior are, and how to maximize mutual gain and minimize potential losses (Ostrom 1990). They also yield shared norms of behavior and reciprocity. Enforcement and compliance are based on trust and expectations rooted in a sense of belonging. Culture mechanisms can become the glue that bonds different actors, not only ensuring compliance with expected norms of behavior but also maximizing the efficiency and effectiveness of other governance mechanisms (Coston 1998b).

Culture governance mechanisms are important throughout the life of a partnership. They are the very foundation of partnerships when the initial decision to partner is based on consensus about values and goals; and culture mechanisms are later used to enforce expectations through moral obligations and professional ethics. They are particularly important during prepartnership collaboration, when organizations work together and negotiate on an ad hoc basis, and again in partnership termination and succession (Lowndes and Skelcher 1998). Culture mechanisms are promoted through the creation and promotion of partnership identity and an associated organization culture with incentive systems specific to partnership objectives and values.

Partnership work is most effective when it relies on a careful mixture of the three governance mechanisms. Actors' preferences and partnership contextual factors determine the mix. Bureaucratic mechanisms are most appropriate where the required intervention is relatively straightforward and the context is politically and technologically simple. The loyalty, trust, and reciprocity of culture mechanisms may not always be appropriate; they may be particularly complex in partnerships based on conflict resolution. Culture mechanisms cannot be forced and will only survive if there is a perceived need and collective will to support them. Complex organizations are weakest at the interface of these different governance mechanisms, where both tension and transaction costs can rise (Machado and Burns 1998). The balance is never simple or sufficient. Additional mechanisms and tools, including incentive systems, can be employed to address these weak points. The parameters and trade-offs of governance mechanisms are summarized in Figure 4.7.

Figure 4.7   Governance Mechanisms: Parameters and Trade-offs

	Market	Bureaucracy	Culture
Functional emphasis	Confidence or exit: establishes the choice of noncompliance or specifies recourse if actors fail to comply.	Confidence, and strategies for trust building and voice.	Trust.
Stages	Partnership initiation and termination.	Partnership design and implementation.	Throughout, especially developing during partnership implementation.
Environment	Information readily available. Appropriate when partners lack mutual understanding (reliance on price mechanism) or there is conflict (exit option).	Predictable/stable. Appropriate when partners lack mutual understanding or there is conflict (reliance on confidence).	Dynamic environment with increasing mutual understanding and harmony among partners.

Incentive systems and values.   The relative emphasis and content of tangible and intangible motivators will influence the type of individuals recruited to the partnership (both from within and in some cases outside of partner organizations), the depth and source of their commitment, and the ability to retain them. Given the additional work and potential stress that partnership work can entail, material rewards are not sufficient and may be harmful if not appropriately balanced with intangible incentives. Intangible incentives are also typically less costly. A primary means to promote intrinsic motivation in the partnership context is to institutionalize the partnership by infusing it with values. Partnership incentive systems require socialization investments that orient staff from all partner organizations to the partnership's objectives and values. The effectiveness of these measures will depend on whether or not partnership negotiation and definition represent a values consensus or shared vision. The degree of socialization investment will also depend on the preferred integration of the partners and the proposed duration of the partnership.

Tangible, material rewards also have their place. Material rewards demonstrate that organizations value skills and individual contributions. Nonfinancial extrinsic incentives can also be employed, such as awards and recognition programs. High-profile external award programs and media coverage may be particularly effective for corporations engaging in corporate citizenship. Because partnership outcomes may not materialize in the short run and attribution is often problematic, extrinsic incentives may be necessary to complement intrinsic incentives and maintain motivation during challenging periods when results may be difficult to identify or relations with partners and constituencies may be tense.

In the absence of material rewards, individuals may identify intrinsic rewards that justify their efforts.[1] Conversely, when material rewards are introduced to individuals who are primarily motivated intrinsically, the perceived intrinsic benefits may diminish accordingly. This is true both at the individual and organizational level. For example, according to NGO advocates, the introduction of contracting and competition within the nonprofit sector, "tilts the [NGO] ethos away from moral commitment towards material reward" (Fowler 1997: 84), much like a self-fulfilling prophecy. This reinforces the rationale for separating discussions of partnership vision, objectives, roles, and responsibilities from financing in the negotiation stage.

Employees and volunteers may self-select to work in environments that reinforce their own values and corresponding preferences regarding tangible and intangible motivators. Tangible (extrinsic/material) and intangible (intrinsic/value) incentives promote external and internal commitment respectively. Internal commitment, once established, is lower in transaction costs and can result in deeper, broader, and a potentially longer duration of employee dedication to the organization (or partnership) and its objectives. Organization citizenship behavior (OCB) posits a role for both types of incentives (see Organ 1990). An actor's value orientation and emphasis on intrinsic reward can attract individuals with a disposition for OCB. Perceptions of fairness with respect to material rewards and implied valuation of individuals' contributions can help to sustain this disposition and retain those who have it. The trade-offs of intrinsic and extrinsic incentives are summarized in Figure 4.8.

If the partnership is not implemented consistent with the normative order it promotes, it will generate cynicism and demotivation and limit

Figure 4.8   Intrinsic and Extrinsic Incentive Trade-offs

Intrinsic/Values	Continuum	Extrinsic/Material
Reinforces team effort.	←——————→	Implies value of individuals' contributions.
Generates internal commitment.	←——————→	Generates external commitment.
Helpful for recruiting those with an OCB disposition.	←——————→	Helpful for retaining those with an OCB disposition through assuring fairness in material rewards.

partnership effectiveness. Such inconsistencies undermine internal commitment and OCB. One way to safeguard against such cynicism, express commitment to partnership principles, and promote this desired behavior is to define and promote representation and participation carefully.

Participation and representation. In the most effective partnerships, voice provides the possibility of introducing new ideas and modifying goals and means, allowing for maximum exploitation of structural holes. Participation also includes collaborative decisionmaking. The quality of participation determines how actors perceive the importance of their contribution to the whole, which in turn determines internal commitment.

During initial negotiation and agreement and in each subsequent meeting among partners, participatory techniques can be used to structure and facilitate meetings, particularly planning meetings. Participation can be largely supported through bureaucratic mandates, specifying representation and participation requirements for decisionmaking quorums, defining participation and representation on the governing bodies of the partnership, and so forth. Partners might also include representatives of their partner organizations on special commissions related to their individual organization or involve partners in other forms of consultation. Greater participation will likely be preferred when actors have a history of distrust or conflict or when transparency systems and associated confidence are lacking.

The parameters of representation must also be considered. For example, representatives might be chosen through election or assigned based on roles and responsibilities. Effective representation from meeting to meeting requires a careful balance between depth and consistency, in order to obtain the incentives and trust of repeated interactions, and breadth to more broadly institutionalize commitment to and understanding of the intricacies of the partnership. A similar balance should be struck regarding the authority of chosen representatives. The breadth and representative authority of partner delegates reflects the degree of trust within the partnership. Partnerships where the "heavies" (only chief executives or senior officers) attend partnership meetings tend to be those with the least trust among the partners; whereas a wider group of individuals are involved when there are greater degrees of trust (Lowndes and Skelcher 1998: 322). Meetings with broad representation also afford better opportunities to capitalize on the benefits of partnership because they draw from a greater variety of inputs and promote a broader sense of ownership and internal commitment. Figure 4.9 summarizes the parameters of participation and representation.

Accountability and transparency. The determination of accountability mechanisms is a test of partnership principles and relates to both of partner-

Figure 4.9   The Parameters of Participation and Representation

Low Participation	Continuum	High Participation
Low tolerance for power sharing.	◄————►	High tolerance for power sharing.
Reluctance to adapt.	◄————►	Willingness to adapt.
High confidence.	◄————►	Conflict and distrust.

Narrow Representation	Continuum	Broad Representation
Low tolerance for sharing power (internally and externally).	◄————►	High tolerance for sharing power (internally and externally).
Reluctance to adapt.	◄————►	Willingness to adapt.
Low trust, both internally and with partners.	◄————►	High trust, internally and among partners.
Relatively mechanistic style of leaders and/or organization structure.	◄————►	Relatively organic style of leaders and/or organization structure.

ship's defining dimensions. With respect to mutuality, accountability systems may be more or less horizontal, based on equality and mutuality of interests, rather than vertical, reflecting power imbalances. Such accountability and transparency mechanisms should be defined jointly, based on a shared understanding of the objectives and purpose of the partnership and any resources in question and with an emphasis on accounting to all partners and stakeholders.

With respect to organization identity, each partner organization has its own accountability and transparency requirements vis-à-vis its constituencies and stakeholders. While partner organizations can cultivate and rely on trust, trust is typically based on experience. Partners' constituencies and stakeholders will require mechanisms that foster confidence. This confidence develops from the definition and implementation of accountability and transparency mechanisms that are typically formal, based on bureaucratic governance mechanisms. Constituency relations may also set limits on the information partners can share. For example, the World Bank is legally bound from publicly disclosing certain types of information such as project appraisal reports.

Information sharing is the foundation for mutual understanding and trust and confidence building. To determine accountability and transparency mechanisms, actors must identify the need for exceptions to existing partner organization requirements and develop new partnership-specific procedures based on an appreciable understanding of each partner's constraints, including limited resources. Figure 4.10 outlines the formality parameters of accountability and transparency systems.

Figure 4.10   Formality Parameters for Accountability and Transparency Systems

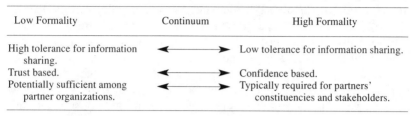

Low Formality	Continuum	High Formality
High tolerance for information sharing.	⟷	Low tolerance for information sharing.
Trust based.	⟷	Confidence based.
Potentially sufficient among partner organizations.	⟷	Typically required for partners' constituencies and stakeholders.

Maintenance and Evaluation

Maintenance concerns two facets of sustainability (see Brinkerhoff et al. 1990): the sustainability of the benefits sought through partnership objectives (Will constituencies continue to benefit from the goods and services produced by the partnership once the partnership ends?) and institutional sustainability, at least for the planned duration of the partnership and potentially beyond. A third facet of sustainability particular to the normative dimension of partnership work is whether at the end of the partnership each partner is better able to survive and thrive in its respective development environment (see Garilao 1987). The primary emphasis here is on partnership institutional sustainability, though some of the discussion applies to all of these facets.

Institutional sustainability is a process, not an end in itself. Institutions naturally become less sustainable over time, owing in part to changes in technologies and professions that necessitate continuous upgrading of staff; turnover of highly trained staff; and "organizational ossification," or the tendency to neglect the physical plant and equipment, to retain outdated or outmoded practices and procedures, and to increase insulation from the environment (Brinkerhoff and Goldsmith 1992: 379). Ensuring partnership maintenance and sustainability requires continuous cultivation of stakeholder and constituency commitment, training and retraining of staff, and the design and implementation of learning and feedback systems. Partnership sustainability depends on the defense of each partner's organization identity. Additional strategies include organizational capacity building and maintenance of each partner, and the development and institutionalization of a partnership organizational culture. These strategies are interdependent. For example, stakeholder relations reinforce culture, and learning enables celebration of success, which empowers employees and deepens their commitment. In fact, learning is essential to and embedded in each of the strategies. It helps to identify relationships that require attention, skills that need to be upgraded, and technologies and approaches that may threaten partner identity.

Maintenance strategies relate directly to addressing environmental hostility. Within the broader environment, partners monitor factors that are beyond the control of the partnership but can influence its effectiveness and sustainability, and they make adjustments accordingly (maximizing related opportunities as they emerge and minimizing threats). In the immediate partnership environment, these strategies focus on appreciating, influencing, and controlling, which includes shifting any of these strategies as needed. Maintenance strategies represent the continuation of strategies initiated at the design stage (see Figures 4.3 and 4.4). Partnerships will encounter new and different constraints as they evolve. A discussion specific to capacity building, culture, and learning and feedback follows.

Capacity building.   Capacity building entails action at three levels: human resource development of each partner organization's staff; partner organizational capacity building; and capacity building of the partnership as a whole. Partnership capacity requires appropriately matching responsibilities with capacity, and, where these do not initially match, investing in capacity building accordingly. New tasks require new capacity and if this capacity is not supported by the influx of additional resources, training, and equipment, capacity displacement will result.

Partnership work affords unique opportunities for mutual learning and interaction through formal staff exchanges, secondment, and apprentice systems. These types of mutual learning are particularly relevant to partnership work, given that so much of it entails learning by doing. A review of training strategies particular to developing countries concludes that of the four types of strategies—formal training, on-the-job training, action training, and nonformal training—the action-training approach holds the most potential for the widest range of training objectives, followed by on-the-job training (Kerrigan and Luke 1987). Representatives from different partner organizations should undergo training together wherever possible.

Addressing the capacity of the partnership as a whole includes ironing out challenging interfaces in respective management systems and technologies. The emphasis on partnership capacity building is often on supporting relationships and operating principles. Conflict resolution, bargaining, negotiation, diplomacy, and consensus-building skills are common targets. Action training and other forms of technical assistance and training can also be directed to generating mutual understanding among the partner organizations and their staff, and cultivating a common partnership culture. Capacity in this sense relates to the internalization of partnership identity, mission, and culture among partner organizations and their staff.

Investments in capacity building and associated capacity-building strategies and content are driven by environmental hostility (e.g., the existence of potential partners with the requisite capacity, previous experience among the partners, and compatibility among partner organizations), objectives (e.g., whether they require new or modified skills, and partnership duration), and preferences (e.g., tolerance for adaptation and associated capacity requirements, and trust and confidence and associated preferences for integration). Implicit in the consideration of these influencing factors is a cost-benefit analysis. Factors that may lead to greater capacity-building investments are:

- Long partnership duration.
- Selection of partner organizations without requisite capacity.
- Significant organizational incompatibilities.
- Preference for high integration with associated requirements for new systems development.
- Priority of trust building, use of culture governance mechanisms, and intrinsic motivation.
- Significant distrust or lack of confidence among partner organizations.
- Little or no mutual understanding or previous experience among partner organizations.

Culture. Organization culture is both a means and a target for changes that have major consequences for partnership commitment, control, and effectiveness. Some of partnership's unifying culture will occur naturally as partner organizations and individuals work together. Organization culture builds directly on values, partnership mission, and partnership principles. To be effective, a partnership's systems, processes, and governance mechanisms should be designed and implemented consistent with its desired organization culture. Culture creation also entails cultivating a common language and terminology; this includes avoiding the use of jargon and "insider" speak that will be unfamiliar to other partner organizations.

Culture can be created and cultivated in many other ways, through leadership, staffing, incentive systems, socialization, rituals, stories, and symbols (Schein 1992). In staffing, organizations should fill pivotal positions with individuals who understand and will promote the culture. Incentive systems should be designed to reward behavior that expresses and confirms the organization culture. This is one of the most important challenges to partnership work within donor organizations, as donor incentive systems tend to favor quantitative results over quality of work, risk taking, and innovation.

Ritual can create a sense of order in chaos, provide meaning in ambiguity, and strengthen the sense of belonging among the staff of the respective partner organizations. It can be formalized through standard operating procedures or it can emerge informally, through trial and error and experience. Stories, symbols, and language can serve either to reinforce partnership organization culture or to aggravate the differences between partner organizational cultures. For example, the use of business language differs considerably from language describing partnership values. Stories and myths can be created around instances where staff of a partner organization spontaneously came forth to assist the staff of another partner organization and perhaps made self-sacrifices in the process. Other symbols with potential significance to partnership culture include relative salaries and, particularly in the international context, standards of luxury and esprit de corps in travel accommodations.

Investments in partnership-organization culture building are based on similar criteria to those for capacity building. For example, the longer the duration, the greater the desired integration; and the more the reliance on culture governance mechanisms and internal commitment, the more likely partners will want to invest in proactive organization culture creation and management.

Learning, feedback, and evaluation.   Learning and feedback are important to partnership work because resources are entrusted to other organizations, and the combination of multiple organizations, respective stakeholders, cultures, and priorities results in even greater uncertainty. The division of labor, with interdependent tasks distributed among multiple organizations, requires learning and feedback, first and foremost to understand who is doing or has done what. Feedback and learning encompass double-loop learning, or the testing of underlying theories and assumptions not only about how the partnership achieves its objectives but also regarding whether or not the objectives are the right ones. Partnership work requires learning and feedback regarding relationships, processes, and objectives at three levels: within each partner organization; across partner organizations; and between each of these and the development context in which the partnership operates. The celebration of lessons learned and successes achieved can also enhance motivation and partnership identity.

Partnership evaluation is extremely complex and has multiple purposes. There is a fine and overlapping line between monitoring and evaluating programmatic methods, outcomes, and impact and monitoring and evaluating the partnership relationship itself.[2] Monitoring and evaluation specific to the partnership approach and process includes the informal aspects of governance, the role of intermediaries, partnership's added value, and outgrowths of partnership work. The synergistic results of partnership work are very difficult to articulate and measure: What did the partnership produce that the individual organizations acting independently could not have attained or produced? Synergistic contributions often relate to building social capital, organizational capacity, and other multipliers noted in

Chapter 1. While synergistic results are often sought and referenced, they are rarely fully articulated and measured. It may be impossible to do so in any quantitative way, but efforts to specify these advantages are important to promoting and learning from partnership approaches.

Each of these monitoring and evaluation components has a different time line, serves a different purpose, and is specifiable and verifiable to varying degrees. Requirements and structure of monitoring and evaluation efforts are negotiated outcomes among the partners, specific to environmental hostility (e.g., requirements for accountability both to partnership constituents and stakeholders, and those of each partner organization), partnership and partner organization objectives (e.g., the partnership may be viewed more as a means than an end with little interest in evaluating the partnership approach), preferences (e.g., the degree of trust and confidence may inspire more or less emphasis on monitoring and evaluation), and cost-benefit analysis.

The who and the how of monitoring and evaluation are also negotiated outcomes. Partners typically monitor and evaluate their own partnership-related activities, as well as their organization identity. More periodic joint evaluations may supplement these efforts, particularly when trust is low. Interorganizational teams may be tasked with specific evaluation questions and issues, whether related to program objectives or partnership processes. Interpartner evaluation might include adherence to voluntary codes of conduct and agreed operating principles. Depending on the objective, it may also be appropriate to include constituency representatives. When an even greater degree of objectivity and neutrality is required or a more formal and extensive evaluation is sought, external evaluations are appropriate. Monitoring and evaluation systems provide another test of mutuality; often, the more powerful partner determines the criteria and methods of evaluation. When there is little trust among partners, more formal, external, or participatory evaluations are likely to be preferred over self- or joint-evaluations. When interorganizational teams are tasked with monitoring and evaluation responsibilities, monitoring and evaluation can also be instrumental to enhancing mutual understanding, consolidating teams, and building trust. Figure 4.11 summarizes the components of partnership evaluation; Figure 4.12 outlines evaluation targets specific to particular evaluation actors and approaches and the circumstances under which these types may be emphasized.

Partnership work poses significant opportunities to enhance the efficiency and effectiveness of evaluation. First, multiple actors with various perspectives lend insight and creativity to observations and analysis and further create checks and balances among the actors, which can enhance the credibility and transparency of the partnership evaluation results. Second, each type of actor may have relatively more experience and skill with par-

Figure 4.11   Partnership Evaluation Components

Partnership Program Objectives	Partnership Relationship
Overall formal structure, division of labor, approach, and technologies. Program design: underlying logic, objectives, assumptions. Self- and interpartner evaluation, including: capacity; expected contributions (including organization identity maintenance); partner selection; and partnership programmatic outcomes and impact.	Informal relations, rules, social norms, organization culture and cohesiveness. Role of intermediary. Partner objectives/drivers. Organization identity maintenance. Synergistic results: social capital, partner organization capacity building, other multipliers. Perceptions of shared risks and rewards. Adherence to agreed operating principles. Stakeholder and constituency participation, as appropriate.

Figure 4.12   Evaluation Actors: Targets and Conditions

	Self-Evaluation	Joint/Interorganizational Evaluation	External Evaluation
Targets	Capacity. Expected contributions. Organization identity.	Capacity. Expected contributions. Organization identity. Adherence to codes of conduct and agreed operating principles. Programmatic targets.	All targets.
Conditions	High trust.	Low trust or confidence-building priority. Priority of enhancing mutual understanding and/or team building/ reinforcement.	Low trust. When objectivity and/or neutrality is a high priority (e.g., end of project evaluation).

ticular evaluation approaches, which can be combined to enhance effectiveness. For example, the public sector specializes in information gathering and analysis; the private sector focuses on technical research and market testing; and NGOs often have expertise in consultative appraisal methods (Prince of Wales Business Leaders Forum 1998). Third, effective partnerships with a strong foundation of trust can make possible and improve the application of different evaluation techniques. For example, partnerships with a high degree of trust can incorporate a listening dimension of evaluation (Salmen 1995), including beneficiary assessments and participatory rural appraisal. Effective evaluation, in turn, can enhance trust among the partners.

Partnership Implementation in Practice

In designing a partnership, actors decide the degree of desired integration and assign mediating functions. The suggested integration trade-offs confirm that both highly integrated and loosely organized models may be effective and efficient, and they imply that partnerships may be structured such that some functions are more integrated than others. This is similarly true for the degree of formality, governance mechanisms, and incentive systems. It is likely that most partnerships will entail a combination of formal and informal processes, a mix of governance mechanisms, and incorporation of both tangible (extrinsic) and intangible (intrinsic) incentives.

Because several of these parameters are difficult to identify and quantify, they may be overlooked or undervalued. Therefore, informal processes, culture governance mechanisms, and intrinsic motivation are emphasized throughout this discussion and in the cases to follow as underutilized tools for partnership effectiveness and efficiency. The functional role of participation and broad representation are also emphasized. Often these are promoted solely or primarily from a normative perspective, which can lead to underestimating their instrumentality for effectiveness and efficiency. This review also proposes that while accountability and transparency are important in any structure or program, these systems should also be informed and complemented by existing trust and trust-building measures among partnership actors.

Notes

1. According to the cognitive dissonance model (see, for example, Weick 1993), particularly in the nonprofit sector, those who engage in committed behavior with minimal or no material reward (volunteers) will emphasize the importance of intrinsic benefits such as the expression of values or the enhancement of self-esteem (see, for example, Clary and Snyder 1993).

2. For a proposed framework for evaluating the partnership relationship itself, see J. Brinkerhoff 2002.

5

Partnership for Public Service: The Barani Area Development Project

How can a partnership approach ensure that local communities are tending to common property and maximizing gains from available government and donor resources? How can it effectively address coordination problems among government agencies and the lack of institutions at the local level? The Barani Area Development Project (BADP) in Pakistan aims to improve public services at the village level in four of the seventeen rain-fed districts of the North West Frontier Province. The Asian Development Bank (ADB) provided $42 million over six years to support the project. The BADP demonstrates how a variety of organizations and sectors, with or without previous experience with each other, can effectively come together to form an organic, confidence- and trust-based interorganizational partnership.

The BADP incorporates several levels of partnership, including partnerships between government departments and local communities; an NGO and local communities; the Barani Development Office (BDO), government departments, and the NGO; and the ADB and the government of the North West Frontier Province (GONWFP). These partnership arrangements seek to build community self-reliance through the creation of permanent local-level organizations to interface with government extension officers, represent community priorities, and manage contributed community resources. The BADP is now in its second phase. This chapter will describe and analyze BADP I (1993–1999).

Great Needs, Many Actors, and the Need for a Partnership Approach

The North West Frontier Province is Pakistan's smallest, with a population of more than 20 million, over 80 percent of which is rural. Most of its cultivated land is rain fed, or *barani*. Barani farms are generally small, subsistence oriented, undercapitalized, high risk, and labor short (ADB 1992). These features, coupled with the lack of investment in the barani areas, contributed to a vicious cycle of low land and livestock productivity, resulting in low on-farm income, exacerbated by a lack of basic physical and social infrastructure, leading to migration and farm labor shortages, cycling back to low productivity (see ADB 1992). Government investment was further challenged by the absence of an effective local forum for collective decisionmaking. Villagers were unaware of the services available. The institutional vacuum at the local level prevented villagers from internalizing the costs and benefits of investing in common property and from benefiting from government and donor agencies (Shah 1998c).

Operationalizing the BADP

The BADP's operationalization consists of a process, corresponding institutional development, and the creation and implementation of a range of coordination mechanisms.

Forming Village and Women's Organizations

Productive investment schemes (PISs) are used to entice villages to form village organizations (VOs) and women's organizations (WOs). The process begins when the NGO, the Sarhad Rural Support Corporation (SRSC), introduces the objectives, scope, and operational procedures for formation and participation of VOs and WOs, and for the implementation of PISs. Once a VO and WO are formed, SRSC representatives and government department specialists discuss with them the potential for productive investment. The VO and WO then identify a scheme and nominate members to assist the SRSC in carrying out the required survey and preparatory work to prepare a feasibility study, detailed design, and engineering cost estimate. The BDO, the coordination unit for the BADP, reviews and sanctions the schemes, whereupon SRSC staff negotiate the scheme's cost (including skilled and unskilled labor) and explain and document the financing terms, (20 percent from the community, and 80 percent through project grants).

All financial matters are discussed and agreed in an open forum, encompassing the whole of the VO and WO (Shah 1998a). The VO and WO must agree to maintain the scheme and abide by additional conditions, such as savings accumulation. Once the VO and WO deposit an average per member sum (300 rupees) into their savings account, the SRSC signs a partnership document with the VO and WO and disburses the first installment (20 percent) of the negotiated cost of the scheme. Subsequent installments are released in accordance with work completed; the final installment is disbursed three months after completion or later, depending on satisfactory functioning of the VO and WO. The VO and WO deposit approximately 25 percent of the labor-cost payments into their savings account to support future productive investment schemes (ADB 1992).

VOs/WOs and Line Departments: Terms of Partnership

Once formed, the VOs and WOs serve as outreach mechanisms for the delivery of goods and services of the government line departments and other outside agencies.[1] Each department enters into a partnership with the VO and WO based on the identified needs and development plans of the community. The partnership is operationalized through negotiated terms of partnership (ToPs) specifying the rights and responsibilities of the project and of the villagers. For example, ToPs may specify project provision of technical and financial assistance for a particular effort, with beneficiary (VO and WO) responsibility for providing local resources, supervision, and operation and maintenance.

Initiating the ToPs required more time than anticipated. Originally, it was expected that these partnership relationships would be established in the first year. In fact, it required two years, along with extensive trainings and orientations (Shah 1998a). This evolution resulted in combining needs assessment and planning into one stage, which includes participation of all line departments, the SRSC, and the VO and WO.

Line Departments and SRSC: Standard Operating Procedures

The BADP requires substantial coordination among the various line departments, participating credit institutions (PCIs), and the NGO. Emphasis was placed on cultivating the partnership between the SRSC and line-department extension staff. According to the project director, partnership skills were developed through mutual flexibility (Shah 1998a). Procedures were modified to facilitate the work between the NGO and the line departments and, by extension, with the communities. The BDO facilitated the establishment of this level of partnership and made both formal and informal efforts to promote cooperation and flexibility. Eventually, it was decided that a more formal, agreed approach would be necessary.

With assistance from the SRSC and contracted consultants, the BDO organized regional-level meetings of the heads of all participating agencies. The project cycle was presented as a process of integrated participatory planning and implementation. The BDO facilitated agreement among the agencies on specific roles and responsibilities at each stage of the project cycle. Identification of village priorities would incorporate participation from all line departments; project preparation would be undertaken by each agency according to its own method, in consultation with beneficiaries; and appraisal of commitment to equity, operations and maintenance arrangements, and other aspects of the ToPs would incorporate joint participation of all line departments and the VO and WO (Shah 1998c).

The process resulted in the formulation of agreed standard operating procedures (SOPs) for an integrated approach to community participation. These SOPs address fund disbursement, interaction processes between the SRSC and government departments, and reporting. These procedures were developed iteratively, in a participatory manner, through subsequent workshops at each level in each district. They do not necessarily constitute "dos and don'ts" or "hard and fast rules." Rather, they are guidelines for enacting implementation efficiently and predictably. Their purpose is to ensure that every implementation actor is clear about respective role functions and responsibilities and that implementers collectively achieve the project objectives "meaningfully, efficiently, and cost-effectively" (Shah 2001). The actors developed the SOPs themselves, based on their direct experience at the local level. Field staff of all line departments receive SOP orientation. The SOPs are based on mutual agreement and encompass flexibility for revision as needed.

Once the SOPs were in place, regional and field-level coordination was assigned to the SRSC. At a higher level, regular field visits by the BDO and its consultants systematically monitor the agreed procedures. The BDO also ensures that annual work plans are made jointly by the SRSC and the government departments, and that changes in the ToPs are made with the agreement of SRSC social organizers and technical specialists.

Coordination at the Operational Level

The BDO also established a mobile Social Organization Unit (SOU) to provide coordination at the operational level. The SOU is an informal arrangement of monthly meetings, which incorporates all government front-line officials and all front-line NGO social mobilizers. These are the individuals working directly with the VOs and WOs. The SOU addresses key issues and assures coordination and quality. The SOU affords extension workers and NGO mobilizers opportunities to discuss and resolve their day-to-day issues, in addition to receiving recognition for their important roles (Shah 1998b).

The SOU is supplemented by village-level conferences. Activists from the VO and WO hold monthly conferences with line-department representatives, whose participation is compulsory. The purpose is to ensure that feedback from the village is regularly provided to the line departments. These conferences have also become a forum for banks and agencies not

directly involved in the project to introduce their programs and seek cooperation from the villages.

Additional accountability expectations and pressure developed as
expectations were raised. The village-level conferences were originally
designed for the purpose of feedback and coordination. They evolved into a
mechanism for village activists to hold line departments accountable for
promises made and quality and timely implementation. Village activists
have also come together to advocate for adherence to the project document.
For example, the project document specifies that one agriculture officer
(AO) should be assigned to each Union Council (an administrative unit
consisting of twenty to twenty-five villages). The village activists
approached the district agriculture extension officer to demand compliance.
They learned that in most instances, the AOs were not available because the
department could not provide them with accommodation. The activists
mobilized the villages to share responsibility for office space. As a result,
not only were represented villages assigned AOs but additional villages
also benefited (Shah 2001). This example indicates a broader operational
culture that encouraged villages to continuously identify weaknesses in
project implementation.

Coordination and Supervision at Higher Levels

In each of the BADP's four districts, District Coordination Committees
(DCCs) meet monthly. The purpose of the DCCs is to review and coordinate ongoing activities in each district. DCCs are comprised of the district-
level representatives of all executing, implementing, and associating agencies. This includes representatives of all line departments, the SRSC, and
the PCIs. The DCC is chaired by the deputy commissioner; the BDO provides secretarial services to the DCCs through the coordinators (of
Agriculture, Livestock, Forestry, and Engineering), who attend the meetings on a rotating basis (ADB 1992).

Similar quarterly review meetings take place at the divisional level.
Divisional Project Review Committees (DPRCs) are chaired by the division commissioners. Through the DPRCs, officials and SRSC representatives directly involved with the work provide input that is synthesized at
the commissioners' level. The purpose of the DPRCs is to review implementation progress and make recommendations on project elements in
accordance with the loan or project agreements and targets. The DPRCs are
quite formal and are required to submit quarterly reports to the Project
Review Board (PRB). DPRCs provide an opportunity to appease political
stakeholders without giving them undue influence over project decisionmaking. The inclusion of local politicians on the DPRC afforded opportuni-

ties for information sharing and mutual accountability, while avoiding political participation on the PRB decisionmaking body.

As with all multisectoral projects in the province, a PRB chaired by the additional chief secretary of the Planning and Development Department is responsible for policy decisions and approval of annual work plans and budgets for the project. The PRB is empowered to take policy decisions on behalf of the government. Its membership includes the heads of all concerned line departments. The chief executive of the SRSC is also invited to participate in the biannual meetings. This is the first time in the province that an NGO is represented on a PRB. The PRB allows the government to review plans at the highest level of decisionmaking.

Learning and Adaptation

A midterm evaluation was conducted in 1996, and some revisions were made to the project agreement. Among these were modification of project cost estimates and related allocations, expansion and intensification of the village-development component to ensure sustainability, substantial reform of the rural-credit component, and agreement to proceed with a second phase, BADP II, immediately upon the closing of the loan in 1999 (ADB 1996). In the course of implementation, other lessons were learned and additional modifications made accordingly. Following is a brief description of the evolution of the village-development component and the evolution of coordination mechanisms and procedures.

Lessons and Adaptations of the Village-Development Component

It was initially expected that the VO and WO would encompass all households of a village. However, SRSC data revealed that VO and WO membership comprised, on average, only 25–30 percent of village households (BDO 1996). This necessitated a review of incentives and costs to ensure equitable benefit and risk of all village members. The PRB confirmed that project-sponsored activities should be extended to all interested households, regardless of formal membership in a VO or WO, according to the ToPs for each development project. The organizations were still considered vital to meeting project objectives and assuring sustainability of benefits; therefore, incentives for VO and WO participation had to be maintained. A tiered pricing and fee system was developed whereby nonmembers who benefit from VO- and WO-sponsored activities (e.g., receiving training and inputs for the development of a nursery) must contribute a portion of related profits to the collective village savings account; and nonmember purchasers of project-related inputs and services must pay a premium (e.g., to member-farmers selling seed through the project's seed multiplication program, or to a paraveterinarian supported by the organizations) (BDO 1996).

It was also expected that all activities would be undertaken collectively by VO and WO members. Experience quickly demonstrated that this was not a realistic day-to-day option, particularly concerning individually owned assets that are enhanced through the project. It was decided that activities aimed at private property (livestock, demonstration plots, nurseries, orchards, and so forth) would be the responsibility of the individual owner. The VO and WO are still responsible for identifying qualified and motivated individuals to pioneer such activities and for negotiating the terms of project support and the structured fee schedule (member/nonmember).

It seemed at the outset that the village-development component would be inhibited by the existing patronage system. In fact, local traditional leaders were the original leaders of the VOs and WOs. However, as envisioned, over time a second generation of village leadership tended to emerge and the local elites faded into the background. The project director credited this to the compulsory transparency mechanisms, which removed opportunities for personal gain (Shah 1998a). Championing the organizations is a lot of work, with *collective* reward. Second-generation leaders, or village activists, receive management training through the project and become representatives to the village-level conferences, the main interface with the line departments. As the activists take on more responsibility, some project-specific incentives are provided. For example, the activist is responsible for credit repayment and receives 2 percent of total recovery.

The BADP, while eventually quite successful, was slow in initial implementation. Field-level activities required the formation and operationalization of VOs and WOs as a matter of policy. Such institutional capacity takes time to develop. The ADB and the provincial Planning and Development Department were unsatisfied with project performance in the first two years. Disbursements and quantifiable outputs were not forthcoming as expected. However, after two years, many VOs and WOs were in place and the SOPs had been established; disbursements and physical outputs escalated accordingly (Shah 1998a). The village-level development component was proving so successful that the BDO proposed increasing the targeted number of community-based organizations (Shah 1998b). The midterm review recommended expanding the village-level component from the original two districts to the four now covered, and continuing the capacity building of the VOs and WOs already established in order to ensure sustainability (ADB 1996). As of June 1999, the BADP had established 1,157 CBOs, including 398 VOs and WOs—153 percent of its target—encompassing a membership of 40,332 households (ASIANICS 1999: 22).[2]

The Evolution of Coordination Mechanisms and Procedures

Many of the coordination mechanisms noted above were not specified in the original project documents but emerged in response to recognized needs in the course of implementation. This is true of the SOPs, the SOU, and the village-level planning processes. While formal review and coordination mechanisms were specified for higher levels of the project implementation (the DCCs, DPRC, and PRB), additional mechanisms and procedures for review, coordination, and implementation were deemed necessary for the operational levels. The SOU ensures monthly review, information sharing, and revision as needed among front-line implementers, while the SOPs inform day-to-day implementation.

Revisions were also made to village-level planning processes. Originally, needs identification and project planning were conceived as two separate activities, the first being facilitated by the NGO intermediary, with participation of the line departments introduced at the planning stage. It was soon realized that the absence of line-department representatives at the initial stages compromised the quality of planning and implementation and resulted in disjointed activities and poor community consultation on sequencing and coordinated implementation of various activities. In some instances, competition among line departments for communities' time and resources would ensue (Shah 2001). The process was, therefore, modified to include representatives of all actors in all of the planning stages. The SRSC would still initiate and facilitate the village-level meetings, but all partners would then "participate as a team" in identification and design of project activities. In fact, it was this "teamwork" that led to the recognition of the need for coordinating procedures, which culminated in the SOPs.

Potential for Success

The BADP's success to date, and its potential for continuing success and sustainability, rests on the formation and capacity of the VOs and WOs, the physical outputs of the project, and multiplier effects. As of June 1999, 338 productive investment schemes had been completed, and 109 were in progress (ASIANICS 1999). This represents steady progress from the 1996 figures of fifty-eight completed and 165 identified (ADB 1996). The 1999 ASIANICS evaluation observed that the quality of the VOs and WOs varies with the level of village participation, and some are more active than others. By 1996, 60 percent of the targeted number of village-level conferences had already been reached (ADB 1996), and most VOs and WOs continued these conferences on a monthly basis (Shah 1998c). Village activities are being carried out by most of the VOs and WOs. The PRB agreed to a target of approximately 30 percent representation by women; by 1998 40 percent had been achieved (Shah 1998b). At the completion of BADP I, success rates of over 90 percent were achieved. Other quantifiable and/or physical indicators of success include:

- An 88 percent loan recovery rate was achieved by 1996, with 100 percent in two of the districts (ADB 1996).
- Yields for most crops increased between 15 and 25 percent due to improved use of technology.
- Cropping patterns were influenced, resulting in improved intensity, an increase in wheat cultivation, and the introduction of oilseed crops.
- The emphasis on fodder production and livestock upgrading improved the incomes and welfare of diverse groups, including landless tenants and women.
- Schemes for distributing small ruminants and poultry benefited the poorest segments of barani society (ASIANICS 1999).

The 1999 evaluation also noted the project's impact in providing direction to and mobilizing rural communities, which has created an amenable environment to the continued introduction and adaptation of new technologies.

In addition to these achievements, the project generated multiplier effects. First, the BADP provides demonstration of an implementable model for effective, integrated, and participatory rural development. The BADP reveals the possibility and a methodology for implementing partnership approaches that encompass government, NGOs, and community organizations (Shah 1998b). First, the BADP's experience confirms villagers' willingness to accept responsibility for their collective interest, overcoming entrenched patronage relations in the process, and exemplifies an integrated delivery mechanism for complex, multiactor cooperation (Shah 1998c). Second, VOs and WOs identified their own priorities and mobilized resources for activities both within and outside of the scope of the project (BDO 1996). Third, the village-level conferences became forums for other agencies to introduce services and opportunities to the VOs and WOs, and the agencies increasingly view those organizations as useful delivery mechanisms for projects such as polio campaigns, public health, water management, and appropriate technology (Shah 1998c). Finally, the project's experience is reflected in other rural-development and poverty-alleviation efforts. The BADP offers implementation assistance and analyses to government, NGOs, donors, and banks (Shah 1998a, 1998c). The potential for the BADP's continued success will depend largely on the stable quality and capacity of its staff; the VOs, WOs, and village activists; and the continued will of the GONWFP, participating line agencies, and the ADB to support its participatory, flexible model.

One of the main risks identified in the appraisal was the potential for implementation delays and lack of technical capacity. The project design assured that annual financial requirements for each component would be within the existing allocations for the sectoral development programs of the provincial government. Additional support and troubleshooting would be provided by the BDO. Other than the adjusted approach and the new actors, all project components were designed to be within the competence of concerned agencies, as demonstrated by their experience with similar projects (ADB 1992). Any other capacity gaps and potential turnover within the lifetime of the project would be addressed through training and capacity-building measures.

Implications and Lessons Learned

The project suggests lessons both for partnership work in general and for partnerships specific to integrated public-service improvements.

Lessons for Partnership Work

1. A significant degree of mutuality can be created, even among multiple and diverse partners. The mutuality that the BADP has achieved in its partnerships is operationalized both structurally and procedurally. Structurally, implementing partner organizations are given representation on the various review and coordination boards, with VOs and WOs providing feedback through the village conferences. Procedurally, SOPs are the result of "mutual flexibility" (Shah 1998a) among implementing partner organizations, and ToPs are jointly negotiated with the VOs and WOs and are consensus based. In the BADP, mutuality includes joint planning and decisionmaking, collaborative policy development (SOPs and ToPs), and joint review and oversight of project implementation (the SOU, DCCs, DPRCs, and PRB). The majority of mutual relationships and intensive interaction appear to take place at the village level, among staff who are most directly involved in day-to-day implementation. Among line-department staff, the NGO, and PCIs, subprojects are implemented jointly or independently, based on mutual agreement with respect to the most rational division of labor based on comparative advantages.

2. Challenges of confidence and trust building, and the potential for misunderstandings, can be addressed both bureaucratically and through culture governance mechanisms. The BADP combined both bureaucratic and culture governance mechanisms to assure confidence and trust and to enhance mutual understanding. Bureaucratically, transparency was mandated; participation of all implementing organizations was compulsory at village conferences, and representation was mandated in the coordination and oversight boards; and the SOPs specified interaction and implementation procedures. Transparency was also instrumental in creating a sense of shared ownership of the project and its activities, particularly at the village level, adding a dimension of social control. Participation in village conferences and in the SOU and other coordination and oversight committees provided frequent, systematic opportunities for face-to-face interaction and reinforced the organization culture of partnership, responsiveness, and shared vision and successes. Finally, while bureaucratic mechanisms were an outcome, the SOPs in their process of development and continued option for adjustment are based on mutual effort and interaction rooted in the organization culture. In all these efforts, interaction is encouraged or required, and there is an emphasis on mutual respect and honest participation in the service of meeting project objectives, which results, with each encounter, in enhanced mutual understanding of each partner's comparative advantages, constraints, and organization identity.

3. *Organization culture can unite multiple and diverse partners when it supports each organization's success.* The BADP's organization culture promoted a shared vision of responsiveness, participation and ownership, and success. When the BADP succeeded, it reflected on all participating organizations. Previously, extension workers had suffered from low morale and defeatism owing to inappropriate technologies and approaches and inadequate equipment, staff, and capacity. Through the BADP, extension workers were made to feel important and began to perceive success as possible. A team spirit was cultivated through the SOU, with joint problem solving and continued focus on common goals. There was a sense of being part of and a significant contributor to something larger and important, and this was reinforced by political buffering and the commitment of the GONWFP and ADB in supporting the BADP's innovative approach and providing the requisite resources and support to make it work.

4. *Flexibility and stability can be combined in support of efficiency and responsiveness.* The BADP's structure and processes can be described as structured flexibility. Stability is secured through provision of basic structures and procedures as outlined in the project design, but flexibility is also incorporated in order to ensure effective responsiveness to the outcomes of participatory processes and to changes in the environment. Annual workplans are generally outlined, with specified PISs and rural infrastructure projects incorporated as possible, once village-level priorities are determined and joint plans are made with implementing agencies for their implementation. Flexibility is maximized at the lowest levels of implementation, with extension staff from line departments directly negotiating ToPs

specific to particular projects, and adjustments in SOPs proposed and determined by front-line staff of participating implementing agencies.

5. *Organization identity can be protected through buffering at multiple levels.* The BADP's complexity, including the number and diversity of partner organizations, posed challenges to resolving needs for particular administrative functions. Complying with these functions may not be a priority for a partner organization, which may detract from its most important contribution or may be beyond its current capacity. The BADP incorporated buffering at various levels to address this challenge: The SRSC buffered the VOs and WOs by collecting information from them, synthesizing it with its own observations, and providing monthly reports to the BDO; the BDO buffered the SRSC by taking that information, synthesizing it along with its own observations and the monthly reports of the various line departments, and formatting it to comply with GONWFP and ADB requirements; and the GONWFP buffered the BDO both administratively, through its location in the Special Development Unit of the Planning and Development Department, and politically, through support from the chief secretary and additional chief secretary, assuring its autonomy and integrity to maintain focus on BADP objectives.

6. *Innovative partnership approaches, requiring substantial changes in business as usual, require political and administrative will to partner.* The BADP reveals the importance of political and administrative will to partner and absorb or create the changes necessary to do so. Shared objectives, along with a realistic understanding of government advantages and limitations, led to recognition of the need for a partnership and to a commitment to adjust standard procedures accordingly. This includes willingness to buffer, to build in the necessary flexibility for responsiveness to the results of participatory processes, and to make sufficient investments in support of participatory processes and effectiveness, including capacity building, material and equipment investments, and institutional development. The many administrative adjustments made reflect the foundation of government will, based on an understanding of the available skills and resources and the nature of the development challenge.

7. *Working with large and powerful partners can result in intraorganizational challenges to interorganizational agreements.* Donors and high-level government partners may create dilemmas with respect to organization and project identity. While one can negotiate partnership arrangements with these entities, once a development effort reaches the implementation stage, the administrators for the partnership typically are not the same individuals or agencies with whom the terms were negotiated (Coston 1998a). This can lead to an orientation toward business as usual, and expectations for more standard procedures and outcomes. This was the case for the

BADP; the emphasis on disbursement and physical output hindered interpretation of the BADPs first two years of implementation. Similar dynamics likely contributed to the final evaluation's relative emphasis on meeting targets as opposed to institutional development processes and outcomes.

8. *Integration trade-offs can be overcome when the partner organizations share distinct identities and comparative advantages and mutuality is emphasized.* The BADP emphasized an integrated approach to public-service delivery and barani development. However, its structure emphasized intensive linkages as well as mutuality. Each partner organization possessed comparative advantages unique within the partnership, some highly technical (such as line departments). These factors enabled the organizations to gain the benefits of integration through intensive linkage, without suffering from the potential downside of diminished comparative advantages and loss of organization identity. In fact, the organization culture emphasized each partner organization's success and integration's role in attaining it.

It is important to distinguish integration from institutional linkage, no matter how frequently such linkage is exercised. It is probable that the BADP's organic organizational structure—with its emphasis on responsive, flexible, and knowledge-based processes—enabled the BADP to avoid integration trade-offs. These processes may be sufficient for counteracting integration's structural features and incorporating some of its advantages, such as predictability and efficiency. An organic organizational structure combined with an emphasis on intensive linkage may produce the benefits of responsiveness and flexibility, as well as efficiency and predictability. Given each partner's distinct specialization and comparative advantage, it is unlikely that such combinations would contribute to organizational homogenization over time.

Lessons for Integrated Public-Service Improvement

1. Public-service improvements take time and the pace of change can be slow, especially if institutional development is a key factor. Partnership organizers and implementers should maintain realistic expectations. The BADP experience demonstrates that projects or partnerships that are based on the development of social processes take time to develop. Field-level activities should not be planned or expected prior to the establishment of the community organizations intended to carry out these activities. While it may take additional time to disburse funds and produce quantifiable outputs, the BADP provides evidence that such projects can yield better results in the longer run.

Innovation implies risk. Particularly in the barani context, the risk to farmers of adopting new, unproved technology is great. Implementing agencies also had to risk adopting new approaches and partners. The final evaluation's findings with respect to farmers' adoption of new technology applies to all levels of the partnership: "small but confident change is better than rapid but unsustainable transformation" (ASIANICS 1999: x).

2. *Institutional development can be pivotal to public-service improvements, necessitating investments for capacity building and institutionalized linkages.* The BADP's emphasis on institutional development will likely prove the basis for its long-term effectiveness and sustainability. Institutional development is not possible without investment, and these investments are likely to be commensurate with the degree of development sought. In the case of the BADP, two new types of organizations were created: the BDO and the multiple VOs and WOs. Existing organizations lacked capacity and equipment to meet the challenges of the new responsibilities. Substantial investments were made for capacity building, training, equipment, consulting, and technical support.

The approach was predicated on linking these various organizations as well. The BADP took a proactive approach, both structurally and procedurally. Substantial time was allowed for ironing out the details of these linkages (particularly the SOPs), and new mechanisms were created and adjusted (the SOU, village conferences, and so forth).

3. *Neutral intermediaries with specialized skills can be instrumental to establishing necessary systems and supporting organization culture.* The BADP recognized the need for a neutral intermediary with specialized skills at two levels. First, the NGO was engaged to mobilize local communities and facilitate relations between them and the government extension officers working in the communities. Second, the BDO operated as a neutral facilitator among government departments and the SRSC. The secondment of technical coordinators facilitated the BDO's role as intermediary, ensuring that it had the necessary technical understanding of the various departments and promoting trust among the line departments that their perspectives were represented.

4. *Public-service improvements should build upon existing government infrastructure and services.* The emphasis on participatory development, with the creation of the VOs and WOs and the engagement of an NGO did not at all negate the need for and work of government departments; rather the partnership enhanced this work through service integration and coordination, input for enhancing the quality and responsiveness of services, and the augmentation of existing services through the activities—design, implementation, and monitoring—of the villages. Existing government infrastructure and services formed the basis for the partnership; NGOs were sought due to their recognized comparative advantage in social mobiliza-

tion; and VOs and WOs were utilized to garner support and input for public services, to collect information, and to employ social norms to regulate their roles in the partnership. Making the line departments and existing government services and systems the foundation of the BADP supported sustainability. None of the assigned responsibilities were beyond the scope of the line departments, either in terms of technical emphasis or existing budget allocations.

Conclusion

The BADP reveals how a partnership can be used to augment and improve public services at the local level; to engage citizens in civic processes, including the design, delivery, and monitoring of development strategies; and to build social capital, broadening the base of legitimate leadership and trusting relationships essential to democratic processes (see Dahl 1971; Evans 1996). It also demonstrates the importance of political and administrative will to partner and to absorb or create the changes necessary to do so. Where actors maintained flexibility and exercised this will to participate in a truly integrated development project, the project broke new ground in introducing cooperative innovations and maximizing results at the village level.

One of the reasons for this relatively smooth cooperation among so many and such diverse actors was the common vision and values supported by a carefully cultivated organization culture. This included careful trust building, through face-to-face contact, the provision of tools and training to support participatory approaches at all levels, the maximization of opportunities for formal and informal partner interaction, and building an ethos of openness and responsiveness. The combination of bureaucratic governance mechanisms to maximize predictability, the trust building inherent to the process and organization culture, and the strong will (both political and administrative) to work in a new way proved effective to building a partnership with significant qualitative and quantitative outcomes. Such a combination demonstrates that it is possible to achieve partnerships even with traditionally entrenched, inflexible bureaucracies.

Notes

1. Participating line departments include the Department of Communications and Works (roads); Department of Irrigation and Public Health Engineering (irrigation and water supply); Department of Forestry, Fisheries, and Wildlife (forestry); Agricultural University (agricultural research); and the Department of Agriculture,

Livestock, and Cooperatives (agriculture and livestock extension) and its Fruits and Vegetables Development Board (horticulture extension).

2. The project appraisal had envisaged the organization of three hundred VOs and WOs over the life of the project (ADB 1992). By 1996, 308 VOs, including 135 WOs had been established, with generated savings of 3.2 million rupees (ADB 1996).

6

Partnership for Corporate Social Responsibility: INMED's "Healthy Children, Healthy Futures" Program in Brazil

How can the many resources of diverse and numerous multinational corporations be applied to support integrated programs to meet complex social needs? The mission of International Medical Services for Health (INMED) is to empower communities to improve their health and quality of life. The international NGO pursues this mission by assembling diverse actors—including multinational corporations—to create and strengthen local programs for preventing and controlling disease.

INMED's work in Brazil is a noteworthy example of its partnership work with multinational corporations, government, local NGOs, church organizations, universities and high schools, teachers, volunteers, and local communities. The composition of each partnership is determined by the needs and interests of various actors in each local community. By partnering with multinational corporations, INMED seeks to "create new money" to address community health needs (Pfeiffer 2000a). In addition to partnering directly with multinational corporations—at both the international and local levels—INMED's Brazilian programs foster partnerships between multinational corporations. These partnerships were initially within the pharmaceutical industry but are expanding to other types of business (energy, information technology, retail, and so forth). INMED's work in Brazil represents a partnership aimed at providing the multiactor, integrated solutions necessary to address community health needs, while at the same time enhancing effectiveness and efficiency by drawing on each actor's comparative advantages and maximizing all available resources.

Salient Needs, Latent Resources, and Self-Interest

Impoverished Brazilian communities suffer from lack of water, poor hygiene, and parasitic infection. The impact on children is particularly devastating. According to the World Health Organization (WHO), intestinal worms is the number-one health problem among school-age children in developing countries (WHO 2001; World Bank 1993). INMED found that parasitic infection, as well as associated nutrient deficiencies, affects up to 85 percent of the children in its project communities (INMED Brasil n.d.). Such infection compromises physical and intellectual growth and development and increases vulnerability to disease. INMED's Healthy Children, Healthy Futures program targets children between the ages of five and fourteen and aims to diagnose and treat parasitic infection and vitamin deficiencies, as well as to address continuing health needs. To do so, it applies a Children as Agents of Change strategy, with three steps:

1. *Treat* children for infection and deficiencies with quality essential medications and vitamins. Children receive semiannual deworming treatment in conjunction with Vitamin A and iron supplements.
2. *Teach* children how to prevent reinfection through participatory educational activities. Educational programs in the schools address family health and hygiene, nutrition, and environmental health, such as washing hands with soap, washing fruits and vegetables before eating, using latrines, and corralling animals. The teaching includes creating and performing plays, music, poetry, and artwork.
3. *Train* children to share these health messages with their families, friends, and communities. It is estimated that each child shares this new health knowledge with an average of four adults.

Parasitic treatment yields results within forty-eight hours. These immediate results are essential to convincing communities to support preventive health measures. Teachers report that children who were previously weak to the point of fainting become alert and physically active following Vitamin A treatment (Capelli 2000). These tangible results gain the confidence of local communities, who are then more willing to implement the preventive health lessons communicated by their children, including improving sanitation.

The Healthy Children, Healthy Futures program began in 1993 in partnership with Interfarma, an association of thirty-three multinational research-based pharmaceutical companies in Brazil. The pharmaceutical industry faced serious image problems at the time. Brazilian laws did not support international patents on intellectual property, and many Brazilian citizens were distrustful of the testing and marketing performed by the companies. The program was consistent with the pharmaceutical industry's efforts to improve the lives and health of people, and its commitment to support social programs through corporate philanthropy.

University, community school, and other NGO partners provided staff and community outreach, and members of Interfarma provided deworming medicines, health-education materials, and financial support for the hiring of a program director based in Brazil. In addition, Interfarma representatives participated in a coordination committee that met regularly to ensure progress toward the program's objectives, as well as the objectives of the individual partners (positive publicity and marketing of the program). The partnership with INMED enabled Interfarma to generate positive visibility and goodwill among consumers and the government; it was believed that this facilitated the passing of a new international intellectual-property patent law in Brazil in 1996.[1]

The partnership with Interfarma lasted from 1993 to 1996. Since then, INMED Brazil, now a separately registered Brazilian NGO, has targeted multinational corporations with a long-term investment in Brazil. These corporations recognize the importance of local philanthropy and social responsibility and consider these to be an expected cost of doing business. Typically, local operations have an allocated budget for this purpose, some of which may go unspent (Pfeiffer 2000b). Multinational corporations seek to contribute to meaningful change and improvements in quality of life that will enhance the image of their business. To do so, they attempt to partner with and support local NGO operations. However, local managers often do not have the time and ability to identify the most worthy and dependable investments. INMED helps these companies to identify ways to contribute to a proven model with high visibility, and minimal time and labor investment.[2] Supporting Healthy Children, Healthy Futures is particularly appealing to multinational corporations due to the range and number of organizations involved and the opportunity to work on a national priority through a legally registered NGO (Pfeiffer 2000b). Most multinational corporations contribute through in-kind and financial contributions that are consistent with their core business.

The program has now grown to address needs beyond those originally targeted through Healthy Children, Healthy Futures, as identified by each local community. In addition, Vitamin A and iron supplements have been added to the standard antiparasitic treatment. Treatment days have now become community events, with music, refreshment, entertainment, and, in some instances, an opportunity for employee volunteerism and corporate publicity. Representatives from the Brazilian Federal Drug Agency and the Ministry of Health may also be invited to sensitize them to the program and the need for import flexibility on donated drugs (Pfeiffer 2000c).[3] In each case, the precise substance, partners, and respective contributions vary. As programs demonstrate success, multinational corporations are motivated to contribute more, either in intensity or for expansion to new areas. In addition, with the growth of the program, its partners, and targeted communities, synergies among partners are increasingly identified, helping to stretch existing resource contributions and further encourage new ones.

The Evolution of Corporate Partnerships

Healthy Children, Healthy Futures has grown into a complex, multifaceted, multilocational, and multipartnership endeavor. Beginning with one partnership of limited duration with an association of multinational corporations, INMED Brazil now works with more than thirteen individual corporate partners, many of whom have made long-term, continuous commitments. The following discussion describes this evolution in greater detail, beginning with a brief history and description of how the partnerships work. It then examines emerging developments within the program and points to evidence of Healthy Children, Healthy Futures' continuing success.

The Interfarma Partnership

The Interfarma partnership grew out of discussions between INMED and several individual corporate members of Interfarma with whom INMED had previously interacted on other programs. These pharmaceutical companies were looking for ways to improve their image in Brazil to assist them in lobbying for a new patent law. INMED had distributed medicines to Brazil in the past and had an existing program, successfully demonstrated in Guatemala, that it was looking to expand. Some of the Interfarma members had contributed medicines to that program. At the same time, the Ministry of Health in Brazil had identified intestinal parasites as the number-one health problem among school-age children. Interfarma and INMED worked closely to define the objectives and respective roles prior to initiating the partnership. As a result, INMED was charged with project implementation and the recruitment of additional community partners as needed.

Coordination occurred at two levels. First, Interfarma, as an association of multinational corporations, coordinated the identification and delivery of individual member corporations' contributions. As an association of thirty-three multinational corporations, this coordination was not easy. It was sometimes difficult for the INMED program director to know to whom to report (Capelli 2000).[4] In essence, these "members" were also competitors; their primary common ground was the desire to foster a better business environment for their work in Brazil. The partnership had to take care to credit the association as a whole, thus supporting the industry in Brazil. Second, in São Paulo, a coordination committee with five Interfarma representatives met once or twice a month with the INMED program director.

These were individuals and companies who had requested to be more involved. The purpose of the meetings was to monitor the progress of the program and confirm the necessary respective contributions. The meetings were held at the various company locations and included representatives from a public relations firm hired by Interfarma to publicize the good works of the partnership.

The program consisted of four steps, from baseline research to final evaluation. First, baseline data indicated that 41 percent of sampled children were infected by one or more types of worms. At this stage, an initial analysis of attitudes and beliefs regarding hygiene practices was conducted through questionnaires and focus groups. In the second phase, children were treated with antiparasitic medicines. Third, at the same time as the treatment, the education phase was implemented, lasting one to three years. These educational programs capitalized on the analysis of hygiene attitudes and beliefs, as well as determined behavior and communication patterns among children and their parents. The information assisted in determining how to structure messages and ways to convey them to maximize existing communication channels. An inventory of existing infrastructure—sanitation and sewage systems, potable water systems, and animal corrals—supplemented the analysis.

Educational programs drew upon existing health-education materials made available by Interfarma members. INMED integrated these and other materials into the curriculum, recruited volunteers from universities and high schools to assist in the training of teachers, and developed and delivered—in 800 classes of the public school system—plays, music, games, poetry, and music to promote health education lessons. High-school students trained all of the janitorial and food-service staff on health and hygiene in the three participating schools in São Paulo.[5] Premedical students from the University of São Paulo trained the teachers and helped to develop songs, skits, and other creative modes of delivery. Children participated in this creative process as well, to help reinforce the messages. For homework, children were tasked with organizing and conducting community assemblies, enlisting the aid of their parents, relatives, and friends.

The fourth phase consisted of additional examinations, covering 50 percent more of the child population. The results of this final examination showed a rate of infection of 23 percent, representing an approximate 50 percent decrease in only three years. The program reached an estimated 150,000 children in both Rio de Janeiro and São Paulo, with an estimated outreach to 400,000 peers, relatives, and neighbors of participating children. In 1995, the first lady of Brazil, Ruth Cardoso, visited one of the program schools in São Paulo and established an informal agreement with INMED, requesting the expansion of Healthy Children, Healthy Futures to all of Brazil's twenty-seven states.[6] INMED Brazil formally registered as a

Brazilian NGO in 1995; the patent law was passed in 1996 and enacted in 1998; and Interfarma subsequently disbanded, though several of its corporate members remain active in the Healthy Children, Healthy Futures program today.

New Partnerships and Programs

The initial partnership with Interfarma established a model, systems, and a track record that could be replicated and expanded. The funding from Interfarma allowed for the hiring of a local program director (now the director of INMED Brazil), thus establishing a continuous INMED presence in Brazil for the first time. The established track record enabled INMED Brazil to register formally as a local NGO and subsequently recruit other donors and partners to continue its programs in other areas in Brazil.

Before the completion of the Interfarma partnership, INMED Brazil had already established a partnership in three program locations with the Pallottines, a Catholic religious order. The Pallottine funding represented the core, as INMED sought to expand its corporate partnerships. An opportunity was presented in the energy sector as early as 1996. Again, the corporate incentive was driven by government policy: the Brazilian government was initiating privatization of the energy sector. INMED began identifying energy companies with a presence in Brazil, and initiated a Tenneco-supported program in Rio de Janeiro in 1996, which worked with a new set of schools. Shortly after El Paso International took over Tenneco, a new partnership was established with El Paso International in Manaus. The program in Manaus built upon an existing Pallottine project and followed the previously established model, in this case finding a 60 percent rate of parasitic infection. The program was initiated with a $25,000 financial contribution comprised of employee contributions and corporate matching funds.

Former Interfarma corporate members, notably Johnson & Johnson and its Brazilian affiliate Janssen-Cilag, continue to provide antiparasitic medicine, as well as Vitamin A and iron. Additional partners have been identified, for example, food companies such as Nestlé to address the nutrition component; and environment and energy companies, retail chains, and auto companies that need to invest in the community from which they draw their labor. Most of the corporate contributions are financial and in-kind, consistent with the Interfarma model. For example, Colgate is a recently added partner, contributing dental kits to the school program. In-kind support also encompasses technical assistance, which includes the loan of medical personnel to assist on treatment days (Johnson & Johnson), planning and marketing training for INMED Brazil staff, and access to a nutrition consultant (Nestlé). Institutional support is also provided for communications and public relations. For example, Johnson & Johnson has provided assistance for compiling and printing project newsletters. Aside from Johnson & Johnson's role in providing medicines, most projects have a leading corporate sponsor, such as El Paso Energy International, the sponsor in Manaus. As multiple corporate partners are sought for each project, their selection is subject to the approval of the leading corporate partner.

In every case, INMED takes care to acknowledge and publicize the contributions and support of all of its corporate partners. For example, while the content of the teachers' manual remains the same throughout the Healthy Children, Healthy Futures program, manuals for specific locations are printed with a customized cover identifying the corporate sponsor (INMED 2000). In Manaus, publicity efforts included targeted meetings with media representatives to negotiate media coverage of the program (public service announcements, television programming directed to the schools, and special newspaper articles), which included agreements to acknowledge corporate sponsorships by name (Jackson 1999).

New corporate partnerships are primarily initiated from INMED's Washington headquarters, based on previous contacts or research that identifies corporations with a vested interest in Brazil. Typically, INMED representatives travel to Brazil to meet with local corporate operations. If they have an interest, a subsequent meeting is set up with the program director from INMED Brazil and a partnership is negotiated. The local corporate manager will usually appoint someone within the company to be the primary liaison with the program director. In some instances, the local manager or contact will agree to match funds secured from the international headquarters of the corporation and vice versa. In other cases, INMED Washington may contact the international headquarters, which will then provide the contact in Brazil.

The engagement of corporate partners and their representatives varies. In some instances, they require only periodic information on the program and its successes. In other instances, they seek to be more involved in the day-to-day operations. Typically, corporate partners make contact at least once every one or two months. INMED Brazil also provides each partner with quarterly reports. Most of the contact goes through the program director in São Paulo, though she may rely on information input from the regional coordinators. Corporate partners who wish to involve their employees are naturally more active; for example, representatives of Termo Norte Energia, the El Paso Energy International affiliate, make site visits to see project implementation and help with treatment days, and Monsanto has supported the children's theatrical performances.

Once a corporate sponsor is identified, locations are selected based on the partner's interests and the receptivity of the community and particular schools. When entering a potential new project community, focus-group meetings are conducted, applying the knowledge, attitudes, and practice (KAP) methodology.[7] The sessions consist of questioning and listening to the community's responses with respect to these three components in relation to the community's health. Focusing on children provides common ground and interest within the community. The KAP sessions form the basis for community empowerment. Leaders are typically identified to help move the program forward, based on priorities identified by the community. While the primary structure of the program—parasitic treatment, vitamin supplements, and health education—remains the same, additional activities may be incorporated at the community level.

INMED Brazil maintains a structure of project directors and regional coordinators based in municipalities in the various program locations. Project directors are specific to large projects sponsored by a particular leading corporate partner. Regional coordinators support multiple projects, often with different corporate sponsors, throughout a particular region. They are trained in the health and nutrition curriculum, train local teachers in participating schools, and coordinate the local programs. Modifications to the suggested curriculum from the education director from INMED Brazil are incorporated into both the training of the regional coordinators and the subsequent training of the local teachers. Pieces of the curriculum may be offered daily, weekly, or monthly.

Additional partnerships emerge on a case-by-case basis, in response to specifically identified needs and to the actors active in the project area. INMED Brazil identifies local partners based on their interests and activities in a project area. For example, INMED Brazil began training the government's health system home visitors in 2000. This affords the opportunity for more broadly disseminating and reinforcing the general hygiene and nutrition curriculum (Jackson 2000; Capelli 2000). In another instance, INMED Brazil partners with a local NGO, Pastorale da Criança. While Pastorale targets children from birth to age two, rather than INMED's targeted age of six to fourteen, there are sometimes opportunities for the organizations to provide mutual support. In 1999, INMED Brazil had more Vitamin A than it needed, so it provided Pastorale with what it needed for its program. In another example, a government hospital provides free fecal exams to participating children. Typically, government hospitals also provide treatment to address any ailments identified through the testing that the program does not already address. On its part, INMED Brazil provides health officials with the data collected through the program. The program recently initiated a dental-hygiene clinic, under construction by Pallottine priests, to be staffed by the local government and dental-student interns.

The program encompasses two types of agreement: one for corporate partners, the other for government. Government agreements primarily describe the project, the sector involved, and the interface that the project will have with government actors or agencies. These agreements are necessary in areas that require approval (e.g., from local health and education officials) for the program's implementation. Partnership agreements (PAs) with corporate partners also include an overview of the project, but more specifically identify the respective responsibilities of each actor, and the "nature of the partnership," including principles of shared commitment, mutual support, transparency, mutual respect, and equality in decisionmaking (see, for example, INMED, INMED Brazil, and Janssen-Cilag 2000). Many other partnerships are managed informally and emerge on an ad hoc basis.

Emerging Directions and Continuing Evolution

The program has expanded substantively through the addition of Vitamin A and iron supplements. In addition, new components are under development, such as an environmental component targeted to corporate partners who are interested in environmental issues and an expanded nutrition component with partners from the food industry. Programmatic expansions are specific to partners' concerns and are tailored to the project context. For instance, INMED Brazil is currently developing a strategy to address HIV/AIDS, drugs, and violence prevention using its participatory education approach. This new component is being developed at the request of teachers and parents from the program's inner-city project locations. Additional innovations, either in progress or foreseen in the near future, address expanding the existing model through new implementation arrangements, adding new dimensions to the partnership approach, and pursuing management-related innovations and plans.

Two new developments seek to expand the existing model with new applications. The "children as agents of change" strategy is premised on an indirect link of reaching communities through their children. INMED has learned that it is also useful to reinforce the lessons through direct interaction with the community. The new agreement to train local government health home visitors is an ideal opportunity to disseminate the health and hygiene lessons more broadly, and directly to parents and community members. Second, corporate volunteer programs are increasingly popular worldwide and have now been introduced in Brazil. Some of INMED's corporate partners have expressed an interest in incorporating employee volunteer programs into their partnerships. In Manaus, employees from Termo Norte Energia are very active on treatment days, assisting with medicine distribution and playing games with the children. INMED expects this to be a growing area within its partnership work, as new corporate partners are requesting employee volunteer components.[8]

INMED is expanding its partnerships and partnership approach in a number of ways. First, INMED is moving beyond its original focus on targeting corporate partners for their potential in-kind contributions or because of their established philanthropic interests. It is also focusing on targeting corporations who want to invest in the local community in which they operate. Most recently, INMED identified a retail chain with a growing number of locations. It is hoped that such partnerships will help INMED to fulfill its agreement with the first lady to expand the program to all twenty-seven states of Brazil. Second, INMED's partnerships with government are becoming more complex. INMED is entering more formal partnership agreements with governments, for example, in the home-visiting program noted above. Third, INMED also facilitates partnerships among its corporate partners. El Paso Energy International and Johnson & Johnson both support the program in Manaus, for example. Finally, as INMED's expertise in corporate partnerships becomes better known, it is being asked to facilitate partnerships and corporate social responsibility programs beyond the scope of Healthy Children, Healthy Futures.[9]

Management-related innovations and plans concern research and evaluation, reporting, coordination, and staffing. The Healthy Children, Healthy Futures program in Brazil incorporated research and evaluation from the outset, through its partnership with Interfarma. To date, evaluation measurements have relied primarily on parasitic-infection rates and other quantifiable health data. These are easily measured and reported. More recently, INMED has begun to explore the use of cognitive studies to determine whether or not the educational and action components of the program have led to changes in cognitive ability, attitude, and behavior. Initially, all of INMED's quarterly reports were based on their own format and assumptions about what the corporate partners would want to know. Increasingly, corporate partners are asking for the completion of standard reports on a par with those expected in the corporate sector.

Until now, project implementers depended on the organizational hierarchy to communicate needs and lessons learned; there has been a significant dependence on the program director in São Paulo for sharing lessons across project locations. INMED is in discussions with potential information technology corporate partners to introduce e-mail and other techniques to facilitate communication among teachers, between teachers and regional coordinators, and among regional coordinators. At the same time, they are discussing setting up a Web page to facilitate communication, post the program curriculum, and eventually assist the children to communicate with each other, for example, to share the songs, skits, and art they have developed through the program.

INMED has also been recognizing a need for more staff, some with particular technical skills. INMED is building a new administrative layer—project and regional coordinators as paid, as opposed to volunteer, staff.

INMED sells this to its corporate partners as an expected cost of running the program. With its continuing expansion, INMED Brazil cannot manage the entire program solely from its headquarters in São Paulo. On the technical side, in order to better meet the needs and interests of its corporate partners, INMED has recently created a new (half-time) position at headquarters—a journalist to assist with publicity and media coverage.

The Success of Healthy Children, Healthy Futures

Healthy Children, Healthy Futures benefited from many early successes. The initial partnership with Interfarma in São Paulo and Rio de Janeiro reached 150,000 children, 8,000 teachers, and an estimated 400,000 family members. Interfarma met its goal of positive publicity and goodwill with consumers and government. Positive visibility included numerous awards from global health and professional organizations, as well as national recognition and endorsement.[10] This recognition included acclaim from Brazil's first lady Ruth Cardoso, whose project site visit was nationally televised (reaching an estimated 30 million viewers). These efforts culminated in the new international patent law in 1996.

The more enduring partnership success is demonstrated in the program's continuing growth and replication. This growth includes programmatic and geographic expansion, an increase in the number and diversity of partners, and the expansion of partner roles to encompass the training of government officials and corporate volunteer programs. At the partnership level, success is revealed in individual partners' renewal and expansion of their participation. INMED has become an established leader in corporate partnership work in Brazil, as evidenced in its facilitation of partnerships among its corporate partners, as well as requests for its facilitation of partnerships beyond the scope of Healthy Children, Healthy Futures. INMED's corporate partners value its holistic approach to health and health education.[11]

Other indicators of success have either not been measured or are intangible. For example, ad hoc and informal reports indicate that school attendance has increased as a result of the program. Parents recognize added benefits to sending their children to school, and the children are in a better position to develop intellectually as their health improves. Studies elsewhere show that Vitamin A supplements reduce the incidence of anemia. Teachers have reported that following antiparasitic treatment and vitamin supplements, children who were previously ill and listless respond, have energy, and are ready to learn (Interfarma n.d.; Capelli 2000). One of the more intangible outcomes derives from the KAP sessions and the program's implications for the community level. Through the KAP sessions, the community is offered an opportunity to identify its primary needs and inventory its strengths and resources available to apply to these needs. At the same time, they experience visible results in terms of health improvements in their children. These experiences instill confidence and empower individuals to become proactive in improving their lives and the quality of life in their community.

The Healthy Children, Healthy Futures program began with a limited number of schools in two cities, São Paulo and Rio de Janeiro. The program was operating in ten states by 2001 and will eventually expand to all twenty-seven states in accordance with INMED's agreement with the first lady. Not only is it proving successful for Brazilian communities, it has established INMED Brazil as a national leader in corporate partnership work, and the model is now being considered for application in other countries.

Implications and Lessons Learned

INMED's Healthy Children, Healthy Futures program in Brazil demonstrates how a great number and diversity of partnerships, whose composition varies in each location, can be designed and implemented for effectiveness and responsiveness to the needs of each community and the interests of each partner. In these respects, the program is an extremely complex partnership that offers lessons for both partnerships in general and those with corporate partners in particular.

Lessons for Partnership Work

1. *Partners can have very different objectives and still work together for effective partnerships. The nature of the partnership relationship may vary from partner to partner within the overall partnership and program.* Effective partnerships require strong partnership drivers for each actor. In Healthy Children, Healthy Futures, these specific drivers vary for each partner and could be seen as contradictory. For example, INMED staff, volunteers, community stakeholders, and government representatives may not have agreed with Interfarma's ultimate objective to establish a new international patent law, and some partners or stakeholders might be uncomfortable with corporate partners' publicity priorities. However, at some point priorities converged, enabling partners to agree to specific partnership objectives and respective contributions. In short, partners are unified around their common aim to improve the health of children and communities, whatever the motivation.

INMED is responsive to each partner's interests and concerns. Publicity and public relations opportunities for corporate partners are fully exploited; however, INMED's work with the Pallottines is kept relatively quiet in deference to their spiritual beliefs and operational preferences. Some partnership relationships are more directly engaging and include corporate volunteer programs and employee matching contributions; others entail only corporate financial contributions and more distant monitoring. Partnership relationships are also more or less formalized and structured. The key is the partners' shared commitment to the overall partnership or program goals and objectives.

2. *Complex partnerships, in particular, require strong champions to ensure responsiveness to each partner, as well as overall program continuity. This championing may be most effective when it entails OCB and values-based incentives.* The program director, Joyce Capelli, champions the program on a day-to-day basis and ensures its success. Capelli is described as the "champion for the people and the cause of children," who also champions ethical practice within the program (Pfeiffer 2000a). Capelli plays the role of mediator, coordinator, and listener to a wide range of individuals, at the national and local levels of multinational corporations; at the local, state, and national levels of government, including interacting with the first lady; and among individual teachers and regional coordinators who may be frustrated with the program's day-to-day challenges. She also strives to allay concerns of stakeholders who may not necessarily be formal partners. For example, in each new project area, she meets with local government officials to introduce the program and subsequently reports to them in order to divert potential opposition. Responding to the needs and concerns of each partner while still ensuring program implementation and success requires an unusual degree of dedication, which Capelli readily gives.

The following quote, delivered with great emotion, demonstrates the depth of Capelli's commitment and values-based incentives:

> For me the most rewarding thing in the project . . . is to go to the field and . . . look at the community and see the change in things that are not even so directly linked to the project but that are outcomes of the project. Like the self-esteem of the kids rising. . . . I think the most important part of the project is that we give [the community] something for free; we give them something without asking; [we give] something back. Because these populations . . . have been very used by politicians. We had a dictatorship in Brazil for so many years. So this is something really new that they can receive something and not pay a high price for it. (Capelli 2000)

Given the difficulties of the work, when asked why she does it, Capelli responded, "To see a better world for people, a better position" (Capelli 2000). She confirmed that this was a common bond among the program staff and volunteers.

3. *When working with diverse partners whose core business may not be*

directly related to the partnership objectives, it may be beneficial to recognize a primary implementer and coordinator. An NGO may have the necessary neutrality and common respect and legitimacy of the partners to fulfill this role. INMED's Healthy Children, Healthy Futures program in Brazil demonstrates that a designated implementer and coordinator can be used to assemble diverse interests and respective contributions without involving partners in implementation arrangements that may not be related to their core business, or may be beyond their intent or capacity to contribute. This is certainly a strength according to Johnson & Johnson, which maintains one of the smallest staffs for giving among multinational corporations (Bzdak 2001). Trusting INMED's model and expertise makes more sense under such circumstances. Corporate partners do not need to develop redundant expertise or onerous oversight. While this may seem to be more relevant for corporate partnerships, one can envision other actors who may also prefer contributing without integrating with their partners, for example, government agencies, individual donors, and foundations.

The designated implementer will depend on the particular actors and individuals involved, their capacity, and perceived legitimacy. NGOs may be logical candidates for this role, given that corporations are frequently criticized for their ultimate perspective to the bottom line, governments for their political motives, and some religious organizations for their proselytizing emphasis. This presumes, however, that the NGO is not affiliated with a particular political agenda or oppositional stance.

4. Buffering of partners and individuals can be helpful at multiple levels. The Healthy Children, Healthy Futures partnership demonstrates a range of buffering efforts. First, the degree of reporting formality is responsive to partners' preferences, but it may be beyond the capacity or priority of particular actors. In response, INMED Washington buffers INMED Brazil in terms of meeting these formal requirements and expectations, acquiring the raw information from the program director and repackaging it to meet the preferences of various partners. National and international buffering also occurs within corporate partners' organizations, for example, in managing local corporate liaisons as needed. More locally, the program director is the primary interface with partners in all locations, buffering local project directors and regional coordinators from this task. This is especially important given that these local implementers may not understand or identify with some of the partners' interests and concerns and they may not share a common language or perspective for the work. Buffering may also entail protecting partners from demands that are not consistent with their comparative advantages. For example, Johnson & Johnson learned that INMED's strength was not in the national distribution of donated drugs. It, therefore, solicited its local affiliate to take on the responsibility, resulting in a more effective and efficient delivery system (Person 2001).

5. Short-term, issue-focused partnerships can be effective and beneficial to all partners; where desirable, can also be used as entrepreneurial opportunities to build capacity for subsequent partnership work; and may be more fruitful if partners are familiar with each other and when some degree of mutual trust or confidence is in place. INMED's experience in Brazil demonstrates the significant advantages of short-term, issue-based partnerships. Interfarma was only interested in a three-year partnership to support its objective of influencing legal reform. Each partner met its respective objectives through the partnership; there were significant health outcomes for targeted children and their communities; and the program ended as scheduled. While it may not have been envisioned from the start, INMED also used this opportunity to build capacity, relationships, and a model with which to build subsequent partnerships (including those with Interfarma members) and an enduring program. The initial Interfarma partnership proved essential for learning how corporate partners think about corporate social responsibility, what their priorities are, and how best to be responsive to these while still promoting the partnership's objectives and INMED's values and identity.

NGOs and other actors can regard short-term partnerships as entrepreneurial opportunities. INMED's experience further suggests that, where possible, NGOs can benefit from starting partnership work with known partners with whom there is already some degree of trust and mutual respect. From there, they can build capacity, systems, and a model on a smaller, more simplified scale, before expanding to new, lesser-known partners, substance, and locations.

6. Partnerships that seek to address complex social problems can benefit from incorporating components that demonstrate immediate results. Preventive health measures, particularly health education, are difficult to promote and sell. Healthy Children, Healthy Futures was able to promote its ultimate objectives of long-term health improvements and community empowerment by gaining the confidence of local communities through the immediate results of antiparasitic treatment. Such immediate results can similarly motivate partners and other stakeholders, instilling confidence in the program, as well as its implementers.

7. The greater the trust among partners and ability to determine partners' compliance with partnership agreements, the greater the potential to rely on informal structures and procedures. Healthy Children, Healthy Futures relies more on partners' trust in INMED Brazil as the implementer and coordinator than it does on confidence mechanisms of highly specified roles and responsibilities and formal reporting requirements. Throughout the program, there is an obvious preference for face-to-face personal contact. This begins with the corporate partners, moves to the KAP sessions with local community members, extends to meetings with local government officials, and encompasses the training and support of regional coordinators, teachers, and other volunteers. The success of INMED's partnership relationships is summarized in a quote from Johnson & Johnson: "Civilization is measured by how many things you can do without thinking about it. Similarly, a good relationship is measured by what you can accomplish without the need for extensive discussion" (Person 2001).

INMED's experience implies that when one initiates a partnership program on the basis of trust and existing confidence, it may be easier to expand that program with informal rather than formal approaches. Reliance on informal processes is further facilitated when it is easier to immediately gauge a partner's compliance with its partnership agreement. In the case of a corporation's contributions, INMED Brazil knows immediately if the corporation has complied with its promised financing and in-kind contributions.

8. Financial and in-kind contributions typically do not require substantial partner integration. Partnerships with minimal integration require less capacity-building investments, and less complex monitoring and evaluation systems. Such partnerships are likely to select partners based on comparative advantages and existing capacity for implementation. Hence, roles and performance are more easily determined. Healthy Children, Healthy Futures requires capacity building for selected roles (training of trainers for the delivery of the health and hygiene curriculum) but not for integrated processes and interface. Each partner has a clearly designated role whose performance is easily measured.

Lessons for Corporate Partnerships

1. Corporate partnerships may be a unique case of partnerships, where organization identity is emphasized, yet mutuality is primarily operationalized at the negotiation phase. In some respects, corporate partnerships such as INMED's could be considered contracting arrangements, given their emphasis on organization identity and its associated comparative advantages, with seemingly minimal integration and opportunities to exercise mutuality. However, relationships such as these differ fundamentally from typical business transaction contracts. Mutuality is exercised, though it is done at the negotiation phase, ensuring mutual input and responsiveness to shared and particular objectives. Partners subsequently remain flexible in order to respond to emerging opportunities and newly identified innovations for program expansion. In the case of INMED's Healthy Children, Healthy

Futures program in Brazil, this mutuality is reinforced through the PAs and the partnership's organization culture, which promotes responsiveness to partners' needs and concerns beyond agreed reporting arrangements.

2. *Partnerships with NGOs can be effective means for corporations to meet their corporate social responsibility objectives. However, they will be most effective where they do not impinge on the organization identity of their NGO partners and where they do not attempt to have their partners represent them.* Healthy Children, Healthy Futures is an effective example of a partnership that maximized organization identity in order to maximize performance and sustainability. INMED was approached as a partner precisely because of its experience in designing and implementing health treatment and education programs in other countries. Rather than impose its own ideas on the program implementation, Interfarma trusted INMED's expertise and capacity to ensure results. Aspects of the program design were mutually developed, with Interfarma contributing its experience and expertise in research and evaluation in particular. Furthermore, when partners have recognized that their demands do not coincide with INMED's comparative advantages, such as in drug distribution, alternative arrangements are made so as not to compromise INMED's capacity and success, keeping it focused on what it does best. At the same time, INMED understands the corporate world and can speak its language; Johnson & Johnson highlights this professionalism and mutual understanding as a key factor in its selection and continuation of INMED as a partner (Person 2001). Corporate partners are also appreciative of INMED's efforts to get the full buy-in of the health and education ministries, schools, and key political figures (Pfeiffer 1999).

INMED's neutrality has been key not only to the program's success in brokering and coordinating its many partnerships but also to maintaining the necessary trust of the program's beneficiaries and stakeholders. For example, if INMED were perceived as a corporate mouthpiece, it likely would not have the same degree of support from government officials, including the first lady's endorsement, especially at a time when INMED's partners were lobbying hard for a change in Brazil's international patent law.

3. *NGOs seeking corporate support for addressing complex social issues would do well to incorporate components with immediate, measurable impact.* As noted above, preventive health measures are difficult to promote and sell, both to targeted participants and to consumers targeted for corporate public relations. Corporations exercising corporate social responsibility will want to focus on those interventions that can provide a compelling story, and they may often prioritize short-term results that can begin to support public relations campaigns as soon as possible. The experience

of Healthy Children, Healthy Futures demonstrates that NGOs seeking corporate support for addressing complex social issues can benefit from incorporating components with short-, intermediate-, and longer-term results. INMED's emphasis on children further enhances its corporate appeal. Johnson & Johnson takes its reputation quotient (Harris Interactive and Fombrun 1999; see also Harris Interactive 2002; Reputation Management 2002) very seriously. One of the six dimensions is emotional appeal.[12]

4. Corporate partnerships with NGOs can stretch resources, create synergies, and maximize comparative advantages. Corporate giving budgets may be limited or already committed; in other cases, the limitations may derive more from minimal staff for oversight. Corporations may also be narrowly focused by their in-kind contributions. In such an instance, supporting existing programs can contextualize contributions, ensuring broader and longer-lasting results. This is the case, for example, with Johnson & Johnson's contribution of deworming medication. Simply providing the donation does not ensure prevention of reinfection or the generation of additional health benefits through education. Through Healthy Children, Healthy Futures, Johnson & Johnson can claim credit for a much broader range of health outcomes and quality-of-life indicators.

Supporting an existing program with a designated implementer creates opportunities for corporations to get a larger return on small investments, as existing programs and models can more readily absorb smaller sums. This was the case, for example, with El Paso Energy International. Because of their employee matching program, it was difficult to foresee the exact contribution amount. INMED could readily absorb whatever amount was eventually made available. Such programs can also enable corporations to be effective with smaller corporate giving staffs, avoiding the need to develop additional expertise related to a program's technology and approach. Johnson & Johnson intentionally seeks longer-term partnerships of this nature.

5. Not only can new resources and synergies be created through partnering with corporations, they can be further enhanced by promoting partnerships between corporations. Despite different industry origins and specific corporate drivers, partnerships that encompass multiple corporate partners can access substantially greater resources. In addition, partnership with one corporation can lend credibility to a program, which can be helpful in attracting additional corporate partners. Such multiple-corporation partnerships enhance the likelihood of effectiveness and sustainability and take the burden off any one partner to fully finance, equip, or supply a program. This is particularly cost-effective when each corporate partner contributes according to its core business and comparative advantages. For example, INMED's continuing partnership with Johnson & Johnson for the antiparasitic medicines was an important selling point for INMED's negotiations with El Paso Energy International.

6. Transnational partnerships can assist multinational corporations to maintain continuity in corporate social responsibility and reinforce a common organization culture among national affiliates and operational branches and international headquarters. This advantage of transnational partnerships has not been sufficiently addressed in the literature on corporate social responsibility, but it should be considered an important advantage and potential selling point for such partnerships. For example, the El Paso Energy International partnership in Manaus relied on employee contributions and corporate matching in Texas and additional contributions, matching, and employee volunteers from Termo Norte Energia, El Paso Energy International's Brazilian affiliate. Reports and associated pictures of the project sites are sent to El Paso Energy International headquarters, where management and employees can see corporate logos both on project materials and on the clothes of employee volunteers. In the case of Johnson & Johnson and Janssen-Cilag Brasil, Johnson & Johnson's credo was reinforced and directly associated with the program and both locations' substantial contributions. Johnson & Johnson's director of corporate giving emphasizes that joint-contribution programs, with matching between international headquarters and local affiliates, help to personalize intracorporation relationships and combat the tendency for local affiliates and their employees to perceive the corporate headquarters as "other" (Bzdak 2001).

Conclusion

Given the nature of the program's objectives and the partners' tolerance for sharing power, willingness to be flexible, and relative emphasis on trust rather than confidence, the Healthy Children, Healthy Futures program is designed as a complex, though minimally integrated, multiactor partnership, with a designated implementer and coordinator, who fulfills its responsibilities flexibly, with informal processes and an emphasis on personal relations. The program encompasses a range of partners that varies with each location and changes with emerging opportunities and the completion of goals.

With the continued growth, emphasis, and expectation of corporate social responsibility, the Healthy Children, Healthy Futures partnership demonstrates a creative, effective, and relatively hassle-free approach for corporations to enact and expand this work. A partnership such as Healthy Children, Healthy Futures can ensure that such contributions (especially when coupled with contributions from other corporations and multisectoral partners) move far beyond welfare approaches to attain a sustainable impact on peoples' lives. This is a great story and nothing could be more advantageous for corporate social responsibility efforts seeking good public relations.

Notes

1. The importance of this law for the pharmaceutical industry cannot be underestimated. In 2000 the Brazilian government declared all patents filed prior to 1997 null and void, enabling it to commence manufacturing generic HIV/AIDS drug cocktails.

2. These advantages are especially noted by INMED's longest partner, Johnson & Johnson (Person 2001).

3. In 2000, the Brazilian FDA became more strict with respect to imported donated drugs due to problems with counterfeiting and donated drugs entering the commercial market (Pfeiffer 2000c).

4. The program director is considered INMED International's Country Director for Brazil. Once INMED Brazil became a separately registered Brazilian NGO, the Healthy Children, Healthy Futures program director also became the director of INMED Brazil.

5. These volunteers came from a prestigious private high school in São Paulo, considered to be the source of many future leaders in Brazil.

6. In 1999, this endorsement and request was formalized in a written agreement.

7. KAP surveys assist in identifying problems and needs and seek qualitative information, such as reasons or causes for nonadoption or inappropriate practice with regard to identified environmental problems. In the Healthy Children, Healthy Futures program, the original KAP manuals were translated, adapted to the Brazilian context, and revised with pictorial explanations, with technical assistance from the University of São Paulo.

8. This relatively new interest may be, in part, due to an article in *VEJA*, a Brazilian magazine, which ranked the top-100 companies to work for in Brazil. High ratings were based on a combination of benefits, work hours, and opportunities to volunteer in the community.

9. For example, a power company in Bahia has operations in areas where people are very poor, and lack basic sanitation systems, potable water, and formal education. The program director is exploring ways the company and the local education department might work together to deliver technical courses for the local population. INMED will only facilitate to initiate the project; it will not remain involved in implementation.

10. For example, the Pan American Health Organization has declared the partnership to be "one of the most effective programs worldwide for improving health and the lives of children" (INMED Brazil n.d.); the organization has also been featured at the WHO conference, received the Brazilian Chapter of the American Chamber of Commerce's Premio Eco award for outstanding corporate-sponsored health-care programs, and been endorsed by the Departments of Health and Education in São Paulo and Rio de Janeiro, as well as by many premier Brazilian universities, academic centers, and foundations.

11. Based on its experience with INMED, when Johnson & Johnson was approached by UNICEF for a deworming medicine donation, it knew what questions to ask with respect to how the program would prevent reinfection and how it

would address longer-lasting benefits through health education (Person 2001).

12. Dimensions include emotional appeal, products and services, financial performance, vision and leadership, workplace environment, and social responsibility (Harris Interactive and Fombrun 1999). Johnson & Johnson has been rated number one for its reputation among the U.S. public in 1999, 2000, and 2001 (Alsop 2001, 1999; Harris Interactive 2002).

7

Partnership for Conflict Resolution:
The World Commission on Dams

How can global public policy be effectively designed, promoted, and implemented when it pits multiple stakeholders against each other with stakes as high as livelihood, economic development, environmental degradation, and death? The World Commission on Dams (WCD) pioneered an experimental answer to this question through its partnership approach to policymaking for regulating the building of large dams worldwide. It offers much hope in terms of resolving the conflict and many lessons in how to implement a seemingly impossible partnership approach.

The WCD was a global partnership with a two-year time frame; it was designed to resolve conflict surrounding large dams by providing thorough and objective analysis of the issues and making corresponding recommendations for decisionmaking guidelines related to large-dam projects. The effort was initiated through a partnership between the World Bank and the World Conservation Union (IUCN) for an initial stakeholders' workshop and grew into a partnership of more than sixty institutions through the WCD.

The Need for a Partnership Approach

To understand the rationale behind the creation of the WCD, and to appreciate its contributions, one must first understand the context of the large-dam controversy and the stakes involved. Large dams are an important vehicle for economic development; they provide electric power, irrigation for agriculture, and residential and industrial water. Critics, however, question the development effectiveness of large dams and fault their promoters for ignoring important social and environmental impacts. The issues involved in large-dam projects are complex and varied; they include technical (engineering and geological), sociocultural (resettlement, cultural heritage), environmental, financial, moral (human rights), and political dimensions. It is clear that no one stakeholder commands the necessary skills and information to understand and incorporate all of these dimensions. These simplistic summaries do not do justice to the severity of the problem and the stakes involved. The history of conflict over large-dam projects includes murder, willful life-threatening protest, international campaigns both on environmental and human rights grounds, resultant stoppage of dam projects, and calls for the decommissioning of existing dams.[1]

Large-dam critics have vowed, "We have stopped dams in the past, and we will stop more in the future" (IRN 1997). At a minimum, potential confrontations introduce uncertainty for governments and the private sector, raising questions regarding political and economic feasibility and stunting the entire hydropower industry (see Armistead 1998). In 1992, the president of the International Commission on Large Dams, the professional association of large-dam engineers, recognized the challenge to its industry posed by "a serious general counter-movement that has already succeeded in reducing the prestige of dam engineering in the public eye, and . . . is starting to make work difficult for our profession" (Khagram 2000: 94; Pircher 1992). The decommissioning of dams is now called for in North America, with particular fervor surrounding the Snake River in the Pacific Northwest of the United States. Additional controversies and continuing protests concerning large dams can be found in the Philippines, Malaysia, Turkey, Brazil, Pakistan, Ghana, Lesotho, Namibia, and Angola to name just a few.

The World Bank and regional development banks (the Inter-American Development Bank, and the Asian Development Bank) are the primary targets for protest against large dams. The World Bank is considered the world's most important large-dam funder to date, having lent approximately $58 billion (in 1993 dollars) to more than ninety-three countries (Pottinger 1997). The controversy, growing awareness of the issues, and international appeal are captured in the movements of several local and international advocacy groups, from the Narmada Bachao Andolan (NBA, Save the Narmada Movement) in India and other similar indigenous yet internationalizing groups, to the International Rivers Network (IRN). Their work has culminated in two critical declarations that encapsulate the movement and its progress: the Manibeli Declaration, adopted in June 1994, and endorsed by 326 nongovernmental organizations and NGO coalitions in forty-four countries; and the Curitiba Declaration, which resulted from the First International Meeting of Dam-Affected People in March 1997. The declarations call for a moratorium on dam building pending certain conditions, including an international independent commission to conduct a comprehensive review of large dams, and a call for environmental restoration and reparations to affected peoples.

Through the WCD, diverse stakeholders sought to move from a no-win situation among multiple actors to a compromise and potential win-win situation for international economies and river ecosystems, and the people who depend on them. The WCD represents the multiactor, integrated solution required by the scope and nature of the problem being addressed. To meet these ends, the WCD was intentionally designed to open decisionmaking processes, proactively seeking input from all stakeholders to the large-dam controversy.

The Evolution of a Global Partnership

The Creation of the WCD

The Operations Evaluation Department (OED) conducted a review of the World Bank's large-dam projects, released for official use only, August 15, 1996 (Liebenthal et al. 1996). The Bank anticipated significant criticism and controversy from its conclusions and knew that any contribution to policy would be dependent on further investigation and consideration of the issues with a broader array of stakeholders. As a result, only a précis of the report was made public (Weaving 1996). As expected, having obtained a leaked copy, the IRN issued a critique of the report, citing seriously flawed methodology and incomplete and inadequate data, and claimed the report "displays a systematic bias in favour of large dam building." They further called the précis "the apex of a process of incremental censorship" (McCully 1997b). In the meantime, the World Bank was planning the second phase of its review, to include participation from all major stakeholder groups. The consultation idea emerged from OED discussions with the World Bank Board of Directors. World Bank senior management supported the idea because of frustration with the status quo and resulting hesitation to consider large-dam options (Liebenthal 1999). The IRN praised this effort, calling it an opportunity for the World Bank to begin "in a credibly and unbiased way" to review its large-dam financing (McCully 1997a).

The World Bank (with support from a Swiss Agency for Development Cooperation trust fund) entered a partnership with the IUCN to organize a multistakeholder workshop to review the findings. The workshop, "Large Dams: Learning from the Past, Looking at the Future," was held in Gland, Switzerland, April 10–11, 1997. IUCN was given veto power on objectives, participants, and agenda items. This resulted in the inclusion of participants that were somewhat uncomfortable for the World Bank, but whose participation was essential to meet the objectives. The selection process resulted in thirty-nine participants with representatives from the World Bank, government agencies, NGOs, the private sector (power companies, engineering firms, and investors), and academics.[2] The workshop was held in a neutral setting, IUCN headquarters; there was no chairperson but rather a neutral facilitator; and hierarchical tendencies were abolished in the organization of small groups and seating arrangements (Liebenthal 1999). The neutral facilitator was credited with creating "the right atmosphere and the right process for an open and constructive debate" (Greene and Picciotto 1997: ii).

This did not totally eliminate tension, especially at the beginning. On the World Bank side there was a feeling that the critics "hadn't been playing fair" but still had to be brought to the table since they were "stopping our projects" (Liebenthal 1998). In introducing themselves the evening before the workshop, others clearly stated their positions and stressed "the legacy of mistrust and acrimony" that would need to be overcome for any measure of success (Dorcey et al. 1997: 9). It was only three days prior to the workshop that NGOs had sent a letter to World Bank president James Wolfensohn condemning the OED report and calling for a moratorium on the Bank's lending for large dams (Box 7.1).

Nevertheless, the ensuing dialogue revealed common ground among the varied stakeholders, including agreement that all were dissatisfied with the status quo and wanted to realize only economically viable and socially and environmentally appropriate dam projects (Liebenthal 1998; McCully 1997c). While some participants criticized OED's conclusion that "the benefits of large dams far outweigh the costs" as based on inadequate data and faulty methodology (McCully 1997c), other participants felt that by providing evidence of both good and bad dam projects, the OED report "provided a useful basis for defining common ground in the discussion that followed" (Liebenthal 2000). The workshop concluded with unanimous agreement to establish an international commission to review global experience with large dams; explore the issues, costs, and benefits; and recommend guidelines for decisionmaking on dams. Participants recognized the need for the commission's work to be "comprehensive in scope, transparent in conduct, and defensible in its analyses" (Dorcey et al. 1997).

The plan was to establish a World Commission on Dams, comprising five to eight members, with an internationally recognized chairperson. The commissioners would have appropriate expertise and experience and would be "widely regarded" for their integrity, objectivity, independence, and representation of the varied perspectives, including the public and private sectors, affected communities, and other advocacy interests. The commission would have a two-year mandate at the end of which a final report and recommendations would be issued. In order to further ensure effective and balanced representation, a consultative group would also be established, comprised of the participants of the workshop and other invited specialists and interested parties. The consultative group would be a sounding board for ideas, and members would join working groups and recommend specialists

Box 7.1   World Commission on Dams Timeline

September 1996	OED's précis on "World Bank Lending for Large Dams: A Preliminary Review of Impacts" released to the public.
April 7, 1997	Forty-nine NGOs from twenty-one countries write to World Bank president James Wolfensohn demanding the World Bank reject the conclusions of the OED review. The NGOs advocate for a comprehensive, unbiased, and authoritative review of past World Bank lending and call for a moratorium on Bank lending for large dams.
April 10–11, 1997	World Bank–IUCN workshop, "Large Dams: Learning from the Past, Looking at the Future," Gland, Switzerland.
April 11, 1997	Participants at Gland workshop unanimously agree to establish, by November 1997, a two-year World Commission on Dams.
May–October 1997	Interim Working Group and Secretariat coordinate the WCD's initial preparatory process.
September 1997	Professor Kader Asmal invited to chair the WCD.
November 24, 1997	Anticipated launch of the WCD; cancelled due to environmental and human rights groups' complaints that the commission lacked fair representation from dam-affected people and dam critics.
February 1998	Save the Narmada Movement activist Medha Patkar added to the list of commissioners. NGOs accept commissioners, with reservation.
February 16, 1998	WCD launched. Development and implementation of work program initiated.
March 25–26, 1999	First meeting of the WCD Forum, Prague, Czech Republic.
July 1999	WCD's interim report released. First-year activities include thirty-two research and consultative efforts.
March 2000	WCD's work program completed. Knowledge base distributed to members of the WCD Forum.
April 6–8, 2000	Second meeting of the WCD Forum, Cape Town, South Africa.
April–August 2000	Synthesis of findings; production of final report.
November 16, 2000	Publication of the WCD's final report.
November 2000–March 2001	Series of workshops to disseminate the final report, organized in conjunction with stakeholder organizations.
February 25–27, 2001	Third meeting of the WCD Forum to explore ways in which representatives will promote implementation of the report's recommendations within and across constituencies.

who might be involved (Dorcey et al. 1997). The objective of the WCD is deceptively straightforward: to review the development effectiveness of large dams and to develop standards, criteria, and guidelines to inform future decisionmaking.

Operationalizing the WCD was not a simple task; in some ways, it embodied the conflict the commission was designed to solve. One of the most outspoken large-dam critics, Shripad Dharmadhikary of the NBA, was keen to remind dam proponents that opposition to large dams—including the intensity of existing campaigns—would not diminish in the interim (McCully 1997c). Despite the workshop's consensus, interpretation of the events was not consistently shared. For example, one NGO representative claimed the creation of the WCD was not the World Bank's initiative, but came as a result of the World Bank finding itself "cornered" at the workshop, where the evident poor quality of its own review forced the Bank to "make concessions," including the establishment of the WCD (see Pottinger 1997).

The process began with the establishment of an Interim Working Group (IWG), comprised of IUCN and World Bank staff, and an associated secretariat. The IWG first selected a chairman for the commission, Professor Kader Asmal. Asmal was selected based on his distinguished track record in water resources management and human rights. As a politician and a lawyer, he seemed ideally suited to understanding both the complexity and the diplomacy required for the WCD. Asmal was appointed chairperson of the WCD in September 1997 and joined the IWG's efforts to select appropriate commissioners.

Selection of the commissioners proved controversial. An extensive consultation process was launched, primarily targeting the initial reference group (participants from the workshop) to solicit nominations. From this consultation, a list of eight nominees was developed. This list, along with the name of the chairman, was sent to the reference group for comment. While there was no opposition to the chairman, the proposed list of commissioners received significant opposition—so much in fact, that the launch of the commission, scheduled for November 24, 1997, had to be postponed. Environmental and human rights groups complained that the list lacked fair representation from dam-affected people and dam critics. The bitter exchange included NGO claims that the World Bank and IUCN "reneged on commitments to a consensus process by selecting the commission members on their own and by disregarding suggested changes from others involved in the process" (McCully 1997d). Representatives of NGOs and the large-dam industry met with the IWG in February 1998 to address the issue. As a result, four additional commissioners were selected, including Medha Patkar, leader of India's NBA.

The WCD consisted of twelve commissioners, including five NGO representatives, and representatives from government agencies, the private sector, and academia. Each commissioner was required to shed her or his institutional affiliation for the purpose of serving the commission, in order to overcome the conflict among positions and to create a new spirit for the work to be carried out by the "team" (Liebenthal 1999). In February 1998, NGOs from the reference group accepted the proposed list of commissioners with reservation.[3] The WCD was formally launched February 16, 1998.

The commission was strictly advisory and would not adjudicate on specific disputes. The WCD's objective was to inform decisionmakers about dams, not to offer a final verdict. Kader Asmal, the WCD chairman, expected its findings to be invoked as a "moral authority" to secure acceptance of its guidelines (Armistead 1998). The group aimed to develop and agree on a framework for an informed and transparent dialogue and decisionmaking process among all stakeholders of particular dam projects (Asmal 1999c). An essential operational objective was to maintain independence and transparency throughout the WCD process and activities.

Implementing the WCD

WCD activities.   The WCD's work program, now completed, reflects views and concerns expressed by the various large-dam stakeholders. The aim of the work program was to establish a knowledge base; it includes seventeen thematic reviews, covering alternatives to large dams, as well as social, environmental, and institutional and governance issues; a 150-dam cross-check survey; ten large-dam case studies; and four regional consultations (South Asia, East and Southeast Asia, Latin America, and Africa and the Middle East). In addition, the commission actively solicited submissions from interested parties, through its newsletter and Web site, and more directly in association with its regional and case-study stakeholder consultations. Submissions enabled the WCD to access existing information, data, and analysis on dams; to ensure a review of a wide range of experience with different dams and river basins; to gain an understanding of the diversity of perspectives on major issues associated with dams; and to attain documentation of good practices and state-of-the-art knowledge on dams and water and energy resource management. A total of 947 submissions informed the WCD's final report (WCD 2001a).

The commission also continues to implement a communications action plan that includes a databank of postal and e-mail addresses of over 2,000 organizations and interested individuals, a state-of-the-art Web site, published information folders in four languages, a newsletter, and media outreach. These communications were considered crucial to keeping the primary stakeholder constituencies informed about the WCD process and

outcomes (WCD 1999d). The Web site will continue until 2003 and will
also be produced and distributed on CD-ROM. According to the WCD, the
Web site is "the most, if not the only, visible, transparent and accessible
evidence of what the WCD is, does and writes . . . on the internet no one
knows or cares if you are pro-dam or anti-dam. It is an equal opportunity,
blind forum for understanding, for feedback, for voicing your opinions"
(WCD 2000a).

The WCD approach.   The commission recognized that there is not always
unanimity in the interpretation of available data or the perceptions of different interest groups. For this reason, WCD's approach was to consult directly with as many stakeholders as possible in an inclusive and transparent
process and to work through teams and task forces that represent experts
from a variety of backgrounds, perspectives, and disciplines. The WCD
process was designed around two concepts: independence from vested
interests and balance in terms of perspectives represented (WCD 1999c).
The WCD aimed to replicate this approach in every activity and at every
level of its implementation, including the WCD Forum, research partnerships, and financing. It also continuously seeks to cultivate and demonstrate a commitment to consultation, and credibility through independence
and transparency. This is noted, for example, beginning with the initial
workshop design (see Dorcey et al. 1997), and included stakeholder consultation for each of the ten case studies and stakeholder reviews of thematic
reports. This approach was not simply a normative one; it was considered
the only option for success under the circumstances, as compliance with the
WCD's final recommendations is voluntary. In short, the process recognized that "differing interests must be understood and respected before genuine agreements can be developed" (Asmal 1999b). The commission itself
operated on a consensus basis.

The WCD Forum.   The WCD Forum was a unique consultative body representing a broad cross-section of interests, views, and institutions to provide
ongoing input into the commission and its work. It included sixty-eight delegates from thirty-four countries, representing multilateral agencies, bilateral agencies, export credit guarantee agencies, government agencies, utili-
ties, research institutes and individual researchers, private-sector firms,
river-basin authorities, engineers, NGOs, environmentalists, and indigenous and affected peoples' groups. Its primary purpose was to maintain
constant two-way communication with representatives of the many interests. It afforded opportunities for focused consultation with various constituencies in the debate and provides a means to disseminate the commission's findings. It was hoped that forum members would assist in building
ownership for the WCD's work among their constituencies and in promot-

ing global adoption of its final report, published in November 2000. Forum members were included as observers to the regional consultations and were invited to participate in working groups to assist in deliberations on strategic questions. The commission formally reported to the WCD Forum, not to the World Bank or any other particular stakeholder.

At its second meeting, April 6–8, 2000, in Cape Town, South Africa, the WCD Forum conducted a critical review of WCD's completed work program, identified gaps in the knowledge base, and expressed support for the value of the anticipated final report. The final forum meeting, February 25–27, 2001, considered how members would promote implementation of the report's recommendations within and across constituencies (WCD 2001b).

Institutional partnerships. The WCD and its secretariat operated through study groups, hearings, task forces, and commissioned studies. A range of institutional partnerships supplemented these efforts (Figure 7.1), providing stakeholder input and liaison, research support (data, analysis, additional cases, information exchange), and operational and functional support. Of particular importance to the WCD's inclusive and consultative process, a global network of NGOs interested in dam-related issues and the work of the WCD designated the Environmental Monitoring Group (EMG) as the NGO liaison or focal point with the WCD. WCD representatives met regularly with the EMG to share information as well as to receive timely NGO input and feedback on the WCD's work program (WCD 1999a).[4] WCD's strategic partnerships were considered critical in terms of rationalizing the WCD's work—avoiding duplication and saving resources wherever possible—as well as carrying on the legacy of the commission's work once its two-year mandate expired (WCD 1999b).

Figure 7.1   WCD Organization Chart

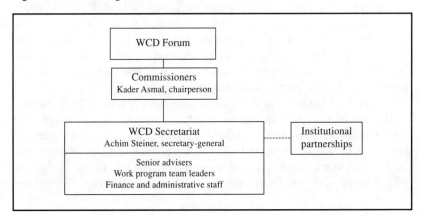

Financing. In order to protect its credibility and independence, every effort was made to secure funding for the WCD from a variety of sources. In just five months, the commission received pledges covering 55 percent of the $9.9 million deemed necessary for it to fulfill its mandate (WCD 1998). The funding success is all the more impressive given that none of the contributors could control the process or outcomes—all contributions had to be made with "no strings attached." Each donor contributed according to its means, with amounts ranging from $800,000 each from the World Bank and the government of Norway (through a trust fund administered by the World Bank), to $2,000 from the U.S. National Wildlife Federation. In May 1999, the UN Foundation announced a challenge grant program, committing to match contributions from other sources up to $900,000. This was accompanied by an additional $800,000 grant through the UN Environment Programme. By June 2000, fifty-one contributors had pledged funds equal to more than three-quarters of the commission's total projected budget (WCD 2001a). Contributors reflect the diversity sought; as of June 1999, they included fourteen bilateral organizations (40 percent), nine private-sector companies (27 percent), eight NGOs (24 percent), and the World Bank (6 percent) (WCD 1999d; Liebenthal 1999).

Challenges and the Potential for Success

The WCD faced continuous criticism and skepticism, which sometimes derailed scheduled meetings and activities and raised questions about the acceptance of its final conclusions. Skeptics and lobbyists questioned the process, not always trusting that their lack of control assured WCD's independence and precluded another stakeholder from controlling the process (Asmal 1999a). Skepticism also surrounded the potential effectiveness of any guidelines or decisionmaking processes that might emerge from the WCD. At least one engineering firm expressed concern that the WCD would end up catering to special-interest groups, resulting in onerous application processes and regulations. NGOs admitted to their own biases and distrust of other actors, noting direct experience with lies and betrayal (Armistead 1998). The WCD was alternatively labeled "anti-dam" and "pro-dam" depending on the beholder (Asmal 1999d), illustrating that its mandate by definition prevented pleasing everyone.

The stakes that defined the conflict continued to plague its operations. Misinformation, fear, and distrust interfered with several of the WCD's well-intentioned consultations and research activities. Among these experiences was the cancellation (and subsequent rescheduling and relocation) of its first regional consultation scheduled for Bhopal, India, September 1998.[5] Suspicion about its intentions and alliances also threatened to derail several case studies. In the case of the Grand Coulee Dam, the WCD responded by assembling a team from outside the region to write a paper establishing the scope of the study. This was followed by a stakeholder workshop to discuss the scoping paper, during which WCD Secretariat staff explained the purpose and independence of the commission's work, and stakeholders were invited to provide input and advice for proceeding with the case study (WCD 1999d). In Thailand, the WCD asked each constituency to nominate a representative to be part of the team to establish the scope of the study and invited their input and perspectives (WCD 1999d). In all case studies, local stakeholders are given the opportunity to comment on final drafts before they are published.

Criticism continued, raising serious questions regarding the actual operationalization of the WCD's well-intentioned approach. For example, in response to the WCD's decision not to pursue a regional consultation in Europe, NGOs organized their own hearing on WCD-related issues, in Bratislava, Slovakia, January 17–18, 2000. Participating NGOs from both European and developing countries sent a letter to the commission documenting their concerns about the WCD process and its subsequent outcomes (Participants 2000). These grievances included concern that the lack of attention to European dam issues would lead to important failings in the WCD report and disappointment that reviewed work products did not reflect anticipated quality and objectivity. Wherever limited information was available, they argued, the burden of proof was on the NGOs. In addition, the signatories argued that few, if any, of the draft work products were referencing NGO submissions.

However, the WCD and its process demonstrated that common ground could be found, even in the midst of high stakes and vehement positioning, and that face-to-face, nonadversarial dialogue was possible, as with the case-study scoping meetings. The broad financial support and voluntary participation from a range of stakeholders demonstrated that there was at least some faith in the process, and, hopefully, some commitment to its outcomes.

The ultimate indicator for the WCD's success will be global acceptance and compliance with its final recommendations, though conflict is likely to continue (Box 7.2). World Bank president James Wolfensohn appealed to the WCD to "use its final report to provide the Bank and the international community with effective entry points for dialogue with governments" (WCD 2000c). Actors increasingly concur that it is governments that will determine the WCD's ultimate success (Box 7.3).

According to the *Economist,* the most problematic challenge to implementing the WCD's findings is the growth of private financing for large dams, the fastest-growing funding source. Less "sensitive" investors will likely be favored over those who seek compliance with the many guidelines

---

Box 7.2   Conflict Is Likely to Continue

According to Bat Schultz of the International Commission on Irrigation and Drainage, "Given [the] required increase in water storage [in the coming years], we should not have the impression that when the work of the WCD is completed, there will be no debates on dams anymore. The debate will continue. The challenge is to see that dams are accepted by society, and do the least damage possible" (WCD 2001b).

Box 7.3   Government's Role in the WCD's Ultimate Success

According to Even Sund, senior energy adviser, Norwegian Agency for International Cooperation, "Considering the fact that it is normally individual governments taking decisions on the implementation of projects within their own territories, the most important outcome of the work of the WCD would be to recommend it to governments, and get acceptance for some fundamental principles to be followed in dam development" (WCD 2000c).

---

and concerns the WCD is likely to promote ("Dam Builders" 1997). Under such circumstances, NGOs' only recourse will continue to be protest and informed advocacy. At a minimum, the WCD's findings may provide an additional tool for these efforts that may help to reduce the incidence of violence in the context of large-dam protests. The WCD's "moral authority" may at least serve to reframe the debate, providing new and better-informed language and a broader constituency for the process.

Even before the release of its final report, the WCD process and completed work program began influencing development practice. For example, in Sri Lanka a committee was appointed "to examine the grievances of dam-affected people and to compensate victims as well as to take action on dam safety issues not undertaken earlier" (WCD 2000c). Additional "ripple effects" have been noted, including possible and enacted replication of the WCD process or portions thereof at the national level in Brazil, Germany, Nepal, Norway, and the United States (WCD 2000b).

The Report and Its Immediate Aftermath

The WCD released its final report on November 16, 2000 (WCD 2001a). The report confirms large dams' contribution to human development, but it finds that historically environmental and social costs have been unnecessarily high. Its review of large-dam experience revealed dismal results, in economic performance, environmental and social impacts, and decisionmaking processes. The WCD acknowledges "deep fault lines" that continue to separate dam critics and proponents; the most intractable are:

- The extent to which alternatives to dams are viable for achieving various development goals and whether alternatives are complementary or mutually exclusive.
- The extent to which adverse environmental and social impacts are acceptable.
- The degree to which adverse environmental and social impacts can be avoided or mitigated.
- The extent to which local consent should govern development decisions in the future (WCD 2001a: 25).

Nevertheless, the WCD proposes a new framework for decisionmaking. The framework emphasizes environmental and social costs and introduces an inclusive "rights and risks" approach that promotes identifying and including all stakeholders in negotiating development choices (Figure 7.2).

Reactions to the report have been both positive and negative. NGOs and indigenous peoples have been very supportive and are already making efforts to promote compliance with the findings (see Bosshard and McCully 2000; James Bay Cree Nation and Pimicikamak Cree Nation 2000). However, representatives of the large-dam industry have questioned the transparency of the final report's preparation and the comprehensiveness and objectivity of the knowledge base from which it draws (ICOLD, IHA, and ICID 2000). The largest threat to compliance is the industry's position that the proposed decisionmaking process would be overly cumbersome and result in stalling any new development projects (see WCD 2001b). Consequently, the International Commission on Large Dams recommends that the report be used only as a starting point for discussions, debate, and negotiations, on a country-by-country basis with consideration to prevailing conditions, traditions, laws, and needs (ICOLD 2000).

Implications and Lessons Learned

The WCD partnership only recently concluded. Former participants continue to disseminate and advocate its recommendations. The WCD had several levels of success indicators ranging from total resolution to the conflict to the creation of a moral authority that would reframe and better inform the debate, creating a broader constituency for a WCD-like conflict resolution process. Most stakeholders do not expect the former outcome; however, evidence with respect to the latter outcome is accumulating. In the mean-

Figure 7.2   The WCD's Proposed Approach for Options Assessment and Project Planning

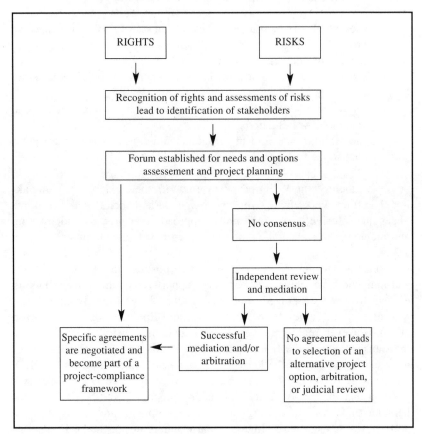

Source: WCD 2001a, figure 7.2, p. 208. Published by Earthscan Publications Ltd. for the World Commission on Yams. Reprinted with permission.

time, the WCD enjoyed significant short-term successes, not the least of which were its very creation, broad and diverse participation, and process demonstration.

The WCD offers important lessons both for partnership work generally and specific to conflict-based partnerships. With respect to the former, the WCD illustrates the relevance of collective-action theory in resolving the challenges associated with partnership. It incorporated incentives and sanctions to appeal to the self-interest of the stakeholders, cultivated a values base for partnership work, and carefully combined formal and informal structure and processes. Regarding conflict resolution, the WCD experience underscores the instrumentality of participation, the essential foundation of confidence, and the importance of agreeing on the process, if not the issues, in order to move the dialogue forward.

Lessons for Partnership Work

1. Partnership duration may lead to differences in investments and outsourcing, but activities normally associated with maintenance and the need to cultivate ownership are still important. The notion of maintaining a partnership—including the necessary activities of stakeholder relations, protection of partner identity, learning and feedback, organization culture, and trust building and maintenance—is relative. Even short-term partnerships will require investments in these activities, depending on their relevance to partnership objectives. In the case of the WCD, all of these activities were essential due to its conflict origins and resolution objectives, and to the fact that the WCD was pioneering a new process among distrustful stakeholders. Stakeholder relations and identity maintenance were essential to WCD's comprehensive, balanced, and inclusive objectives for its review and to subsequent compliance with its findings. Organization culture and trust building were necessary to attain the quality participation needed by all of the stakeholders. Finally, learning and feedback proved essential to generating trust among stakeholders, and learning how to best introduce and demonstrate the WCD process in each new activity setting. Because its activities were repeated in different venues, the WCD took the opportunity to reflect on its experience and make subsequent adaptations in its approach as necessary.

Despite its short duration, the WCD placed heavy emphasis on cultivating broad ownership of its process and outcomes. This emphasis was driven by the commission's objectives. All stakeholders understood that ownership was crucial to the WCD's ultimate effectiveness. The duration of the partnership was irrelevant to this necessity.

However, the WCD experience also suggests that a partnership's duration will determine the need for certain managerial systems and procedures (evaluation, training, and motivation) and structures (financial management). The WCD demonstrates the potential effectiveness and cost and time savings of outsourcing these components to qualified, neutral parties, and meeting capacity needs through institutional partnerships. For time-sensitive partnerships, for example, those facing critical deadlines or needing to immediately capitalize on partnership momentum, outsourcing may be critical to the partnership's success. The WCD also demonstrates that for short-term partnerships, careful selection criteria can substitute for capacity building, especially when such partnerships are accompanied by strong socialization and organization culture.

2. The need for and utilization of institutional linkages and stakeholder relations can best be rationalized through a combination of relying on existing structures and actors and initiating new structures and activities. Clearly, institutional linkages and stakeholder relations are essential to meeting the WCD's objectives and were instrumental in its success thus far. The WCD met these needs both by creating new mechanisms and activities (for example, the WCD Forum, the submission process, and communications strategy) and by identifying and relying on existing ones. Where possible, the WCD relied on existing stakeholder intermediary organizations and entities, such as the International Commission on Large Dams and the International Commission on Irrigation and Drainage, or it designated new roles to existing organizations with the requisite relationships, such as the NGO liaison activities of the EMG, the IRN, and the NBA. The rationalization of institutional linkages was also reflected in the WCD's many institutional partnerships.

3. The use of selection criteria is an important means to furthering partnership objectives and maximizing efficiency and effectiveness. The WCD applied selection criteria to most facets of its institutional design and work program. This included the selection of participants for the Gland workshop, the selection of WCD commissioners, the composition of the WCD Forum, the identification of case studies, and the selection of study teams. Criteria included credibility with particular stakeholder groups, representativeness of the issues, balance among interests, and, with respect to institutional partnerships, targeted comparative advantages. In applying these criteria, the WCD contributed to meaningful participation and ownership—important objectives in their own right, in addition to maximizing effectiveness and efficiency through relying on comparative advantages.

4. The degree of a partnership's integration may vary depending on the function. The WCD was internally integrated and externally diffuse. It combined James Coleman's emphasis on trust within the commission with Ronald Burt's exploitation of structural holes in its external relations (see Chapter 4). The distinction between internal and external relations is relative because the WCD was not designed to integrate the various stakeholder groups. Relatively greater integration may have been required for the deliberations of the commissioners in generating their final report and recommendations, while diffusion was essential to assembling the diversity of perspectives and expertise required to grasp the complexity of large-dam issues and to maintaining the organization identity essential to eventual resolution and ownership.

5. Formal structure is not incompatible with informal processes and culture mechanisms. The WCD's design and implementation included highly specified governance mechanisms and a well-articulated approach and process. Its formal design reflected its operational objectives of independence and transparency, with reporting arrangements carefully crafted. The WCD was structured to maintain accountability to all stakeholder groups by reporting directly to the WCD Forum.

However, the WCD remained flexible to emerging challenges and responsive to particular stakeholder concerns. This is evidenced in its expansion from eight commissioners to twelve and in the iterative and inclusive processes applied to its case studies. This flexibility afforded opportunities to build trust in the process and its eventual outcomes and enabled stakeholder groups to establish and defend their organization identity, for example, in the case-study scoping meetings.

Formal structures were also supplanted and supported through a well-established reliance on particular operating principles and a related partnership culture. The WCD succeeded in inculcating a strong vision and associated culture for its work, which espoused values consistent with its guiding principles, and discouraged retreat into polarized positions. Values were an explicitly articulated component of the WCD since its inception, with the discussion of values separated from the issues or any judgment of who is right or wrong. The values emphasized were for the most part operational: transparency, balance, inclusiveness, independence, and rationality. The WCD encouraged all stakeholders to separate the issues from the actors, always search for common ground, and remain respectful during face-to-face dialogues. Such precedents were set during the Gland workshop and institutionalized into the WCD's continuing work. Those who spoke on behalf of the commission reinforced these values in their public statements.

6. *The stronger an organization's partnership drivers, the easier it will be to overcome that partner's organizational constraints.* Despite the mechanistic orientation of some participating organizations, these organizations were still willing to share power and adapt in the context of the WCD partnership. Such organizational culture constraints can be overcome if there are sufficiently strong drivers. Most stakeholders appeared committed to the WCD process—despite outside skeptics—recognizing that if the process failed, it was unlikely to be attempted again in the future, owing to the distrust that would likely result. Commitment to success encouraged each WCD actor to remain transparent in any action in order to avoid shedding doubt on the comprehensiveness, defensibility, and objectivity of the commission's findings. For some stakeholders the resolution of the conflict would lead to less-encumbered opportunities for material gain; for others, the process and its outcome were motivated by the desire to protect livelihoods, communities, and the environment.

7. *Individuals play a crucial role in championing partnership efforts.* The WCD experience strongly supports the importance of individuals to partnership processes. Several individuals played critical roles in creating the right conditions for the WCD process, creating the organizational cul-

ture that appears to be the foundation for its success and securing the commitment of important stakeholder groups. First, the Gland workshop facilitator was credited with creating "the right atmosphere and the right process for an open and constructive debate" (Greene and Picciotto 1997). Second, NGO advocates and large-dam critics expressed faith that only World Bank president James Wolfensohn's leadership could guarantee an independent large-dam review (McCully 1997a). This faith could arguably have encouraged NGOs to enter into the WCD process in the first place. Third, the WCD chairperson, Kader Asmal, seemed uniquely qualified to chair the commission and has tirelessly embodied and promoted its organization culture. In addition, each commissioner selected was an individual able to command respect and instill confidence in objectivity. In particular, the inclusion of Medha Patkar from the NBA sufficiently resolved the selection conflict to enable the establishment of the WCD based on stakeholder consensus.

8. *Narrow representation can be efficient and may contribute to the cultivation of partnership and stakeholder group leaders.* Narrow representation is an efficient means to allocating responsibility and developing expertise and potential leadership. While representation in the work program was relatively broad, representation in more formal structures, such as the WCD Forum and the commission itself, was much more narrow, reflecting the pragmatism of assigning delegates who can report back to their home institutions. Through such consistent participation, individual representatives may take on important leadership roles in the forums in which they participate, as they acquire expertise, nurture personal and professional relationships, and gain respect and trust. Such leadership may be recognized outside of these forums, for example, within particular stakeholder groups. Such was the case, for example, with Patrick McCully of the IRN, and Shripad Dharmadhikary from the NBA, who were already considered outspoken leaders among their constituencies.

Lessons for Conflict Resolution

1. *Conflict resolution requires confidence among the partners, and their commitment to the process. A shared understanding and agreement on values are an important foundation for conflict resolution and can be promoted through organizational culture.* The WCD demonstrates the importance of confidence, built through transparency, and values. Confidence can substitute for trust in the initial stages of building a partnership. In the case of a conflict-based partnership, where trust may never be forthcoming, confidence plays a critical role in substituting for mutual trust and, to some extent, mutual respect and understanding. When such trust is lacking or impossible, commitment to jointly determined operational values can

bridge differences and assure commitment to the partnership. Relying on organizational culture is also an important mechanism for creating a shared understanding on an operational and process level that can ensure that the process moves forward in a meaningful way. Essential in this process is strict adherence to stated values and objectives. Rhetoric without follow-through could have jeopardized the WCD's success, as implied by the European NGO hearing in January 2000.

2. *Conflict intensity can contribute to resolution processes.* The WCD is built upon a realistic recognition of the conflict and an explicit acceptance of the one basis for common ground: the need for resolution. While seemingly counterintuitive, it is possible that the more intense the conflict—and consequently the more painful its implications—the easier it may be to bring the stakeholders to the table and attain some agreement on process. In the case of the WCD, it was clear that all stakeholders had strong drivers that not only encouraged them to attend the Gland workshop but also provided incentives for the proposal and mutual agreement on the establishment of the WCD, subsequent participation in its work program and processes, and adherence to transparency to maintain confidence.

3. *Mediation may be required at multiple levels.* The severity of the conflict, the diversity of the stakeholders, and the necessity for compliance among all interested parties required mediation at multiple levels: in the context of each stakeholder meeting (starting with the Gland Workshop, in meetings related to the work program, and in the WCD Forum meetings); within stakeholder groups (intermediary organizations such as the International Commissions on Large Dams and on Irrigation and Drainage, and the NGO intermediaries, EMG, IRN, and NBA); and in the final deliberations (the commission itself).

4. *Democratic processes are instrumental.* Democratic processes include the incorporation of representation and participation, open decisionmaking processes, transparency, accountability, and responsiveness. While these components may contribute to more effective policy outcomes and more responsive public services generally, they are particularly salient to conflict resolution. The WCD design, experience, and stakeholders' actions and statements emphasize that inclusive, transparent, and balanced participation were not pursued for moral reasons, but for the very fact that without them resolution of the large-dam conflict would be impossible.

5. *Perception is everything.* Like any public good, global policy on large dams is vulnerable to the free-rider problem, both in its formulation and its implementation. Stakeholders must perceive that the process is advancing in good faith, abiding by stated values and principles, or they will have no incentives to comply with the findings. This has not always been the case. Perceptions of noninclusiveness, and unbalanced representation already yielded criticisms during the implementation of the work pro-

gram; and transparency and objectivity were questioned in the drafting of the final report. This does not bode well for the acceptance of and potential compliance with the WCD's findings.

6. *Conflict resolution is not a one-time effort for all.* No matter the WCD's commitment to inclusiveness and balance, some stakeholders may choose not to participate or continue to hold stringent perspectives that preclude any negotiation. Conflict resolution requires that all parties share the objective of resolution. This may not always be the case. Similarly, the eventual acceptance and subsequent operationalization of the WCD's findings is yet to be determined. Even the World Bank, a primary initiator of the process, would not accept the findings sight unseen (Liebenthal 1999). These features imply that conflict resolution may necessarily be an iterative process that may not immediately embrace all parties to the issue. Kader Asmal recognizes this in his stated hope that the WCD become at a minimum a moral authority, its process a demonstration of what can be.

7. *Partnership is an effective and efficient approach to resolving conflict.* The principles of partnership are the foundation for the WCD's proposed solution to the large-dam conflict. First, the WCD recognized that the issue required a multistakeholder approach to address the complexity of large dams, attaining the necessary technical, regional, social, and political information to inform its studies and findings. Second, the entire process was predicated on the participation of all stakeholders and representation of their interests in order to attain ownership of the process outcomes and eventual compliance with its outcomes. These two objectives—technical information and political buy-in—would not be possible without incorporation of mutuality and maintenance of organization identity. These attributes determined stakeholders' entry into the process and continued participation. Furthermore, partnership's value orientation can facilitate the cultivation of a partnership operating culture to unite stakeholders, at least on process agreements, and to reinforce trust in the resulting processes.

WCD's Potential Global Impact

The WCD is a hopeful demonstration of the potential of partnerships, especially in resolving conflict. According to WCD chairman Kader Asmal, "The Commission is pushing the boundaries of what participation, transparency, and openness imply in a global dialogue on public policy issues" (Asmal 2000). The UN has recognized the WCD as an important model to follow, as noted in the secretary-general's Millenium Report (Annan 2000), which builds on Wolfgang Reinicke and Francis Deng's analysis: "The case of the WCD demonstrates how an almost archetypical tri-sectoral (government, private sector and civil society organizations) network operating at the global level can contribute to building consensual knowledge and overcoming stalemate in a policy arena riven with conflict" (Reinicke and Deng 2000: 30).

However, the WCD's success as a model and process for conflict resolution and global public policy debate rests not solely on its trisectoral nature. The participating representative stakeholders were far more diverse than a simple trisectoral image would suggest. More important, the WCD was more than a vague network; it was a partnership that maximized organization identity and mutuality, governed, in large part, by an organizational culture that emphasized inclusion, balance, and transparency.

Notes

1. For example, the Rio Negro community in Guatemala was targeted for resettlement under the Chixoy Hydroelectric Project and hence was opposed to it. In 1982, more than half of the community was reported massacred (Witness for Peace 1996). Proposed dam projects in India's Narmada Valley have prompted serious protests on a global scale, with affected peoples declaring *satyagraha*, or a search for truth. The satyagrahis vowed that they would rather drown than leave their homes as the floodwaters rise. In a test of submergence (September 1999), the satyagrahis stood in increasing backwaters—peaking at neck-height—for fifteen to forty-eight hours (Sangvai 1999).

2. NGO participants included the International Rivers Network, Narmada Bachao Andolan (Save the Narmada Movement, India), Movement of People Affected by Dams (Brazil), the Alliance for Energy (Nepal), and the Berne Declaration (Switzerland) (McCully 1997c).

3. Continuing concerns included underrepresentation of technical experience on environmental issues and large-dam alternatives, the exclusion of critics of large dams with engineering backgrounds, and the lack of a Latin American "who is trusted by NGOs and affected people's groups" in the region (IRN 1998).

4. The IRN and the NBA were also closely involved in monitoring the WCD and assisting to coordinate NGO input.

5. The meeting was to take place in the context of one of the most controversial large-dam standoffs, the Narmada Valley. Misinformation raised questions about the nature and purpose of the commission's visit. A climate of confrontation was created, where, according to the state of Gujarat, the presence of commissioners "known for their anti-dam views" eliminated any possibility for the WCD's impartiality.

8

Partnership for
International Development:
From Rhetoric to Results

Given the multiple actors, objectives, environments, and preferences, no two partnerships will ever look alike. For this reason, some have argued that it may be impossible to generate a more scientific understanding of how to maximize partnership returns, especially through attempting to examine partnerships comparatively. Rigid prescriptions could not account for all of these variables and could undermine instinctive strategic management approaches. However, in describing the terrain and specifying the parameters over which actors must decide, we come closer to appreciating the circumstances under which one approach may be more fruitful than another, whether due to objectives, opportunities and constraints, or actors' preferences. Incorporating the preferences of actors acknowledges the reality of partnership work: that it is voluntary and rarely, if ever, based on equal power relationships.

This chapter reviews the lessons from the cases, particularly as they relate to the initiation, design, and maintenance hypotheses and trade-offs. Lessons for operationalizing partnership's defining dimensions are also discussed. The second part of the chapter takes a forward look at the implications of the findings for partnership work and the continuing role of partnership in an increasingly globalized world. The chapter concludes with final comments for partnership practitioners and scholars.

Lessons for Effective Partnership

Partnerships usually stem from one primary driver, though more or all of the four drivers identified in Chapter 1 frequently play a role. In the three cases reviewed here, partnership was used to provide the multiactor, integrated solutions required by the scope and the nature of the problems being addressed: provision of integrated, expanded, and higher-quality public services (the BADP), including those to address community health needs (INMED), and global-level conflict among multiple and diverse actors (the WCD). In addition, partnership enhanced efficiency and effectiveness through a reliance on comparative advantages and a rational division of labor. In the case of INMED, this rationale was specifically applied to create or activate new and latent resources. The WCD explicitly focused on moving from a no-win situation among multiple actors to a compromise and potential win-win situation for international economies and river ecosystems and the people who depend upon them. The WCD also sought to open decisionmaking processes to promote a broader operationalization of the public good. Similarly, the BADP proactively sought to open decisionmaking processes at multiple levels to ensure sustainability of the innovations and investments introduced.

The three cases confirm the design and implementation trade-offs and suggestions (Chapter 4) and specify lessons for effective partnership. All three cases confirm the proposed general responses to addressing partnership challenges. Each built on self-interest and instrumental rationality and incorporated values, moral incentives, and a combination of formal and informal processes. The pragmatic as well as the normative, values-based ends of the democratic values associated with partnership work were also confirmed. All three partnerships exhibited characteristics of learning organizations. They were outward looking in their orientation, recognized and sought to capitalize on interdependencies, and achieved both internal and external commitment, encompassing individuals and champions with personal mastery and a disposition for OCB. Finally, each partnership emphasized the softer side of interorganizational management, explicitly recognizing and promoting values, incorporating moral as well as material incentives, and supporting these through the cultivation of a partnership identity and associated organization culture.

Initiation

Preferences, objectives, and environmental hostility informed the partnerships' initiation. These, in turn, informed partner selection and related criteria. In all three cases, actors demonstrated a strong willingness to accommodate mutuality. This willingness immediately set the stage for pursuing a partnership approach, as opposed to other interorganizational options. Additionally, the maintenance of partner identity was essential to meeting objectives. This was due to the expertise required for the BADP, the representational functions essential to the WCD, and the legitimacy and neutrality required for INMED as an implementer. In the BADP, government's realistic understanding of its advantages and limitations led to its recognition of the need for and potential benefits of a partnership, and to a commitment to adjust standards and procedures accordingly—including in ways that would accommodate mutuality. INMED explicitly seeks to create new money and resources and sees partnership approaches as the most effective way to do so. Its corporate partners find the approach a win-win situation, where they can meet their public relations objectives without having to duplicate existing expertise and relational comparative advantages. The WCD recognized that the technical information and political buy-in required to resolve the conflict over large dams would not be possible without incorporating mutuality and respecting organization identity. In each case, actors had strong drivers for working with other actors and for partnering in particular.

These experiences confirm the importance of preferences (Figure 4.2). Actors' tolerance for sharing power and willingness to adapt to partnership needs led to more organic (rather than mechanistic) partnership structures, where the division of labor was fluid and authority was based on knowledge, expertise, and information needs rather than position; and decisions were made through participation, rather than hierarchically. While some aspects of the partnerships' work was formalized and supported through bureaucratic governance mechanisms, as in the BADP, these could be modified in response to changing needs. This was less possible for the WCD, where process consistency was essential to confidence; however, process rules were jointly determined among partners. In the INMED partnership, the specification of division of labor and rights and obligations were not always formally defined. They were jointly determined, with INMED taking a leading role in proposing a framework, and the relationship remained more horizontal and mutual than vertical and hierarchical. The increasing demand for more formal and standardized reporting is more a reflection of the corporate partners' need to respond to their constituencies and stakeholders than it is a reflection of a reduced flexibility or power sharing.

These findings imply that effective partnerships may be relatively more organic in their structure and operations. However, partnerships may still encompass partners with mechanistic structures (e.g., multilaterals, governments, and multinational corporations). These partners may be willing to operate relatively organically vis-à-vis the partnership, even if their own organization remains internally mechanistic. Within the partnership, the organizational structure may also vary with each relationship and with some tasks.

Preferences with respect to confidence and trust largely determined the partnerships' general approach to design. The WCD, where trust among partners was not an option, is the most explicit example. Confidence had to be prioritized throughout the partnership's design and implementation, which led to a much greater reliance on formal processes and structures and a much stronger emphasis on bureaucratic governance mechanisms than the other partnerships exhibited. Full information disclosure and a universal right to participate further supported confidence building. INMED, however, relied much more on trust mechanisms, where values and culture governance mechanisms support interrelationships. Corporate partnerships were originally initiated through the trust built from previous mutual experience and familiarity, and subsequently through the confidence produced by demonstrated processes and success. Today, trust has evolved through accumulated experience with each partner, with a continuing emphasis on culture governance mechanisms; and confidence is reinforced through partners' option to leave the program if they are dissatisfied. The BADP, too, sought to cultivate and rely on trust among partners, particularly with its community partners, and relied heavily on culture governance mechanisms. However, confidence and greater efficiency were also generated through the standardization and clarity implied by the BADP's reliance on bureaucratic governance mechanisms, most notably the SOPs. The process of developing the SOPs was instrumental to developing trust among the partners, as well as creating and supporting the partnership's organization culture.

While the literature often refers to trust as an essential component for partnership effectiveness, the cases here demonstrate that confidence can substitute for, lay the foundation for, and supplement trust. Confidence and trust can be mutually reinforcing, particularly when one's introduction and design supports the other. These findings should encourage actors to pursue the partnership option even in the absence of initial trust, and under circumstances of extreme distrust such as conflict resolution.

Objectives also influenced design and implementation approaches. INMED's experience confirms that short-term, issue-focused partnerships can be effective and beneficial to all partners; used, where desirable, as entrepreneurial opportunities to build capacity for subsequent partnership work; and more fruitful when partners are familiar with each other and some degree of mutual trust or confidence is in place. INMED's experience also illustrates the benefits of incorporating programmatic components that demonstrate immediate results, particularly when the partnership seeks to address complex social problems or when it entails a corporate partnership. Because many partnerships seek to address complex and seemingly intractable issues (thus justifying the more demanding interorganizational approach) results will often take a long time to materialize. This is especially true with respect to public service improvements, where the pace of change can be particularly slow. Partnership actors and stakeholders should take care to maintain and promote realistic expectations. Partnerships can address multiple and diverse objectives, each posing unique opportunities and constraints. The cases illustrate how presumed constraints can be addressed or transformed into opportunities.

Cost-benefit analysis with respect to environmental factors informed the approach of partnership initiation and design. Such analysis was most explicit in the case of BADP, where, as a multilateral project, the project appraisal included a risk assessment and proposed response. In all three cases, the partnerships were designed in response to environmental threats and opportunities. In the BADP, capacity deficiencies were identified and subsequently addressed through a reliance on respective comparative advantages, as well as an explicit capacity-building strategy, which included training on participatory processes. INMED sought to capitalize on changing environmental factors that would provide incentives to potential corporate partners (for example, the pharmaceutical industry's concerns regarding Brazil's international patent laws, and the privatization of the energy sector), or provide more general support to its corporate partnership approach (First Lady Ruth Cardoso's endorsement and promotion of inter-sectoral partnerships). The WCD's environment proved both challenging and fortuitous. The intense conflict actually provided stronger drivers for stakeholders to participate in the partnership, and the partnership benefited from a convergence of facilitative factors, such as the existence of partnership champions, an existing partnership agreement between the World Bank and IUCN, and a targeted trust fund for resolving the large-dam conflict. In all three cases, actors were proactive in assessing and responding to their environments, with cost-benefit analysis (whether implicitly or explicitly) informing their approach.

The cases also suggest several lessons about partner organizations and their selection. Selection criteria proved important in all three cases, for maximizing comparative advantages, minimizing risks, and, by extension, generally furthering partnership objectives and maximizing efficiency and effectiveness. INMED, for example, specifically targeted corporate partners who had relevant resources to offer to the program, such as in-kind contributions (medications, vitamin supplements) or financing and labor. Corporate partners were also identified based on their vested interest in a target community or in Brazil more generally. The WCD demonstrates the efficiency and effectiveness advantages of selection criteria, particularly with respect to the selection of its institutional partners and the inclusion in its work program of particular stakeholder groups and representatives who could provide technical and contextual information.

All three cases offer lessons related to the risks associated with particular partner organizations. The BADP provides a cautionary perspective with respect to working with large and powerful partners. Its experience with the ADB and its emphasis on short-term quantifiable results illustrates that working with such partners can result in internal challenges to interorganizational agreements. It further confirms the need for political and administrative will to partner, particularly with respect to making the adaptations necessary for partnership effectiveness. The greatest challenge with these partners is institutionalizing the partnership culture beyond individual representatives. Since this is a daunting challenge with partner organizations as large and powerful as multilateral banks, an alternative and supplementary approach is to ensure that the organization's representative acts as a champion and strong advocate within the organization. The existence or potential for cultivating partnership champions should be considered in cost-benefit analysis and selection criteria where possible.

The WCD experience also teaches a lesson in partnership drivers: the stronger an organization's partnership drivers, the easier it will be to overcome that partner's organizational constraints. In this case, the World Bank was willing to be flexible in its approach given the substantial conflict that was inhibiting its operations and public relations. These drivers greatly facilitated the efforts of the partnership champions from the OED. While partnership literature and practice frequently emphasize partner compatibility and strong drivers, INMED's work in Brazil suggests that effective partnerships are possible even when their objectives do not directly relate to a partner's core business. Under such circumstances, and particularly when there are multiple and diverse partners involved, it may be beneficial to recognize a primary implementer, coordinator, and mediator.

Design Trade-offs

The three cases exhibit variations in formality, autonomy, flexibility, and trust at three levels: operational (day-to-day management), collective (collective decisionmaking that structures behavior at the operational level), and constitutional (the overall framework for how decisions are made) (see Kiser and Ostrom 1982). By far, the most flexibility and informality is found at the operational level. Here, the WCD modified the implementation of its case studies to respond to local stakeholders' interests and concerns, particularly for objectivity. INMED also maintains flexibility at the operational level, selecting partners and programmatic emphases directly responsive to the local context and partner drivers (including the results of the KAP sessions). The BADP took an interesting approach to its collective level. Here, the process was highly participatory, building on and cultivating trust, as extension officers and social mobilizers mutually determined and agreed to standard operating procedures.

At the constitutional level, the BADP represents the most formal and noninclusive approach. The overall framework for the program was set out in the ADB's project appraisal report and was agreed by the government of Pakistan and the GONWFP. The degree of mutuality and participation in that process was presumably low. INMED provides a particularly interesting approach at the constitutional level. While the initial framework was developed in conjunction with Interfarma, INMED subsequently presented the constitutional framework to new partners as given, based on its successful track record. This framework is agreed on mutually and, in most cases, partners can readily appreciate its advantages. It is also likely that agreement at this level is facilitated by the mutual design process at the collective level and implementation at the operational level.

The three cases suggest that differentiating between these three levels may be useful on a number of fronts. First, actors can be flexible and responsive to partners' concern for participation, flexibility, and autonomy at each level. Partners may prioritize mutuality and the expression of organization identity at one level more than at others. Understanding these priorities can assist partner organizations to design the partnership more effectively and responsively. Second, differentiating between these levels can call attention to the need for partnership and participation at all three levels. This can assist partnership champions in avoiding one of the most common downfalls for partnership effectiveness—overreliance on partnerships with individuals, as opposed to organizations. Attention to all three levels of action can help to institutionalize the partnership. Finally, the three levels point to three distinct targets for evaluating the extent to which an interorganizational alliance is operating as a partnership.

Degree of integration.   The design approaches to all three partnerships confirm the integration trade-offs continuum (Figure 4.5). INMED is the least integrated of the three partnerships. It relies primarily on trust among the actors and seeks to maximize opportunities afforded through the respective identities and corresponding comparative advantages of its many partners. The INMED experience also implies that financial and in-kind contributions do not requi , ubstantial partner integration, and, by extension, will require minimal capacity-building investments and less complex monitoring and evaluation systems. The BADP sought more integration, particularly through its SOPs. Here, predictability and efficiency were maximized, incorporating trust building as well as confidence. The WCD represents a hybrid in the sense that a substantial degree of integration would not have been possible at the macro level, where each stakeholder group was in conflict with the others. A low degree of integration characterized its general work program and process, which maximized the range of information, knowledge, and skills of each partner. Integration was sought only in the commission itself, and trust was rooted in the mediator (the commission) rather than the other stakeholder groups. The WCD and INMED cases also suggest that when low integration is desired, market and culture governance mechanisms can substitute for bureaucratic ones.

Effective partnerships may require a combination of high and low integration, depending on the level of action and the particular function. While none of the cases was examined over a sufficiently long time frame to determine the impact of integration on organization identity, common sense and other documented experiences would suggest that partnerships seeking high integration need to take particular care in protecting the organization identity of their partners so as not to gain the advantages of social capital at the expense of structural holes. The degree of integration is directly determined by actors' preferences with respect to willingness to share power and adapt. However, the three cases suggest that actors would also do well to consider the operational advantages of various degrees of integration with respect to each level of collective action, and the particular functions and activities at the operational level.

Mediation.   Mediation is essential to any partnership. All three cases relied heavily on mediation, particularly by individuals acting as partnership champions. In the case of the WCD, the commission acted as a social network mediator (see Moore 1996). The WCD experience demonstrates that, particularly in partnerships designed for conflict resolution, mediation may be required at multiple levels (in this case, the commission, the WCD Forum, within stakeholder groups, and in the context of discrete activities). The BADP similarly illustrates both institutional and individual mediation. The SOU, for example, was an important mediating body; mediation also occurred through buffering from administrative requirements that could be overly burdensome and distracting from actors' comparative advantages. However, institutional buffering did not substitute for the important role played by the project director, who championed the process. In addition to similar administrative buffering, the INMED case uniquely demonstrates how one partner can play the primary mediating role within a partnership. In this case, INMED Brazil brokered partnerships locally, with INMED International brokering and initiating partnerships with multinational companies outside of operational locations.

Degree of formalization.   All three cases combined formal and informal processes (see Figure 4.6). The WCD was perhaps the most formal partnership, and INMED the least. The WCD suggests that when confidence is overwhelmingly emphasized over trust, formalization may be necessary. However, this does not preclude flexibility, as the case demonstrates, nor is it incompatible with the use of culture mechanisms. The BADP similarly demonstrates that flexibility and stability can be combined in support of efficiency and responsiveness. INMED relied more on trust and an ultimate exit option, which created an acceptance of informality. This approach was more acceptable given the relatively high specificity and identification of program outcomes. Informal structures and procedures were buttressed by a strong partnership organization culture and emphasis on values, which cultivated a shared understanding of expected behavior. The cases confirm that formalization is neither exclusively good nor bad. Rather, its degree should be determined by actors' preferences and the nature of the task. The three cases confirm that formalized structures and activities should encompass sufficient flexibility to respond to changing environmental opportunities and constraints, and partners' preferences.

Governance mechanisms.   The cases differ in their relative emphasis on various governance mechanisms (see Figure 4.7). However, they all confirm the instrumental role of the frequently undervalued culture governance mechanisms. In each case, a clear partnership identity and organization culture was cultivated, emphasizing shared values (such as self-help and the importance of preventive health services, particularly for children) and organizational processes (such as participation, inclusion, objectivity, and flexibility for responsiveness). These mechanisms and emphases are compatible with the other governance mechanisms. Indeed, some of these were mandated or reinforced through bureaucratic measures (the BADP SOPs and WCD transparency) or market mechanisms (INMED's exit option).

Each case demonstrates a unique combination of governance mechanisms, with changing emphasis as the partnership evolves. The objective of the partnership, and the nature and preferences of its composite partners, will determine this emphasis at different stages. In the BADP, the mechanisms evolved from bureaucratic to a combination of bureaucratic and culture mechanisms from initiation to consolidation and program delivery. The bureaucratic starting point reflects the partnership's initiation from and involvement of a large multilateral organization (the ADB), which requires specificity, formality, and accountability; and the public-sector emphasis, which rests on an authority system, not a market where there are options for exit (with the exception of the SRSC, which in principle had the option to exit from its contract). The INMED case roughly follows Vivien Lowndes and Chris Skelcher's (1998) anticipated sequencing (from culture to bureaucratic, to market, and back to culture mechanisms, from initiation to termination). However, there is very little emphasis on bureaucratic mechanisms at all (even the partnership agreements and reporting requirements are quite informal), and culture mechanisms are the glue that holds each partner relationship together throughout its evolution. The WCD best exemplifies Lowndes and Skelcher's anticipated evolution of governance mechanisms, and it is the case where one can recognize the continuing importance of culture mechanisms as the partnership is terminated. The findings suggest a great flexibility in terms of potentially effective combinations and evolutionary paths of governance mechanisms. They further emphasize the importance and potential contributions of culture mechanisms throughout the life of a partnership and beyond.

Incentives and values.   The partnerships' incentive systems emphasize the importance of considering the full range of potential incentives—both tangible and intangible (see Figure 4.8). The greatest incentive to participate in the WCD process and comply with its findings was the potential resolution of the large-dam conflict. For some stakeholders, this simply meant achieving economic benefits with fewer encumbrances. For others, the resolution would relate directly to intrinsic values related to compassion, respect for human rights, and environmental protection. Participation was voluntary. It mattered not if this volunteerism was based on tangible or intangible incentives. What mattered was that the incentives were instrumental; they contributed to meeting the WCD's objectives of participation and compliance.

In keeping with the use of culture mechanisms and the cultivation of partnership identity noted above, the values-basis of incentives played a role in each case. Values were specifically identified, cultivated, and supported. This enabled recruiting and retaining key personnel. Coupled with the emphasis on participation in all three cases, the partnerships successfully nurtured internal commitment among their stakeholders, beneficiaries, and staff. In recruiting key personnel, the partnerships were able to employ individuals with a high disposition for OCB. This was true, for example, for INMED Brazil's program director, the BADP's project director, and the WCD commissioners. Each of these individuals displayed an unusual degree of vision and commitment to the partnership's success, which was not at all rooted in material rewards.

Participation and representation.   The cases generally support the proposed participation and representation continuums (see Figure 4.9). However, the degree of each depends on the partnership's level of action. The WCD was generally highly participatory, reflecting the conflict and distrust it sought to address. At the same time, within the commission itself, representation was quite narrow. This narrow representation fulfilled an important function in that it facilitated the development and reinforcement of stakeholder group leaders who could mediate with their group and, hopefully, promote compliance with the WCD's findings. The BADP represents the broadest representation, as demonstrated in the SOU and the ToPs development. This reflects actors' high tolerance for sharing power and willingness to adapt. The INMED case illustrates how instrumental participation can be phased; the partnerships are most participatory in the design phase, both at the community level and in the context of the corporate partnerships. With respect to corporate partnerships, INMED subsequently becomes the implementer with partner participation limited to specified contributions and employee volunteerism as designed. The degree of participation does not have to remain consistent throughout the partnership's evolution (as INMED demonstrates); nor is consistency required among its different levels of operation and functions (as is the case with the WCD). The cases confirm the instrumentality of broad participation and representation, particularly in terms of cultivating internal and widely shared commitment.

Accountability and transparency. The three cases also confirm the formality continuum with respect to accountability and transparency systems (see Figure 4.10). Both INMED and the BADP are relatively informal in these systems, reflecting their high tolerance of information sharing and their trust basis. INMED further demonstrates that while informal systems may be sufficient among the partners, more formal mechanisms may be required for responsiveness to partners' stakeholders—in this case the corporations' responsiveness to their constituents. The WCD, however, required highly formal transparency and accountability mechanisms, emphasizing the importance of perception to conflict resolution and reflecting the partnership's reliance on confidence, as opposed to trust. Regardless of the degree of formality, all three cases emphasized accountability and transparency and reinforced them through the partnership organization culture. This suggests that despite their required presence in any effective partnership (essentially by definition), these characteristics do not necessarily have to be formal.

Maintenance Activities

Activities normally associated with partnership maintenance are important to partnership success regardless of the partnership's anticipated duration. This is most apparent in the WCD, where organization culture and learning proved instrumental to its effectiveness to date, and in the continuity of INMED's organizational culture despite changing partners. Investments in addressing environmental hostility, capacity building, partnership organization culture, and learning, feedback, and evaluation should be based on rational responses to environmental opportunities and constraints; actors' strengths, weaknesses, and preferences; and strategies to maximize partnership effectiveness and efficiency.

Addressing environmental hostility. In all three cases, individuals played key roles in responding to environmental hostility, taking initiatives to mediate among stakeholders and partners, and generally championing the partnership. This included designing effective management systems and carefully balancing the degree of integration and formalization and the mix of governance mechanisms and incentives systems according to environmental demands and actors' preferences. Responses did not always require creating new systems and functions; they also included responding to opportunities in the environment and those presented by partners' compara-tive advantages. Examples include the WCD's institutional partnerships, and the BADP's clear strategy to rely on existing government infrastruc-ture, personnel, and services. In other instances, new actors and sometimes capacity building were required, such as the inclusion of the SRSC in the BADP partnership and its training on participatory processes; or new roles were established, such as INMED's designation as implementer and media-tor. Selection criteria further buttressed a rational approach to opportunities and constraints in the immediate and distant partnership environment and were used in all three cases. These criteria encompassed a wide range of concerns (including capacity, relationships, legitimacy, and partner drivers) and maximized return on investments in program activities.

A major factor in responding to environmental hostility was other part-ners and their commitment to the partnership. INMED's experience sug-gests that, where possible, partnerships should try to identify components and activities with immediate and measurable impact to secure partners' and stakeholders' commitment. The WCD recognized the importance of stakeholders' perceptions, and this led to a strong emphasis on transparen-cy, as well as objectivity, inclusion, and balance. In all three cases, environ-mental response strategies were continuous and adapted to changing con-texts and actors' preferences.

Organization culture.   Partnership organization culture was built on the foundation of explicit values statements and organizational processes that were consistent with these values. Pivotal positions were filled with indi-viduals who understood and championed the organization culture, such as Kader Asmal and Medha Patkar of the WCD and the directors of the BADP and INMED Brazil. Socialization was structured through training and ori-entation programs, as in the case of the BADP's training program in partici-patory processes, and in special events such as the WCD's forum meetings and INMED's treatment days. Stories and myths were also created. For example, the WCD articulated partnership successes in ways that rein-forced the organization culture's underlying values. INMED also recounted stories of spontaneous giving, such as a doctor's initiative to arrange for free fecal exams or INMED Brazil's provision of surplus Vitamin A to an NGO partner. In both cases, these stories are told with an emphasis on shared values and goals, that is, the principle of helping others, particularly children. This reinforces an overarching lesson among the cases: organiza-tion culture can unite multiple and diverse partners when it supports each organization's success. Investments in establishing and maintaining a part-nership organization culture can be instrumental regardless of a partner-ship's anticipated duration.

Capacity building.   Capacity building is determined by partnership duration, as well as the availability and capacity of potential partners. For
example, the BADP selected the SRSC based on its comparative advantages, which corresponded to characteristics deemed necessary for partnership effectiveness. Substantial investments were still made in capacity
building, in introducing new technical skills, developing new procedures,
and cultivating trust and organization culture. In this sense, the BADP best
illustrates the proposed factors suggesting greater capacity-building investments (see Chapter 4, p. 93). The other cases called for less capacity building, in the WCD due to its limited mandate and duration and in INMED
due to the designation of an implementer with demonstrated capacity and
the preference for minimal integration.

The findings reinforce the cost-effectiveness of relying primarily on
selection criteria to identify existing organizations with the requisite characteristics and capacity, and secondarily looking to capacity-building
options. However, capacity building is likely to be required or at least beneficial, despite the application of such criteria, for serving other objectives,
such as introducing skills specific to the partnership's approach or for
inculcating a shared partnership organization culture and building trust
among partners.

Learning and feedback.   Learning and feedback can occur without formal
monitoring and evaluation, and formal learning and evaluation tasks can be
outsourced. However, precisely because partnership and organization culture tend to be difficult to identify, outsourcing evaluation runs the risk that
evaluators will misunderstand the importance of certain relationship features and their direct contribution to program effectiveness; this was the
case with the BADP. In addition, outcomes are not always quantifiable and,
given partnerships' reliance on relationships for success, outcomes may be
slow in coming. This reinforces the benefits of identifying activities with
short-term success (even if they do not represent the core objectives and
desired outcomes of the partnership) and the need to be patient and realistic
in terms of expectations. Finally, monitoring and feedback may vary
according to the specific relationship within the partnership, as INMED's
reporting demonstrates.

In all cases, evaluation stressed programmatic effectiveness only. With
the exception of the WCD, none of the actors expressed or acted on a
strong interest to evaluate and learn formally from the relationships encompassed by the partnerships. And none of the partnerships can articulate
quantifiable and easily attributable partnership synergistic benefits. One
exception is Johnson & Johnson's recognition that by partnering with
INMED, it will be able to help prevent reinfections, improve learning, and

help communities become better off. This suggests one or both of two things. One, partnership actors, like any others, concentrate scarce resources and attention on expediency; and two, these synergies may be impossible to identify in any verifiable way. To the extent such value-added can be qualitatively described and promoted through organization culture, specifically myths and stories, actors are more likely to pursue new partnerships, remain committed to current partnerships, and commit to future ones. As these synergies are not easily described, it would behoove partnership actors to seek creative ways to tell the story. These experiences suggest a continued need to study partnership relationships in the context of program effectiveness. This would include attention to the development of indicators that may capture the synergies produced by partnerships.

Partnership Dimensions

The three cases offer different emphases and perspectives on operationalizing mutuality and organization identity. Like partnership design more generally, the operationalization of these dimensions can be more or less formal, and it may be reinforced through various combinations of the three governance mechanisms. Culture mechanisms, however, play a large role in maintaining the defining dimensions in all three cases, as they are likely to do in all aspects of partnerships. This is due, in part, to the voluntary nature of partnerships and the fact that partners will not be equal in size, resources, and power. It does not mean, however, that the other governance mechanisms cannot be used effectively with respect to mutuality and organization identity; the other two mechanisms may be the foundation on which culture mechanisms build. For example, mutuality is introduced bureaucratically in the BADP's SOU, the WCD and the WCD Forum, and in INMED's PAs. Exit, or market mechanisms, plays an essential role in INMED's partnerships and with respect to WCD compliance.

All three cases demonstrate that mutuality can be created even among multiple and diverse partners. However, the emphasis on mutuality may vary with the level of action or the partnership's stage of implementation. For example, mutuality was minimal at the constitutional level of the BADP, and narrow in the WCD's final deliberations. In INMED it was emphasized primarily in the design phase.

Organization identity was essential to each partnership's success. As designated implementer and coordinator, INMED could maximize effectiveness based on its comparative advantages and minimize inefficiencies by avoiding acting at cross-purposes with other potential implementers. In partnerships with a designated implementer, autonomy, trust, and protection of organization identity are essential to effectiveness and efficiency. This designated role does not imply that other partners' organization identities are any less important. Part of INMED's implementation role was to incorporate and respond to the interests and concerns of the other partners. Since maintaining organization identity is so important to continuing effectiveness, partnership actors must take care to avoid subtle encroachments on their identities. Such dangers are commonly addressed through buffering techniques, which require proactive monitoring, and an awareness of respective organization identities and ways that their combinations could impinge on one another. Organization identity can also be reinforced through culture mechanisms, such as the WCD's stated and enacted expectations that each stakeholder group continue to advocate on behalf of its members.

In sum, partnership's defining dimensions are the basis for pursuing partnership approaches. However, partnership effectiveness and sustainability are predicated on their sustenance, which requires proactive attention and response. In the cases reviewed here, partners took responsibility for both their own organization identity and that of their partners, initiating and implementing buffering approaches, as relevant, and supporting respective identities through culture mechanisms.

While partnership actors can ultimately exercise exit options to protect their identity, it is unrealistic to rely exclusively on such mechanisms. Doing so would imply that threats to organization identity must become exceedingly serious before actors might respond. More important, by the time such threats become obvious an actor may already have substantial vested interest in remaining in the partnership. This might include expectations of and accountability requirements to its stakeholders. Power is socially structured and may be exercised by shaping the needs of others (Lukes 1974). Actors may come to believe that serving the interests of more powerful partners is consistent with their own interests. The limitations and risks associated with relying on exit options imply that partnership actors would do well to establish organization identity, respect, and maintenance parameters bureaucratically (e.g., in partnership agreements such as INMED's) and subsequently reinforce these through culture mechanisms. Such efforts should encourage proactive attention to buffering needs and flexibility that may be required for partners to remain responsive to their constituencies (e.g., INMED's formalizing reporting requirements).

The Future of Partnerships

Globalization Trends

Globalization has led to closer integration among the countries of the world, increasing recognition of challenges and implications that cross national borders and demand cross-border solutions and continuing efforts to refine the processes for establishing public policy at global and national levels. Citizens are increasingly coming together and organizing to represent their own interests, express their views, and undertake actions to assist themselves and others, independent of, in conflict with, or in partnership with governments and other actors. The emergence of a transnational civil society and activist national civil societies, with their demonstrated successes in influencing national, donor, and international policy, can improve the outcomes of public policy. This can occur due to the information civil society can bring to inform policymaking; the ownership engendered through participation, which may result in greater commitment and follow-through on implementation (see Brinkerhoff with Kulibaba 1996); civil society's unique advantages in addressing social exclusion (see Badelt 1999); and the monitoring role civil society can play (see Coston 1995). However, the emergence and growing strength of these sometimes well-organized, sometimes disparate advocates may exacerbate conflict and complexity, which may preclude the identification of workable solutions.

A new global consensus has emerged, which encompasses (among other things) market-oriented policies, effective institutions and law, integration with the world, a global economic system, and the provision of global public goods (Summers 2000). The greater reliance on markets has often translated into decreases in public funding for public services and a greater reliance on other actors (the commercial and nonprofit sectors), who may or may not receive corresponding increases in their own funding streams. There are also increasing expectations for democratic practice, with demands for accountability, transparency, and participation in public policy processes. All of this occurs in a context of global trends—economic and financial, technological, environmental, and sociopolitical (Brinkerhoff and Coston 1999)—which create both new opportunities and new challenges for enacting this global consensus, and doing so democratically as demanded by transnational society and other societal actors at the national and local levels (see Mudacumura 2000). The need for policies to address the negative externalities and public goods on a global scale is increasingly recognized (Bailey 1999). Conflict—locally, nationally, and transnationally—is inevitably emerging across and within sectors, as actors attempt to determine and enact their roles specific to each context and issue addressed. At the same time, other actors look on, scrutinizing these interpretations and actions.

The challenge of coping with the dual demands of substance and process is captured by the concept of governance gaps. These include an operational gap, in which policymakers and public institutions do not have the information, knowledge, and tools to respond to the complexity of policy issues, and a participatory gap, where the complexity prevents a common understanding and agreement on critical policy issues (Reinicke and Deng 2000). The result is a political economy where actors can no longer assume their traditional roles are sufficient and must, therefore, expand their conception of self-interest to embrace (1) the accountability, transparency, and, in some cases, participation, increasingly expected of them and (2) the need to actively collaborate with other actors to attain the knowledge, information, and tools required for effectiveness.

Partnership, the Rational Response

Partnership is a rational response to this complexity and represents an effective means for operationalizing, promoting, and providing socialization for the participation and democratic values increasingly expected. The cases demonstrate partnership's effectiveness in three different public policy realms, each of which is grappling with the constraints and opportunities posed by globalization and the global consensus. The WCD demonstrates how partnerships can address global public policy processes and resolve global conflict. The case is all the more salient considering the depth of the conflict, the diversity of stakeholders, and the implications globalization has had in terms of linking these stakeholders into powerful forces for accountability.

The Healthy Children, Healthy Futures partnership explores the expanding role of the private sector in addressing public service needs through corporate social responsibility. As the flow of private-sector resources into development activities and service delivery has increased dramatically, overshadowing official development assistance, questions have been raised with respect to how these resources will be applied effectively. While some multinational corporations, such as Shell International, devise formal internal strategies and administration for this purpose, the INMED case illustrates the potential cost-effectiveness of partnerships that rely on a designated NGO implementer. Such an approach exploits comparative advantages, avoiding redundant capacity building and maximizing all available resources.

Finally, the challenges addressed by the BADP are not necessarily new to developing countries (or industrialized ones for that matter). However, globalization and the global consensus have led to diminished public-sector resources and capacity. The case illustrates how partnerships can effectively address this scarcity within public sectors and maximize existing resources and capacity. The partnership essentially operated both internal to the provincial government structure (i.e., among various departments), and externally, with the SRSC and local communities. New resources and efficiencies were created through the participation of external actors, and the synergies cultivated among internal actors. The BADP's ultimate success is predicated on the self-reliance and ownership of local communities that will ideally sustain current improvements and take initiatives for further ones, reducing dependency on the public sector in the longer term.

Implications for Partnership Implementation

Global trends both necessitate and facilitate partnership approaches. The recognition of interdependencies, and even associated conflict, assists previously disparate actors in finding common ground and shared concerns. This process is facilitated by technological developments, most notably advancements in information, telecommunication, and transportation technologies, which provide for communication and the development of virtual communities.

Partnerships address traditional needs and concerns, such as effective public service delivery (the BADP), as well as newly emerging issues, such as the growing needs for global public policy processes, especially those that seek to resolve conflict (the WCD) and to maximize the efficiency and effectiveness of relatively new actors in engaged service arenas and international development, such as multinational corporations (INMED). While there are other interorganizational relationship options available, partnership will become the collaborative mode of choice for those who recognize the extent of its benefits. Wider recognition of these benefits will lead to a greater willingness to adapt and share decisionmaking power in order to exploit comparative advantages fully and maximize available resources.

Is partnership universally good? The practical answer is a confident no. Actors' preferences will shape the selection of the partnership option, as well as the partnership's design and implementation. Because partnerships are complex and sometimes subtle in their operationalization, they require substantial investments in effort, if not always in resources. It is essential to justify these investments based on a shared belief in partnership's value-added, which rests on its defining dimensions of mutuality and organization identity. Only with such a justification and belief will actors be sufficiently willing to make the necessary adaptations, share power, and be proactive in maintaining mutuality and protecting respective organization identities.

Refining the Practice

Partnership remains an evolving concept and practice. Its defining dimensions will inform continued theory building. Practical experimentation can help to refine these defining dimensions, develop indicators of effective partnership practice, and enhance responsiveness to actors' expectations of partnership. The identification of mutuality and organization identity as partnership's defining dimensions both reflects the expectations of partnership and serves to distinguish partnership from other relationship types, forming the basis for identifying its value-added. The operationalization of these dimensions, as well as their indicators, is subject to interpretation, most important by the partners themselves. Specifying these dimensions provides a basis for discussion when creating partnerships, points to strategic areas of attention in implementation, and highlights areas of inquiry for process documentation and evaluation.

The lessons for managing partnership reinforce the determining role of actors' preferences and call attention to the need for environmental responsiveness and informed decisionmaking with respect to partnership's many implementation trade-offs. Cost-benefit analysis presumes a thorough understanding of the partnership's context, actors' preferences, and the sources of synergistic benefits. A keen understanding of partners' organization identities and corresponding requirements for constituency responsiveness will greatly contribute to trade-off and maintenance strategies that can safeguard partnership effectiveness for the longer term.

This book also emphasizes the softer side of partnership design and implementation, encouraging actors to be more proactive about establishing and reinforcing a values basis for partnership work and a corresponding partnership identity. This values basis will assist in recruiting and retaining individuals with a disposition for OCB, cultivating internal commitment to partnership objectives, maximizing the effectiveness and efficiency of incentives systems by recognizing intangible and particularly values-based incentives, and supporting an organizational culture and maximizing the use of culture governance mechanisms as a means for both efficiency and effectiveness. Normative and instrumental values are not necessarily contradictory. In fact, normative values can, themselves, become instrumental. This is most obviously demonstrated with respect to the advantages of democratic values and processes, but it is also inherent in the cited cases' reliance on other values specific to partnerships and to particular service objectives.

Semantics, Friend or Foe?

There remains one more, essential caveat—power. Power is an unavoidable dimension in any relationship, whether between individuals or among organizations. Some scholars and practitioners have argued against the use of partnership rhetoric, let alone attempts to pursue partnership approaches. In her analysis of power within partnership, Sarah Lister (2000) implies that true partnership may be impossible due to the exercise of power inherent to international development (see also Postma 1994). She argues that power can be exercised to shape the needs of others, influencing them to pursue behavior in the interests of the powerholder. Thus, consensus may in actuality be a deeply ingrained power play. So "adopting partnership as a dominant concept may be doing more harm than good in improving system credibility and performance" (Fowler 2000a: 1; see also Fowler 2000b).

Why insist on referring to *partnership* given its potential impossibility, due to the purported (and probable) masking of power relations? Wouldn't *network* be a more neutral term that better captures the variety of interorganizational relations, while still capturing the benefits upon which they are based?

There is a good argument to be made for using the term *network*. The literature on networks tends to be the most analytic and potentially useful of the writings related to partnership for international development, and I hope this book will be seen as a contribution to that literature. However, specification of the partnership dimensions of mutuality and organization identity serves to better distinguish partnerships as a particular type of network and to identify and support the attainment of their value-added. Moreover, this study is oriented to applied research, and aims to influence practice. While use of partnership terminology holds the potential for masking power relations and discrediting organizational systems and sustainability as Lister (2000) and Alan Fowler (2000a) suggest, it can also be an important vehicle for potentially weaker players or "partners" to enter relationships and promote improvement and accountability. The emergence, evolution, and successes of transnational civil society confirm an effective path of lobbying for improved policy and rhetoric, which then become the basis for accountability and improved practice (see Florini 2000; Fox and Brown 1998).

Partnership's defining dimensions identify essential targets for accountability and analysis when evaluating the authenticity of partnership rhetoric. The model is not intended to reinforce the overuse of partnership rhetoric but to improve actual partnership work. Such analytic work can help to balance the boosters versus the naysayers of partnership for international development. While empty rhetoric can lead to deeper cynicism, simply criticizing the rhetoric will not encourage enhanced understanding and application of partnership's potential contributions to development outcomes.

ACRONYMS

ACVFA	Advisory Committee on Voluntary Foreign Aid
ADB	Asian Development Bank
A/I/C	Appreciate/Influence/Control
AO	agricultural officer (BADP, Pakistan)
BADP	Barani Area Development Project
BDO	Barani Development Office
BPD	Business Partners for Development (International Finance Corporation)
CBO	community-based organization
CSO	civil society organization
DAC	Development Assistance Committee
DCC	District Coordination Committee (BADP, Pakistan)
DPRC	Divisional Project Review Committee (BADP, Pakistan)
EMG	Environmental Monitoring Group
GDA	Global Development Alliance (USAID)
GONWFP	Government of the North West Frontier Province (Pakistan)
KAP	knowledge, attitudes, and practice
INMED	International Medical Services for Health
IRN	International Rivers Network
IUCN	World Conservation Union
IWG	Interim Working Group (WCD)
NBA	Narmada Bachao Andolan [Save the Narmada Movement]
NGO	nongovernmental organization
NPI	New Partnership Initiative (USAID)
NWFP	North West Frontier Province (Pakistan)
OCB	organization citizenship behavior
OED	Operations Evaluation Department
PAs	partnership agreements (INMED)
PCIs	participating credit institutions (BADP, Pakistan)

PISs	productive investment schemes (BADP, Pakistan)
PRB	Project Review Board (BADP, Pakistan)
PVC	Office of Private and Voluntary Cooperation (USAID)
PVO	Private Voluntary Organization (USAID)
SOPs	standard operating procedures
SOU	Social Organization Unit (BADP, Pakistan)
SRSC	Sarhad Rural Support Corporation (NGO, BADP, Pakistan)
ToPs	terms of partnership (BADP, Pakistan)
UN	United Nations
UNDP	United Nations Development Programme
UNHCR	United Nations High Commissioner for Refugees
USAID	United States Agency for International Development
VOs	village organizations (BADP, Pakistan)
WCD	World Commission on Dams
WHO	World Health Organization
WOs	women's organizations (BADP, Pakistan)

BIBLIOGRAPHY

ACVFA (Advisory Committee on Voluntary Foreign Aid). 1997. "Assessment of the State of the USAID/PVO Partnership." Washington, D.C.: U.S. Agency for International Development.

ADB (Asian Development Bank). 1992. "Appraisal of the North-West Frontier Province Barani Area Development Project in Pakistan." Islamabad: Asian Development Bank.

———. 1996. Aide-Memoire: Mid-Term Review Mission (Loan No. 1179PAK: NWFP Barani Area Development Project). Islamabad: Asian Development Bank, September 1.

Alexander, Nancy C. n.d. *The World Bank's New Strategic Alliances.* Washington, D.C.: Development Bank Watchers' Project, Bread for the World Institute.

Alsop, Ronald. 1999. "Corporate Reputations Are Earned with Trust, Reliability, Study Shows." *Wall Street Journal*, September 23.

———. 2001. "Harris Interactive Survey Indicates Fragility of Corporate Reputations." *Wall Street Journal*, February 7.

Annan, Kofi. 1998a. Secretary-General's Address to the 51st Annual DPI-NGO Conference (Commemorating the Universal Declaration of Human Rights). New York: United Nations.

———. 1998b. Statement of the Secretary-General to Parlatino. São Paulo: United Nations.

———. 2000. *We the Peoples: The Role of the United Nations in the 21st Century.* New York: United Nations.

Annis, Sheldon. 1987. "Can Small-Scale Development Be a Large-Scale Policy? The Case of Latin America." *World Development* 15 (Supplement): 129–135.

Anonymous. 2000. "The PRSP Process in Bolivia: Civil Society and Government Relations." December 1999/January 2000. Washington, D.C.: Poverty Group, Social Development Family, World Bank.

Argyris, Chris. 2000. *Flawed Advice and the Management Trap: How Managers Can Know When They're Getting Good Advice and When They're Not.* New York: Oxford University Press.

Armistead, Thomas F. 1998. "Dam Conflicts Threaten Growth: Global Group Seeks New Consensus on Megaproject Risks and Rewards." *Engineering News Record*, September 14.

Ascher, William, and Robert Healy. 1990. *Natural Resource Policymaking in*

181

Developing Countries: Environment, Economic Growth, and Income Distribution. Durham and London: Duke University Press.

ASIANICS. 1999. NWFP Barani Area Development Project (Pakistan: Loan No. 1179–PK). Project Benefit Monitoring and Evaluation. Evaluation and Baseline Survey. Peshawar, Pakistan: ASIANICS, for the Barani Area Development Office, GONWFP, August.

Asmal, Kader. 1999a. "Message from the Chair." *World Commission on Dams Newsletter* 2, March [Retrieved January 24, 2000, from www.dams.org/newsletters/newsletter2.htm].

———. 1999b. Editorial. *World Commission on Dams Newsletter* 3, June [Retrieved January 24, 2000, from www.dams.org/newsletters/newsletter3.htm].

———. 1999c. Preface. *World Commission on Dams Interim Report.* Cape Town, South Africa: World Commission on Dams, 2–3.

———. 1999d. "An Opportunity for the WCD and ICID to Interact." Address to delegates of the Seventeenth Congress of the International Commission on Irrigation and Drainage, Granada, Spain. *World Commission on Dams Press Release,* September 14.

———. 2000. "Message from the Chair: Seattle, Washington, and the WCD . . ." *World Commission on Dams Newsletter* 6, April [Retrieved January 24, 2001, from www.dams.org/newsletters/newsletter6.htm].

Austin, James E. 2000. *The Collaborative Challenge: How Nonprofits and Businesses Succeed Through Strategic Alliances.* San Francisco: Jossey-Bass.

Badelt, Christoph. 1999. *The Role of NPOs in Policies to Combat Social Exclusion.* Social Protection Discussion Paper no. 9912. Washington, D.C.: World Bank, Social Protection, June.

Bailey, Elizabeth E. 1999. "A Regulatory Framework for the 21st Century." *Eastern Economic Journal* 25: 253–263.

Bauman, Robert P., Peter Jackson, and Joanne T. Laurence. 1997. *From Promise to Performance.* Boston: Harvard Business School Press.

BDO (Barani Development Office). 1996. NWFP Barani Area Development Project: Progress Review of October 1996. Peshawar, Pakistan: Barani Development Office, Special Development Unit—Planning, Environment and Development Department, GONWFP.

Bebbington, Anthony, and Roger Riddell. 1997. "Heavy Hands, Hidden Hands, Holding Hands? Donors, Intermediary NGOs and Civil Society Organizations." In David Hulme and Michael Edwards, eds., *NGOs, States and Donors: Too Close for Comfort?* New York: St. Martin's, 107–127.

Beckmann, David. 1991. "Recent Experience and Emerging Trends." In Samuel Paul and Arturo Israel, eds., *Nongovernmental Organizations and the World Bank: Cooperation for Development.* Washington, D.C.: World Bank, 134–154.

Bilbao, Arantza, and Susana Pachano. 1997. *Successful Experiences in Poverty Reduction: Horizontal Cooperation in Latin America and the Caribbean. Self-Help for Housing in Barrio Santa Cruz, Venezuela.* Caracas, Venezuela: Venezuela Competitiva (National Center for Competitiveness) for Partnerships for Poverty Reduction, World Bank.

Börzel, Tanja A. 1998. "Organizing Babylon—On the Different Conceptions of Policy Networks." *Public Administration* 76: 253–273.

Bosshard, Peter, and Patrick McCully. 2000. "From Commission to Action: An NGO Call to Public Financial Institutions (Endorsed by 109 NGOs from 39

Countries)," November 16 [Retrieved January 23, 2001, from www.irn.org/wcd/ngocall.shtml and www.dams.org/report/reaction_ngo.htm].

Bradach, Jeffrey, and James R. Eccles. 1991. "Price, Authority, and Trust: From Ideal Types to Plural Forms." In Grahame Thompson, Jennifer Frances, Rosalind Levacic, and Jeremy Mitchell, eds., *Markets, Hierarchies, and Networks: The Coordination of Social Life*. London: Sage.

Bratton, Michael. 1990. "Non-Governmental Organizations in Africa: Can They Influence Public Policy?" *Development and Change* 21: 87–118.

Brinkerhoff, Derick W. 1991. *Improving Development Performance: Guidelines for Managers*. Boulder: Lynne Rienner.

———. 1997. "Integrating Institutional and Implementation Issues into Policy Decisions: An Introduction and Overview." In Derick W. Brinkerhoff, ed., *Policy Analysis Concepts and Methods: An Institutional and Implementation Focus*. Greenwich, Conn.: JAI, 1–18.

———. 2002. "Government-Nonprofit Partners for Health Sector Reform in Central Asia: Family Group Practice Associations in Kazakhstan and Kyrgyzstan." *Public Administration and Development* 22: 51–61.

Brinkerhoff, Derick W., and Jennifer M. Brinkerhoff. 2001. "Cross-Sectoral Policy Networks: Lessons from Developing and Transitioning Countries." In Myrna Mandell, ed., *Getting Results Through Collaboration: Networks and Network Structures for Public Policy and Management*. Westport, Conn.: Quorum, 167–189.

Brinkerhoff, Derick W., and Jennifer M. Coston. 1999. "International Development Management in a Globalized World." *Public Administration Review* 59: 346–361.

Brinkerhoff, Derick W., and Arthur Goldsmith. 1992. "Promoting the Sustainability of Development Institutions: A Framework for Strategy." *World Development* 20: 369–383.

Brinkerhoff, Derick W., Arthur A. Goldsmith, Marcus D. Ingle, and S. Tjip Walker. 1990. "Institutional Sustainability: A Conceptual Framework." In Derick W. Brinkerhoff and Arthur A. Goldsmith, eds., *Institutional Sustainability in Agriculture and Rural Development: A Global Perspective*. New York: Praeger, 19–48.

Brinkerhoff, Derick W., with assistance from Nicolas P. Kulibaba. 1996. "Perspectives on Participation in Economic Policy Reform in Africa." *Studies in Comparative International Development* 31: 123–151.

Brinkerhoff, Jennifer M. 2002. "Assessing and Improving Partnership Relationships and Outcomes: A Proposed Framework." *Evaluation and Program Planning* 25: 215–231.

Brown, David L., and Darcy Ashman. 1996. "Participation, Social Capital, and Intersectoral Problem-solving: African and Asian Cases." *World Development* 24: 1467–1479.

Brown, David L., and David C. Korten. 1991. "Working More Effectively with Nongovernmental Organizations." In Samuel Paul and Arturo Israel, eds., *Nongovernmental Organizations and the World Bank: Cooperation for Development*. Washington, D.C.: World Bank, 44–93.

Burns, Tom, and George M. Stalker. 1961. *The Management of Innovation*. London: Tavistock.

Burt, Ronald S. 2000. "The Network Structure of Social Capital." In Robert I. Sutton and Barry M. Staw, eds., *Research in Organizational Behavior* 22. Greenwich, Conn.: JAI.

Bush, Richard. 1992. "Survival of the Nonprofit Spirit in a For-Profit World." *Nonprofit and Voluntary Sector Quarterly* 12: 391–410.

Bzdak, Michael (Director of Corporate Contributions, Johnson & Johnson). 2001. Interview by author, April 12.

Capelli, Joyce (Program Director, INMED Brazil). 2000. Interview by author, October 10.

Carvahlo, Soniya (Operations Evaluation Department, Sector and Thematic Evaluation Division, World Bank). 1998. Interview by author, July 16.

Carvajal Foundation. 1997. "Autoconstruccion de Obras de Infraestructura de Servicios Publicos con Entrega de Materiales" (Self-Construction of Public Service Infrastructure Works with Delivery of Materials). Colombia: Fundacion Carvajal, Universidad del Valle, for Partnerships for Poverty Reduction, World Bank, in collaboration with the Inter-American Foundation and UNDP.

Chambers, Robert. 1988. *Managing Canal Irrigation: Practical Analysis from South Asia.* Cambridge: Cambridge University Press.

Charles, Chanya L., Stephanie McNulty, and John A. Pennell. 1998. "A User's Guide to Intersectoral Partnering." Presented at Mission Director Conference, U.S. Agency for International Development, Washington, D.C., November.

Chisholm, Donald. 1989. *Coordination Without Hierarchy: Informal Structures in Multiorganizational Systems.* Berkeley and Los Angeles: University of California Press.

Clark, John M. 1991. *Democratizing Development: The Role of Voluntary Organizations.* West Hartford, Conn.: Kumarian.

———. 1997. "The State, Popular Participation and the Voluntary Sector." In David Hulme and Michael Edwards, eds., *NGOs, States and Donors: Too Close for Comfort?* New York: St. Martin's, 43–58.

Clary, E. Gil, and Mark Snyder. 1993. "Persuasive Communication Strategies for Recruiting Volunteers." In Dennis R. Young, Robert M. Hollister, Virginia A. Hodgkinson, and associates, eds., *Governing, Leading, and Managing Nonprofit Organizations: New Insights from Research and Practice.* San Francisco: Jossey-Bass, 121–138.

Coleman, James S. 1988. "Social Capital in the Creation of Human Capital." *American Journal of Sociology* 94: S95–S120.

———. 1990. *Foundations of Social Theory.* Cambridge, Mass.: Harvard University Press, Belknap Press.

Cooper, Terry L. 1980. "Bureaucracy and Community Organization: The Metamorphosis of a Relationship." *Administration and Society* 11: 411–444.

Coston, Jennifer M. 1995. *Civil Society Literature Review: Democratic Governance and Civil Society's Theoretical Development, Contemporary Conceptualization, and Institutional, Economic, and Political Implications.* Washington, D.C.: U.S. Agency for International Development, Global Center for Democracy and Governance.

———. 1998a. "Making Development Partnerships Work." Proceedings publication. Building Effective Partnerships to Meet the Challenge of Equitable and Sustainable Development, Learning and Leadership Center and the NGO Unit, Social Development Department, World Bank, Washington, D.C., May 19–21.

———. 1998b. "Administrative Avenues to Democratic Governance: The Balance of Supply and Demand." *Public Administration and Development* 18: 479–493.

———. 1998c. "Consultative Meeting on Partnerships: Joining Hands with

Government and Non-Government Development Organizations and Local Communities." Synthesis report. Building Effective Partnerships to Meet the Challenge of Equitable and Sustainable Development, Learning and Leadership Center and the NGO Unit, Social Development Department, World Bank, Washington, D.C.

———. 1999. "Building Effective Partnerships to Meet the Challenge of Equitable and Sustainable Development: Case Examples." Building Effective Partnerships to Meet the Challenge of Equitable and Sustainable Development, Learning and Leadership Center and the NGO Unit. Washington, D.C.: Social Development Department, World Bank.

Dahl, Robert. 1971. *Polyarchy: Participation and Opposition.* New Haven: Yale University Press.

"Dam Builders and Dam Busters: Should Dams Be Built?" 1997. *Economist*, April 19, 79–80.

Da Silva, Samantha. 1998. Malawi Social Action Fund. Presentation to the Training Workshop on Making Development Partnerships Work, NGO Unit and Learning and Leadership Center, World Bank. Elkridge, Md., May 19–21.

Deen, Thalif. 1999. "NGOs Barred from Speaking at Special Session." *Inter Press Service*, July 2.

De Leva, Adreana. 1998. Community Project in Mali. Presentation for the Training Workshop on Making Development Partnerships Work, NGO Unit and Learning and Leadership Center, World Bank. Elkridge, Md., May 19–21.

DeSimone, Livio D., and Frank Popoff, with the World Council for Sustainable Development. 2000. *Eco-Efficiency: The Business Link to Sustainable Development.* Cambridge, Mass.: MIT Press.

Development Committee (Joint Ministerial Committee of the Boards of Governors of the World Bank and the International Monetary Fund on the Transfer of Real Resources to Developing Countries). 1999. *Building Poverty Reduction Strategies in Developing Countries.* Washington, D.C.: World Bank Development Committee, September 22.

Dorcey, Tony, Achim Steiner, Michael Acreman, and Brett Orlando, eds. 1997. *Large Dams: Learning from the Past, Looking at the Future: Workshop Proceedings, Gland, Switzerland, April 11–12, 1997.* Cambridge, U.K., and Washington, D.C.: IUCN (World Conservation Union) and World Bank.

Doz, Yves L., and Gary Hamel. 1998. *Alliance Advantage: The Art of Creating Value Through Partnering.* Boston: Harvard Business School Press.

Ellinger, Alexander E., Scott B. Keller, and Andrea D. Ellinger. 2000. "Developing Interdepartmental Integration: An Evaluation of Three Strategic Approaches for Performance Improvement." *Performance Improvement Quarterly* 13: 41–59.

Elliott, Charles. 1987. "Some Aspects of Relations Between the North and South in the NGO Sector." *World Development* 15 (Supplement): 57–68.

Eriksson, John R. 1998. "An Institutional Framework for Learning from Failed States." In Robert Picciotto and Eduardo Wiesner, eds., *Evaluation and Development: The Institutional Dimension.* New Brunswick, N.J., and London: Transaction: 218–230.

Etzioni, Amitai. 1988. *The Moral Dimension: Toward a New Economics.* New York: Free Press.

———. 1991. "The Case for a Multiple-Utility Conception." *A Responsive Society: Collected Essays on Guiding Deliberate Social Change.* San Francisco: Jossey-Bass, 418–451.

Evans, Peter. 1996. "Government Action, Social Capital and Development: Reviewing the Evidence on Synergy." *World Development* 24: 1119–1132.

Evans, Rodney K. 1999. "From Small Farms to Supermarkets." In Steven A. Breth, ed., *Partnerships for Rural Development in Sub-Saharan Africa*. Geneva: Centre for Applied Studies in International Negotiations, 103–110.

Fischer, Rosa Maria, and Andres Pablo Falconer. 1999. "An Example from Brazil of Tradition and Modernity in Intersectoral Partnerships: Liceu de Artes e Ofícios da Bahia and Fundação Odebrecht." Presentation to Civil Society Business Cooperation Program, Institute for Development Research. Boston, July.

Fischer, Rosa Maria, and Luciana Jacques Faria. 1999. "Changes in Social Action of Privatized Enterprises: The Case of a Corporate Foundation in Brazil." Presentation to Civil Society Business Cooperation Program, Institute for Development Research. Boston, July.

Fiszbein, Ariel, and Pamela Lowden. 1998. *Working Together for a Change: Government, Business and Civic Partnerships for Poverty Reduction in LAC*. Washington, D.C.: Economic Development Institute of the World Bank.

Florini, Ann, ed. 2000. *The Third Force: The Rise of Transnational Civil Society*. Washington, D.C.: Japan Center for International Exchange and Carnegie Endowment for International Peace.

Fogle, Catherine (Task Manager, India Population Project VIII, Health Population and Nutrition, World Bank). 1998. Interview by author, July 9.

Forester, John. 1993. *Critical Theory, Public Policy, and Planning Practice: Toward a Critical Pragmatism*. Albany: State University of New York Press.

Fowler, Alan. 1992. "Distant Obligations: Speculations on NGO Funding and the Global Market." *Review of African Political Economy* 55: 9–29.

———. 1995a. "Sample Criteria for Assessing the Capacity of CBOs." In Carmen Malena, ed., *Working with NGOs: A Practical Guide to Operational Collaboration Between the World Bank and Non-governmental Organizations*. Washington, D.C.: Operations Policy Department, World Bank.

———. 1995b. "Strengthening the Role of Voluntary Development Organizations: Nine Policy Issues Facing Official Aid Agencies." *Strengthening Civil Society's Contribution to Development: The Role of Official Development Assistance. Report on a Conference for Official Development Assistance Agencies*. Pocantico Hills, N.Y.: Overseas Development Council and the Synergos Institute, September 26–28, 21–33.

———. 1997. *Striking a Balance: A Guide to Enhancing the Effectiveness of NGOs in International Development*. London: Earthscan.

———. 1999. "Bad Aid to NGOs—A Case of Partnership or Conspiracy?" @lliance 4: 20–23.

———. 2000a. "Introduction—Beyond Partnership: Getting Real About NGO Relationships in the Aid System." In Alan F. Fowler, ed., *Questioning Partnership: The Reality of Aid and NGO Relations. IDS Bulletin* 31: 1–13.

———, ed. 2000b. *Questioning Partnership: The Reality of Aid and NGO Relations. IDS Bulletin* 31.

Fox, Jonathan, and David Brown, eds. 1998. *The Struggle for Accountability: The World Bank, NGOs, and Grassroots Movements*. Cambridge, Mass.: MIT Press.

Frank, Robert H. 1990. "A Theory of Moral Sentiments." In Jane J. Mansbridge, ed., *Beyond Self-Interest*. Chicago: University of Chicago Press, 159–171.

Frischtak, Leila L. 1994. *Governance Capacity and Economic Reform in Developing Countries*. World Bank Technical Paper no. 254. Washington, D.C.: World Bank.

Frumkin, Peter, and Alice Andre-Clark. 2000. "When Missions, Markets, and Politics Collide: Values and Strategy in the Nonprofit Human Services." *Nonprofit and Voluntary Sector Quarterly* 29: 141–163.

FUNDE (Fundación Nacional para el Desarrollo). 1997. Case Study: Comite Ambiental de Chalatenango (CACH). San Salvador, El Salvador: FUNDE for Partnerships for Poverty Reduction, World Bank, in collaboration with the Inter-American Foundation and UNDP, June.

Gagliardi, Pasquale. 1986. "The Creation and Change of Organizational Cultures: A Conceptual Framework." *Organization Studies* 7: 117–134.

Garilao, Ernesto D. 1987. "Indigenous NGOs as Strategic Institutions: Managing the Relationship with Government and Resource Agencies." *World Development* 15 (Supplement): 113–120.

Garrison, John. 1999. "Reconciling Diverse Forms of Civil Society Engagement in Brazil." In Kerianne Piester, ed., *Food for Thought: Proceedings from Brown Bag Lunch Series. Civil Society Papers*. Washington, D.C.: World Bank: 28–33.

Gioia, Dennis A., Majken Schultz, and Kevin G. Korley. 2000. "Organizational Identity, Image and Adaptive Instability." *Academy of Management Review* 25: 65–81.

Global Policy Forum. 1999. "NGOs and the United Nations: Comments for the Report of the Secretary General," June [Retrieved April 13, 2000, from www.globalpolicy.org/ngos/docs99/gpfrep.htm].

Goldsmith, Arthur A. 1996. "Strategic Thinking in International Development: Using Management Tools to See the Big Picture." *World Development* 24: 1431–1439.

Greene, George, and Robert Picciotto. 1997. Preface. In Tony Dorcey, Achim Steiner, Michael Acreman, and Brett Orlando, eds., *Large Dams: Learning from the Past, Looking at the Future: Workshop Proceedings, Gland, Switzerland, April 11–12, 1997*. Cambridge, U.K., and Washington, D.C.: IUCN (World Conservation Union) and World Bank, ii.

Harris Interactive. 2002. Harris Interactive Reputation Quotient. Harris Interactive [Retrieved February 7, 2002, from www.harrisinteractive.com/pop_up/rq/index.asp].

Harris Interactive and Charles Fombrun. 1999. Harris-Fombrun Reputation Quotient. Harris Interactive [Retrieved April 13, 2001, from www.harrisinteractive.com/pop_up/rq/20.asp].

Hernández, Lisette, Rafael Portillo, and Domingo Méndez. 1997. "Successful Experiences in Poverty Reduction: Horizontal Cooperation in Latin America and the Caribbean." Caracas, Venezuela: Universidad de Zulia for Partnerships for Poverty Reduction, World Bank, in collaboration with the Inter-American Foundation and UNDP, August.

Hino, Toshiko. 1996. *NGO–World Bank Partnerships: A Tale of Two Projects*. Human Capital Development (HCD) Working Papers. Washington, D.C.: World Bank, June.

Hodson, Roland. 1997. "Elephant Loose in the Jungle: The World Bank and NGOs in Sri Lanka." In David Hulme and Michael Edwards, eds., *NGOs, States and Donors: Too Close for Comfort?* New York: St. Martin's, 168–187.

Hulme, David, and Michael Edwards. 1997a. "NGOs, States and Donors: An

Overview." In David Hulme and Michael Edwards, eds., *NGOs, States and Donors: Too Close for Comfort?* New York: St. Martin's, 3–22.

———. 1997b. "Too Close to the Powerful, Too Far from the Powerless?" In David Hulme and Michael Edwards, eds., *NGOs, States and Donors: Too Close for Comfort?* New York: St. Martin's, 275–284.

Huxham Chris. 1993. "Pursuing Collaborative Advantage." *Journal of the Operational Research Society* 44: 599–611.

———, ed. 1996. *Creating Collaborative Advantage.* London: Sage.

ICOLD (International Commission on Large Dams). 2000. ICOLD open letter to the WCD chair, November 30 [Retrieved January 23, 2001, from www.dams. org/report/reaction_icold2.htm].

ICOLD, IHA (International Hydropower Association), and ICID (International Commission on Irrigation and Drainage). 2000. Open letter from ICOLD, IHA, and ICID on the final report of the World Commission on Dams, November 13 [Retrieved January 23, 2001, from www.dams.org/report/reaction_icold_et_ al.htm].

INMED. n.d. "Healthy Children, Healthy Futures. A Program of INMED and INMED Brazil." Brochure. Sterling, Va.: INMED.

———. 2000. "Healthy Children, Healthy Futures." Proposal to El Paso Energy for a New Projeto Comunitário in Porto Velho, Randônia, Brazil. Sterling, Va.: INMED, February.

INMED, INMED Brazil, and Janssen-Cilag. 2000. Partnership agreement among INMED, INMED Brazil, and Janssen-Cilag Pharmaceutical. São Paulo, Brazil, December 1.

INMED Brazil. n.d. "INMED Brazil . . . Improving the Health of Brazil's Children, Families and Communities." Brochure. São Paulo: INMED.

Interfarma (International Federation of Pharmaceutical Manufacturers Association). n.d. "Partners in Healing." Video. São Paulo: Interfarma.

International Center for Not-for-Profit Law. 1997. *Handbook on Good Practices for Laws Relating to Non-Governmental Organizations.* Washington, D.C.: World Bank.

IRN (International Rivers Network). 1997. "Curitiba Declaration: Affirming the Right to Life and Livelihood of People Affected by Dams." Approved at the First International Meeting of People Affected by Dams, Curitiba, Brazil, March 14 [Retrieved January 24, 2001, from www.irn.org/programs/curitiba. html].

———. 1998. "Status Note on World Commission on Dams: Agreement Reached on List of Commissioners." *International Rivers Network Press Release*, February 9 [Retrieved January 24, 2001, from www.irn.org/programs/review/ status980209.html].

Isofo, Egbe (Task Manager, West Bank and Gaza Education and Health Rehabilitation Project, World Bank). 1998. Interview by author, July 17.

Jackson, Thad (Executive Vice President, INMED). 1999. Letter to Gregory Bafalis, President, El Paso Energy International do Brazil Ltda. March 25.

———. 2000. Interview by author, October 10.

James Bay Cree Nation and the Pimicikamak Cree Nation. 2000. Statement on the occasion of the release of the World Commission on Dams final report, November 16 [Retrieved January 23, 2001, from www.dams.org/report/ reaction_cree.htm].

Judge, Anthony. 1999a. Statement by the Union of International Associations on secretary-general's report on NGOs, May 21 [Retrieved April 13, 2000, from www.globalpolicy.org/ngos/docs99/uia99.htm].

————. 1999b. Response to GPF's report "NGOs and the United Nations," June 25 [Retrieved April 13, 2000, from www.globalpolicy.org/ngos/docs99/judge. htm].

Kanter, Rosabeth Moss. 1994. "Collaborative Advantage: The Art of Alliances." *Harvard Business Review* 72: 96–108.

————. 1995. "Thriving in the Global Economy." *Harvard Business Review* 73: 151–160.

Kellner, Peter, and Rachelle Thackray. 1999. "A Philosophy for a Fallible World." *The New Statesman* 12 (March 19): R22–R25.

Kerrigan, John E., and Jeff S. Luke. 1987. *Management Training Strategies for Developing Countries*. Boulder: Lynne Rienner.

Khagram, Sanjeev. 2000. "Toward Democratic Governance for Sustainable Development: Transnational Civil Society Organizing Around Big Dams." In Ann M. Florini, ed., *The Third Force: The Rise of Transnational Civil Society*. Washington, D.C.: Japan Center for International Exchange and Carnegie Endowment for International Peace, 83–114.

Kiser, Larry L., and Elinor Ostrom. 1982. "The Three Worlds of Action: A Metatheoretical Synthesis of Institutional Approaches." In Elinor Ostrom, ed., *Strategies of Political Inquiry*. Beverly Hills: Sage, 179–222.

Kolzow, David R. 1994. "Public/Private Partnership: The Economic Development Organization of the 90s." *Economic Development Review* 12: 4–6.

Lambert, Douglas M., Margaret A. Emmelhainz, and John T. Gardner. 1996. "Developing and Implementing Supply Chain Partnerships." *International Journal of Logistics Management* 7: 1–17.

Langseth, Petter (Task Manager, Governance and Anti-Corruption Program, Economic Development Institute, Regulatory Reform and Private Enterprise Division, World Bank). 1998. Interview by author, July 8.

Liebenthal, Andres. 1998. "Partnership Case Studies: Large Dams." Presentation at the Training Workshop on Making Development Partnerships Work, SDV/LLC and NGO Unit, World Bank. Elkridge, Md., May 19–21.

————. 1999. Interview by author, October 4.

————. 2000. Communication with the author, June 13.

Liebenthal, Andres, et al. 1996. "The World Bank's Experience with Large Dams: An Overview of Impacts." Washington, D.C.: Operations Evaluation Department, World Bank, August 15.

Lipsky, Michael, and Steven Rathgreb Smith. 1989–1990. "Nonprofit Organizations, Government, and the Welfare State." *Political Science Quarterly* 104: 625–648.

Lister, Sarah. 2000. "Power in Partnership? An Analysis of an NGO's Relationships with Its Partners." *Journal of International Development* 12: 227–239.

Lowndes, Vivien, and Chris Skelcher. 1998. "The Dynamics of Multi-Organizational Partnerships: An Analysis of Changing Modes of Governance." *Public Administration* 76: 313–333.

Luengo, Nestor Luis, and María Gabriela Ponce. 1997. "Successful Experiences in Poverty Reduction: Horizontal Cooperation in Latin America and the Caribbean." Instituto Radiofónico Fe y Alegría. San Joaquin, Venezuela: Institute for Economic and Social Research, Catholic University Andrés Bello, for Partnerships for Poverty Reduction, World Bank, in collaboration with the Inter-American Foundation and UNDP, June.

Luhmann, Niklas. 1988. "Familiarity, Confidence, Trust: Problems and Perspectives." In Diego Gambetta, ed., *Trust: The Making and Breaking of Cooperative Relations*. Oxford: Basil Blackwell.

Lukes, Steven. 1974. *Power: A Radical View*. London: Macmillan.

Machado, Nora, and Tom R. Burns. 1998. "Complex Social Organization: Multiple Organizing Modes, Structural Incongruence, and Mechanisms of Integration." *Public Administration* 76: 355–386.

Madhavan, Ravindranath, Balaji R. Koka, and John E. Prescott. 1998. "Networks in Transition: How Industry Events (Re)Shape Interfirm Relationships." *Strategic Management Journal* 19: 439–459.

Malena, Carmen. 1995. "Relations Between Northern and Southern Non-Governmental Development Organizations." *Canadian Journal of Development Studies* 16: 7–29.

Mansbridge, Jane J., ed. 1990. *Beyond Self-Interest*. Chicago: University of Chicago Press.

Mawer, Richard. 1997. "Mice Among the Tigers: Adding Value in NGO-Government Relations in South East Asia." In David Hulme and Michael Edwards, eds., *NGOs, States and Donors: Too Close for Comfort?* New York: St. Martin's, 243–253.

Mazur, Laurie Ann, and Susan E. Sechler. 1997. "Global Interdependence and the Need for Social Stewardship." Global Interdependence Initiative, Rockefeller Brothers Fund Paper no. 1. New York: Rockefeller Brothers Fund.

McCully, Patrick. 1997a. "World Bank Dam Evaluation 'Seriously Deficient': NGOs Demand Independent Review and Moratorium on World Bank Support of Large Dams." *International Rivers Network Press Release*, April 7 [Retrieved January 24, 2001, from www.irn.org/programs/finance/pr970407.html].

———. 1997b. "A Critique of 'The World Bank's Experience with Large Dams: A Preliminary Review of Impacts.'" International Rivers Network, April 11 [Retrieved January 24, 2001, from www.irn.org/programs/finance/critique.htm].

———. 1997c. "Independent Commission to Review World's Dams." *World Rivers Review* 12 [Retrieved January 24, 2001, from www.irn.org/pubs/wrr/9706/9706cover.html].

———. 1997d. "NGOs Condemn World Bank/IUCN Dam Building Commission." *International Rivers Network Press Release*, November 25 [Retrieved January 24, 2001, from www.irn.org/programs/review/pr971125.html].

Mercier, Jean-Roger (Africa Technical Family, Environment, World Bank). 1998. Interview by author, July 16.

Merrey, Douglas J. 1986. "Reorganizing Irrigation: Local Level Management in the Punjab (Pakistan)." In Douglas J. Merrey and James M. Wolf, eds., *Irrigation Management in Pakistan: Four Papers*. IIMI Research Paper no. 4. Colombo, Sri Lanka: International Irrigation Management Institute.

Migdal, Joel S. 1988. *Strong Societies and Weak States: State-Society Relations and State Capabilities in the Third World*. Princeton: Princeton University Press.

Mitchell, Ronald K., Bradley R. Angle, and Donna J. Wood. 1997. "Toward a Theory of Stakeholder Identification and Salience: Defining the Principle of Who and What Really Counts." *Academy of Management Review* 22: 853–886.

Moore, Christopher W. 1996. *The Mediation Process: Practical Strategies for Resolving Conflict*. 2d ed. San Francisco: Jossey-Bass.

MSC (Marine Stewardship Council). 2000. Homepage [Retrieved April 13, 2000, from www.msc.org].

Mudacumura, Gedeon M. 2000. "Participative Management in Global Transformational Change." *International Journal of Public Administration* 13: 2051–2083.

Murphy, David F, and Jem Bendell. 1997. *In the Company of Partners: Business, Environmental Groups and Sustainable Development Post-Rio.* Bristol, U.K.: Policy Press.

Najarro, Juan Carlos Rivas. 1997. Alliances for Poverty Alleviation and Local Development Study Case: FUNDACOATEPEQUE (Coatepeque Foundation). San Salvador, El Salvador: Salvadoran Foundation for Economic and Social Development, for Partnerships for Poverty Reduction, World Bank, in collaboration with the Inter-American Foundation and UNDP, June.

Nassif, Natividad, and José Mussi. 1997. "Case Study, Partnerships for Poverty Reduction: Ramón Abdala Neighborhood, Rosario de la Frontera." Salta, Argentina: Universidad Nacional de Santiago de Estero for Partnerships for Poverty Reduction, World Bank, in collaboration with the Inter-American Foundation and UNDP.

Nelson, Jane. 1996. *Business as Partners in Development: Creating Wealth for Countries, Companies, and Communities.* London: Prince of Wales Business Leaders Forum.

Nicholson, Norman (Senior Management Adviser, Policy and Program Coordination and Development Policy, U.S. Agency for International Development). 1999. Interview by author, November 16.

ODII (Organizing for Development: An International Institute). 2000. "AIC: The Process." [Retrieved June 16, 2000, from www.odii.com].

Olson, Mancur. 1965. *The Logic of Collective Action.* Cambridge: Harvard University Press.

Organ, Dennis W. 1990. "The Motivational Basis of Organizational Citizenship Behavior." *Research in Organizational Behavior* 12: 43–72.

Ostrom, Elinor. 1990. *Governing the Commons: The Evolution of Institutions for Collective Action.* Cambridge: Cambridge University Press.

Ouchi, William G. 1979. "A Conceptual Framework for the Design of Organizational Control Mechanisms." *Management Science* (September): 833–848.

————. 1980. "Markets, Bureaucracies and Clans." *Administrative Science Quarterly* 25: 129–141.

Overseas Development Council and Synergos Institute. 1995. *Strengthening Civil Society's Contribution to Development: The Role of Official Development Assistance.* New York: Overseas Development Council and Synergos Institute.

Parker, Andrew, and Rodrigo Serrano. 2000. "Promoting Good Local Governance Through Social Funds and Decentralization." Thematic Groups on Decentralization, Municipal Finance, and Social Funds, Washington, D.C., World Bank, August.

Participants of the European NGO Hearing on WCD-related Issues. 2000. Letter to all commissioners, the World Commission on Dams, Bratislava, Slovakia, January 19.

Passow, Sam. 1995. "Infrastructure: A Model Government–Private Sector Partnership." *Institutional Investor* 29: SS28.

Perera, Jehan. 1997. "In Unequal Dialogue with Donors: The Experience of the Sarvodaya Shramadana Movement." In David Hulme and Michael Edwards, eds., *NGOs, States and Donors: Too Close for Comfort?* New York: St. Martin's, 156–167.

Person, Conrad (Director of International Programs, Johnson & Johnson). 2001. Interview by author, April 12.

Peters, B. Guy. 1998. "Managing Horizontal Government: The Politics of Co-ordination." *Public Administration* 76: 295–311.

Peterson, D. J. 1997. "The NGO/Donor Workshop: Highlights of the Discussion." In Eliza Klose and Irmgard Hunt, eds., *NGO/Donor Workshop, Szentendre, May 12–14, 1997: A Summary Report.* Szentendre, Hungary: ISAR: Clearinghouse on Grassroots Cooperation in Eurasia and the Regional Environmental Center for Central and Eastern Europe in collaboration with ECOLOGIA and the Environmental Partnership for Central Europe, with support from the U.S. Agency for International Development; the Environmental Ministries of Austria, Finland, and the Netherlands; and the World Bank.

Pfeiffer, Linda (Executive Director, INMED). 1999. INMED memo re: El Paso Energy, May.

———. 2000a. Interview by author, October 10.

———. 2000b. Interview by author, August 3.

———. 2000c. INMED memo re: Johnson & Johnson Meeting, June 30.

Pircher, Wolfgang. 1992. "36,000 Large Dams and Still More Needed." Paper presented at the Seventh Biennial Conference of the British Dam Society, University of Stirling, June 25.

Pollack, Elaine. 1995. "Partnership: Buzzword or Best Practice?" *Chain Store Age Executive* 71 (August 25): 11A–12A.

Postma, William. 1994. "NGO Partnership and Institutional Development: Making It Real, Making It Intentional." *Canadian Journal of African Studies* 28: 543–553.

Pottinger, Lori. 1997. "Dam Industry Faces Judgment Day." *World Rivers Review* 12 (June) [Retrieved January 24, 2001, from www.irn.org/pubs/wrr/9706/9706comment.html].

Prince of Wales Business Leaders Forum. 1998. *Managing Partnerships: Tools for Mobilising the Public Sector, Business and Civil Society as Partners in Development.* London: Prince of Wales Business Leaders Forum.

Reinicke, Wolfgang, and Francis Deng, with associates. 2000. *Critical Choices, The United Nations, Networks and the Future of Global Governance.* Ottawa: International Development Research Centre.

Reputation Management. 2002. "Welcome to Reputation Management." [Retrieved February 7, 2002, from www.reputations.org].

Rice, Andrew E., and Cyril Ritchie. 1995. "Relationships Between International Non-Governmental Organizations and the United Nations: A Research and Policy Paper." *Transnational Associations* 47: 254–265.

Robinson, Mark. 1997. "Privatising the Voluntary Sector: NGOs as Public Service Contractors?" In David Hulme and Michael Edwards, eds., *NGOs, States and Donors: Too Close for Comfort?* New York: St. Martin's, 59–78.

Sagawa, Shirley, and Eli Segal. 2000. *Common Interest, Common Good: Creating Value Through Business and Social Sector Partnerships.* Boston: Harvard Business School Press.

Salmen, Lawrence F. 1995. "The Listening Dimension of Evaluation." *New Directions for Evaluation* 67: 147–154.

Sangvai, Sanjay. 1999. "Narmada Satyagraha Concludes with Reassertion of Resolve to Dare Unjust Submergence: Villagers Gear Up for Nav-Nirman. People Hold Government Guilty of Violation of Laws and Constitution, Demand Punishment." Narmada Bachao Andolan press release, October 15.

Savoie, Donald J., and B. Guy Peters. 1998. *Programme Review in Canada and the United States*. Ottawa: Canadian Centre for Management Development.

Schein, Edgar H. 1992. *Organizational Culture and Leadership*. 2d ed. San Francisco: Jossey-Bass.

Scott, W. Richard. 1995. *Institutions and Organizations*. Thousand Oaks, Calif.: Sage.

Senge, Peter M. 1990. *The Fifth Discipline: The Art and Practice of the Learning Organization*. New York: Doubleday Currency.

Shah, Qaim (Project Director, Barani Area Development Project). 1998a. Barani Area Development Project (Pakistan). Presentation for the Training Workshop on Making Development Partnerships Work, NGO Unit and Learning and Leadership Center, World Bank. Elkridge, Md., May 19–21.

———. 1998b. The Barani Area Development Project. Presentation for the Consultative Meeting on Partnerships: Joining Hands with Government and Non-Government Development Organizations and Local Communities, NGO Unit and Learning and Leadership Center, World Bank. Washington, D.C., May 13–14.

———. 1998c. NWFP Barani Area Development Project (Pakistan): Project Case Study. April 25.

———. 2001. Interview by author, March 5.

Shah, Janat, and Nitin Singh. 2001. "Benchmarking Internal Supply-Chain Performance: Development of a Framework." *Journal of Supply Chain Management* 37: 37–47.

Smillie, Ian. 1995. *The Alms Bazaar: Altruism Under Fire—Non-Profit Organizations and International Development*. Ottawa: International Development Research Centre.

Smith, William E. 1991. *The AIC Model: Concepts and Practice*. Washington, D.C.: Organizing for Development.

Sternberg, Elaine. 1994. *Just Business*. London: Little, Brown.

Stoker, Gerry. 1997. "Local Political Participation." In Robin Hambleton and Associates, eds., *New Perspectives on Local Government*. York, U.K.: York Publishing Services.

Summers, Lawrence H. 2000. "Development and Integration: A New Global Consensus." *Presidents and Prime Ministers* 9: 7–9.

Tandon, Rajesh. 1991. *NGO-Government Relations: A Source of Life or a Kiss of Death?* New Delhi: Society for Participatory Research in Asia.

Tonkiss, Fran, and Andrew Passey. 1999. "Trust, Confidence and Voluntary Organisations: Between Values and Institutions." *Sociology* 33: 257–274.

UN (United Nations). 1998. Arrangements and Practices for the Interaction of Non-Governmental Organizations in All Activities of the United Nations System. New York: Report of the Secretary-General, United Nations.

———. 1999. *Partners with the United Nations*. [Retrieved September 23, 1999, from www.un.org/partners].

Universidad de West Indies. 1997. Case study on COMAND [Community Organizations for Management and Sustainable Development]. Montego Bay, Jamaica: Universidad de West Indies.

USAID (United States Agency for International Development). 1995a. Core Report of the New Partnerships Initiative. Washington, D.C.: USAID, New Partnerships Initiative.

———. 1995b. "New Partnership Initiative: Democratic Local Governance." Core Report of the New Partnerships Initiative. Washington, D.C.: USAID, New Partnerships Initiative.

————. 1995c. "New Partnerships Initiative: NGO Empowerment." Core Report of the New Partnerships Initiative. Washington, D.C.: USAID, New Partnership Initiative.

————. 1995d. "New Partnership Initiative: Small Business Partnership." Core Report of the New Partnerships Initiative. Washington, D.C.: USAID, New Partnership Initiative.

————. 1997. *NPI Resource Guide: New Partnerships Initiative: A Strategic Approach to Development Partnering*. Washington, D.C.: USAID, New Partnerships Initiative.

————. 2001. GDA conceptual framework [Retrieved February 7, 2002, from www.usaid.gov/gda/gda_framework.html].

USAID/SA (USAID Mission to South Africa). 1999a. "News Flash: Civil Society Program Design Progress Report." Report 1. Pretoria: USAID/SA.

————. 1999b. "News Flash: Civil Society Program Design Progress Report." Report 2. Pretoria: USAID/SA.

Van der Heijden, Hendrik. 1987. "The Reconciliation of NGO Autonomy, Program Integrity and Operational Effectiveness with Accountability to Donors." *World Development* 15 (Supplement): 103–112.

Van Sant, Jerry. 1996. "Governance as Stewardship: Decentralization and Sustainable Human Development." Staff Working Paper. UNDP, Research Triangle Institute, Center for International Development, October.

Viswanath, Vanita. 1995. "Building Partnerships for Poverty Reduction: The Participatory Project Planning Approach of the Women's Enterprise Management Training Outreach Program (WEMTOP)." World Bank Technical Paper no. 265. Washington, D.C.: World Bank.

Waddock, Sandra A. 1993. "Lessons from the National Alliance of Business Compact Project: Business and Public Education Reform." *Human Relations* 46: 777–802.

Wambia, Joseph (Task Manager, Pakistan National Drainage Project, South Asia Rural Development Sector Unit, World Bank). 1998. Interview by author, July 16.

Watanabe, Eimi (Director, Bureau for Development Policy and Assistant Administrator, UNDP). 1998. "Broadening Partnerships for Sustainable Development." Keynote address at the Partnerships in Development Conference, Lyon, France, November 10.

WCD (World Commission on Dams). 1998. "Early Success in Fundraising." *World Commission on Dams Newsletter* 1 (December) [Retrieved January 24, 2001, from www.dams.org/newsletters/newsletter2.htm].

————. 1999a. "WCD Establishes Regular Briefing Meeting with NGO Network." *World Commission on Dams Newsletter* 2 (March) [Retrieved January 24, 2001, from www.dams.org/newsletters/newsletter2.htm].

————. 1999b. "Foundation Announces Million-Dollar Funding for Partnership in Global Policymaking on Dams." *World Commission on Dams Press Release*, May 19 [Retrieved January 24, 2001, from www.dams.org/press/pressrelease_20.htm].

————. 1999c. "World Commission on Dams Meeting at Tarbela." *World Commission on Dams Press Release*, June 22 [Retrieved January 24, 2000, from www.dams.org/press/pressrelease_22.htm].

————. 1999d. *Interim Report, July 1999*. Cape Town, South Africa: World Commission on Dams.

————. 2000a. "The Future . . . News Beyond the Life of the Commission: The

Eternal Website." *World Commission on Dams Newsletter* 8 (December) [Retrieved January 24, 2000, from www.dams.org/newsletters/n8_contents. htm].

————. 2000b. "Even Before Releasing Its Report the WCD Process Is Having Ripple Effects Worldwide." *World Commission on Dams Newsletter* 7 (August) [Retrieved January 24, 2000, from www.dams.org/newsletters/ n8_contents.htm].

————. 2000c. "68-Member Forum Gives Nod of Approval to WCD's Progress." *World Commission on Dams Newsletter* 6 (April) [Retrieved January 24, 2000, from www.dams.org/newsletters/n8_contents.htm].

————. 2001a. *Dams and Development: A New Framework for Decision-Making. The Report of the World Commission on Dams.* London: Earthscan [Retrieved January 24, 2000, from www.dams.org/report/wcd_overview.htm].

————. 2001b. *Final WCD Forum: Report, Responses, Discussions and Outcomes. Third WCD Forum Meeting, The Spier Village, Cape Town, South Africa, 25–27 February, 2001* [Retrieved February 7, 2002, from www.dams.org].

Weaving, Rachel. 1996. "World Bank Lending for Large Dams: A Preliminary Review of Impacts." OEC Précis no. 125, September. Washington, D.C.: World Bank.

Weick, Karl E. 1993. "Sensemaking in Organizations: Small Structures with Large Consequences." In J. Keith Murnighan, ed., *Social Psychology in Organizations: Advances in Theory and Research.* Englewood Cliffs, N.J.: Prentice Hall, 10–37.

WHO (World Health Organization). 2001. "Intestinal Parasites." [Retrieved January 8, 2001, from www.who.int/ctd/intpara/disease.htm].

Witness for Peace. 1996. "A People Dammed: The Impact of the World Bank Chixoy Hydroelectric Project in Guatemala," May [Retrieved October 20, 1999, www.witnessforpeace.org/apd.html].

Woodward, Craig. 1994. "Partnership: More Than a Buzzword." *Economic Development Review* 12: 66–68.

World Bank. 1993. "Disclosure of Operational Information" (BP 17.50). *The World Bank Operational Manual: Bank Procedures.* Washington, D.C.: World Bank.

————. 1996. *Pursuing Common Goals: Strengthening Relations Between Government and Development NGOs in Bangladesh.* Dhaka, Bangladesh: University Press.

————. 1997. World Bank Corporate Citizenship Conference, Washington, D.C., May 21–22, 1997, World Bank.

————. 1999. "Business Partners for Development." [Retrieved September 23, 1999, from www.worldbank.org/bpd/index.htm].

Zartman, I. William. 1995. "Introduction: Posing the Problem of State Collapse." In I. William Zartman, ed., *Collapsed States: The Disintegration and Restoration of Legitimate Authority.* Boulder: Lynne Rienner.

INDEX

Accountability: corporate, 69; as dimension in partnerships, 89–90, 91*box;* donor requirements for, 64; flexibility and, 8, 153, 169
Acesita Foundation for Social Development, 32*box*
Action training, 92
Actors: CBOs as, 54–57; donors as, 62–66; environmental influences in partnerships, 34, 37–40, 45; as evaluators, 95–97; governments as, 58–62; NGOs as, 48–54; preferences of, 74–77; private sector as, 66–71; risks in partnerships to, 48; types of, 47
Adult education, 68*box*
African Environment Consultative Meetings (World Bank), 39*box*
Agriculture: horticultural products, 67*box;* rain-fed, 99–100; risk of new technology, 112. *See also* Barani Area Development Project (BADP)
Agriculture officers (AOs), 103
AIDS. *See* HIV/AIDS
Alliance for Energy (Nepal), 157*n2*
American Chamber of Commerce, 134*n10*
American-Jewish Joint Distribution Committee (JDC), 37*box*
Angola, 138
Annan, Kofi, 10–11, 156
Appreciate/Influence/Control (AIC) model, 77
Argentina, 37*box*
Artificiality, 33–34, 36*fig,* 43

Asian Development Bank (ADB), 99, 105, 109, 138, 163, 167
Asmal, Kader, 141*box,* 142–143, 145*fig,* 154, 156, 170
Awards, 87–88

Bangladesh, 44*box*
Barani Area Development Project (BADP): achievements, 106–107; adaptations in, 104–106; Barani Development Office (BDO), 99–105, 108, 110, 112; coordination, 102–104, 106; design trade-offs, 164–169; District Coordination Committees (DCCs), 103, 106, 108; Divisional Project Review Committees (DPRCs), 103, 106, 108; evaluation of, 104, 106–108; future potential, 106–108; initiation of, 160–163; leadership in, 105; lessons for partnership work, 108–111; lessons for public-service improvement, 111–113; local community role in, 175–176; operationalization of, 100–104; Project Review Board (PRB), 103–104, 106, 108; scope of, 3, 99; Social Organization Unit, 5; transparency in, 105, 109, 160; trust among partners, 162
Berne Declaration, 157*n2*
Bolivia, 42*box,* 49*box*
Boycotts, 69
Brazil: children's health, 115–116; corporate philanthropy, 32*box;* dam con-

197

ABOUT THE BOOK

In the search for institutional models that can deliver more and better development outcomes, partnership is among the most popular solutions proposed. But the evidence of partnerships' contributions to actual performance has been for the most part anecdotal. *Partnership for International Development* bridges the gap between rhetoric and practice, clarifying what the concept means and providing a roadmap for how to achieve meaningful partnership results. The discussion is enhanced by case studies of partnerships for public service, corporate social responsibility, and conflict resolution.

Jennifer M. Brinkerhoff is assistant professor of public administration at George Washington University.